POWER,
POLITICS
AND
PROGRESS

POWER, POLITICS AND PROGRESS

SOCIAL CHANGE
IN RURAL PERU

WILLIAM FOOTE WHYTE

AND GIORGIO ALBERTI

ELSEVIER

New York/Oxford/Amsterdam

ELSEVIER SCIENTIFIC PUBLISHING COMPANY, INC.
52 Vanderbilt Avenue, New York, N.Y. 10017

ELSEVIER SCIENTIFIC PUBLISHING COMPANY
335 Jan Van Galenstraat, P.O. Box 211
Amsterdam, The Netherlands

Library of Congress Cataloging in Publication Data

Whyte, William Foote, 1914–
  Power, politics and progress: social change in rural Peru.
  Bibliography: p. 301
  1. Peru—Rural conditions.   2.   Peasantry—Peru.
3. Social change.   I.   Alberti, Giorgio, 1936–
joint author.   II.   Title.
HN343.5.W48   301.35′2′0985   76-25193
ISBN 0-444-99028-3

Manufactured in the United States of America

Designed by Loretta Li

TO JOSE MATOS MAR

CONTENTS

III   JUNIN

IV   THE CHANCAY VALLEY

V   THEORY, METHODOLOGY, AND PRACTICE

PREFACE

This book grows out of a research program carried out in collaboration between the Instituto de Estudios Peruanos and Cornell University, with José Matos Mar codirector for IEP and William F. Whyte and Lawrence K. Williams codirectors for Cornell. Julio Cotler served as research coordinator for IEP from 1965 to 1973. Oscar Alers served as coordinator for Cornell in Peru for two years beginning in 1965, followed by Williams for one year, and Alberti from 1968 through 1975. The IEP-Cornell relationship has been a partnership of equals in every sense of the word. We jointly planned the research. The fieldwork was carried out primarily by Peruvian professors and students of sociology and anthropology, but Alers and Alberti actively participated. We were jointly responsible for data analysis and for writing of research reports. As the bibliography of our program indicates, up to this point we have published more in Spanish in Peru than in English elsewhere. This book, then, represents our effort, for the benefit of English-speaking readers, to distill what we have learned throughout the course of our research program in Peru.

Whyte was introduced to Peru through the late Allan R. Holmberg, well known for his Vicos project. Eileen Maynard and Mario Vázquez, then working with Holmberg, provided valuable assistance in developing and applying the 1964 questionnaire. Hernan Castillo worked with Whyte in applying that survey in Cuzco and Virú and in analyzing some of the data.

For the 1964 surveys, José Matos Mar, then professor of anthropology at San Marcos National University, was in charge of the Chancay valley project; he was assisted by Heraclio Bonilla and Cesar Fonseca. Victor Antonio Rodríguez Suy Suy, professor of anthropology at the University of Trujillo, was in charge of the Virú project. Oscar Núñez del Prado, then professor of anthropology at the University of Cuzco, was field director for the surveys of Cuzco.

For the 1969 resurveys, the IEP staff carried out the surveys in the Chancay valley and was responsible for directing the surveys in the other areas, working with students from the regional universities in those cases. The IEP staff members principally involved at this point were José Portugal, Luís Soberón, Fernando Fuenzalida, Dennis Chavez, and Rodrigo Sánchez.

So as to avoid having innumerable footnote citations in the text, we indicate here the individuals particularly responsible for research and publications that were the sources of each section of the book. A detailed bibliography is given at the back of the book.

Within our own program, Part II (Cuzco) is based primarily upon the work of Oscar Núñez del Prado and on the field reports of Angel Garmendia, Juan Núñez del Prado, Daniel Raguz, Alfredo Valencia, Jaime Bonet Yepez, Miguel Aragón, Olinda Celestino, and Peri Paredes. For Chapter 4 ("The Opening Up of Sicuani") we utilized the doctoral thesis of Benjamin Orlove. For Chapters 5 and 6, dealing with the Convencion valley movement, we relied upon the writings of Hugo Blanco, Wesley Craig, Eduardo Fioravanti, and Enrique Gallegos Venero.

Part III (Junín) is based primarily upon the field research and publications of Alberti and Rodrigo Sanchez. Dale Nelson, Josefina Pereira, and José Portugal participated in the fieldwork with them. In 1964, field reports on the three Mantaro valley communities were written by Rose Mejía Cordova and Edy Waidhofer.

Part IV (The Chancay Valley) was already an area of major fieldwork directed by José Matos Mar at the time of the launching of our program, so that the research reports and publications are particularly plentiful for this area.

For the study of Aucallama, we drew particularly upon the work of Heraclio Bonilla; for La Esperanza, José Portugal. Carlos Ivan Degregori and Jürgen Golte wrote the book that is the major source of our information on Pacaraos. The book on Huayopampa by Fernando Fuenzalida, José Villarán, and Teresa Valiente was the main source of our data for that community. The Lampián chapter is entirely based upon the book by Olinda Celestino.

Lawrence K. Williams had the main planning responsibility for our survey program and guided much of the data analysis. John Lawrence French was also very helpful to us in the survey-data analysis.

We received helpful criticisms and suggestions for revision of our manuscript from Irving Louis Horowitz, Liliana de Soberón, and Samuel Bacharach.

We are especially indebted to Kathleen Whyte, whose skillful and painstaking editorial work on the third draft of this book made it possible for us to reduce our words by almost one-third without sacrificing essential ideas or information. She also drew the maps.

Finally, special recognition is due to José Matos Mar, director of the Instituto de Estudios Peruanos. Whyte and Cornell had nothing to do with the establishment of IEP in early 1964, but the collaborative project in the Chancay valley directed by Matos and Whyte led to an invitation from Matos Mar to bring our program into IEP and make it a joint IEP-Cornell responsibility. From September 1964 to September 1975, our program office was with IEP. In effect, this meant that Matos Mar carried the main administrative burdens and responsibilities while he also participated fully in the total process of planning and directing fieldwork and in data analysis and report writing. Without his strong support and enthusiastic collaboration, it would not have been possible to develop and maintain such a large-scale international cooperation during a period of increasing political tensions between Peru and the United States. Matos's drive and vision also created within IEP what has come to be regarded as one of the most important publishers of social science books in Latin America. IEP has published and is publishing many books having no relation to our joint research program, but we were fortunate in being able to publish the results of much of our work within Peru through IEP. We are also indebted to Rosalía Avalos de Matos and to Rogger Ravines for skillful and dedicated editorial work in preparing our reports for publication.

The main sources of financial support for the program have been the National Science Foundation and the National Institute of Mental Health. Between grants, we have had smaller yet vital support from Cornell University's Latin American Program and from the New York State School of Industrial and Labor Relations.

With great skill and dedication, Katherine Anderson served as administrative secretary at Cornell throughout the program. She took care of everything from human problems and financial records to typing. Donna Updike typed the final draft of the manuscript.

April 1, 1976   William Foote Whyte
                                                  Cornell University

                                                  Giorgio Alberti
                                                  University of Bologna

INTRODUCTION I

Prologue to an 1
Intellectual Exploration

This is a report on a long-term intellectual exploration carried out in rural Peru. Our program began in late 1963 and continued for approximately 10 years, with the rewriting and rethinking extending many months beyond the field work.

We have reported in detail on our findings in Peru in the publications listed in our bibliography. Our present purpose is to use the Peruvian data as a vehicle for reporting the lessons we have learned in regard to social theory, methodology, and the practical implications of our research findings.

In the course of explaining the process of social change in rural Peru, we came to make major changes in our theoretical framework and research design. In our last chapter, we focus directly upon this process of intellectual change as we try to answer the questions: Where did our ideas come from? And how did they change in response to our field experiences and our efforts to explain what we found? As we set forth on this intellectual exploration, let us simply summarize the evolution of our thinking.

We began within a framework of "modernization" theory, which put great emphasis on personality aspects of the development process: changes in values, attitudes, beliefs, and perceptions. Implicit in modernization theory is what we now call "the myth of the passive peasant": the assumption that the peasant is naturally tradition-bound, fatalistic, and inclined to resist change. This view focuses attention upon the psychological orientations of peasants and upon the forces leading to change in these orientations. The questionnaire or survey is the appropriate method for such psychological measurements, but it supplies only indirect information on the human experiences that shape and change these orientations. We were therefore committed from the outset to combining surveys with anthropological studies of social processes and social structures.

We began at the microlevel of community studies, viewing the areal, regional, national, and international contexts simply as useful background for the understanding of local-level events. Similarly, we viewed history simply as background information useful for understanding current events. In fact, the first guidelines for the field studies suggested that 50 years of history would be ample for such understanding.

Our research design called for the study of a number of villages exhibiting a wide range of wealth, education, and homogeneity-heterogeneity of occupations. In 1964, we surveyed 23 villages and 3 haciendas in five areas of Peru. In 1969, for practical reasons, we reduced the study areas to four and the villages resurveyed to 12, while we resurveyed the 3 haciendas and added 3 more. For the survey data, the present book concentrates primarily on the 12 villages that were surveyed on both occasions. We aimed at a 20 percent sample of adults by directing field workers to select every fifth household and to try to survey every adult living there. In order to increase the numbers of respondents in the smallest communities, we expanded the percentage of households sampled; in the larger communities, we were satisfied with less than a 20 percent sample.

We began our anthropological field studies at the same time as we applied the 1964 surveys. These field studies continued with varying intensity and coverage for almost a decade.

4

PERUVIAN DEPARTMENTS
Containing Main Research Areas

As we worked closely with our Peruvian associates in planning and directing the field studies and in data analyzing and report writing, we learned through discussions with each other as well as from what our studies told us about the countryside.

In the course of this experience, we abandoned the modernization framework and came to focus on *structural* change. Discarding the myth of the passive peasant, we came to see peasants as men and women in motion in response to forces they generated among themselves as well as in response to external forces. Community studies were no longer our central concern, and we came to view villages simply as convenient locations for the study of structural change at the microlevel.

No longer did we see space and time information simply as background for a community study. In order to explain local events, we had to identify the external forces that impacted upon the community.

We now see local events as being the results of the interaction between local conditions and external forces. According to this view, history should take us beyond understanding and enable us to discover those external conditions most relevant in the determination of local events.

Our aim in this book is to link together the microlevel of community with the larger geographical, political, and economic units of area, region, and nation. Since the nature of these links only becomes clear as we study changes over time, historical research became an important element in our evolving program strategy.

In Chapter 2, we have selected from the historical events of Peru the principal structural changes at the national level that opened the way for the processes of peasant mobilization and community development that we will examine in subsequent chapters.

Parts II, III, and IV follow an organizational scheme in which local-level events are fitted into a regional context and are linked to preceding events at local, regional, and national levels. In Parts I and II, we begin by examining the disintegration of the monolithic structure of power that prevailed in most of the department of Cuzco. Moving to the central highlands in Part III, we focus primarily on politics and community development in the villages of the Mantaro valley, where the monolithic power structure of Cuzco never fully developed. Following the Chancay valley in Part IV from highlands to coast, we focus on villages very much within the orbit of the metropolitan area of the capital city of Lima.

In Part V, we examine the implications, for research methods, theory, and practice, of what we learned in the course of fieldwork and in the long process of analysis and reanalysis of our data. Our experience of more than a decade in this program has led us to rethink the nature of social science and to question what we take to be the standard model of sociological research. We present this reformulation in our final chapter.

Rural Peru in the Context 2
of National Development

Peasant activism is not a recently emerging phenomenon in Peru. From the colonial period into the twentieth century, history records a large number of areal and regional peasant movements. Although some of the earlier movements may have had long-term effects, they had one feature in common: they all failed to bring about the major changes for which the peasants were struggling. It was not until the 1950s and 1960s that peasant movements began to win lasting victories.

What made it possible for the peasants to begin winning? The general answer is that society, on both national and rural levels, was undergoing profound changes that created conditions more conducive to both peasant insurgence and peasant success than those that had existed in earlier periods. In this chapter, we focus on those aspects of national history that are especially relevant in the determination of conditions and events in rural Peru.

7

IMPACT OF THE CONQUEST

The history of modern Peru begins with the conquest that superimposed Spanish rule on an ancient and highly developed Indian civilization.

The patterns of conquest and settlement in North and South America were drastically different, and these differences laid the foundations for different social structures and different lines of economic development.

When the English landed in North America, they found the land sparsely populated by relatively primitive tribes who roamed over wide areas. Settlement and European expansion did not bring about amalgamation of races and cultures. The Indians were simply pushed out of the way and suffered as outsiders in their native land. They were not included in the white man's society either as slaves or as serfs.

The *conquistadores* came to South America in search of gold and other treasure to advance their social and economic positions back in Spain. Since the first Spaniards left their women at home, racial amalgamation began even in the early years after the conquest.

Pizarro and his men did not encounter scattered Indian tribes but a centrally controlled empire. At the time of the conquest in 1532, the Incas ruled a vast territory extending from what is now northern Ecuador, through Peru, into northern Chile, and into much of Bolivia. In the centuries before the conquest, the Incas had extended their military and public administration system over a number of peoples who had already reached a high level of civilization, as evidenced in arts and crafts, construction, and agriculture, based upon an irrigation system that produced abundant crops and controlled land erosion. The Indian population at the time of the arrival of the white man has been estimated at approximately 1 million for the continental United States, but in Pizzarro's time there appear to have been over 8 million people within what is now Peru.

When later Spaniards did come to settle, they ruled over a subjugated population. In the rural areas, the crown rewarded favored subjects and church orders with extensive land grants. The priests were given responsibility for the care of the souls of the Indians, while the laymen exploited their bodies. Since manual labor was then beneath the dignity

8

of the Spanish gentleman, the conquerors devised systems of forcing the Indians to work the fields and mines.

DIFFERENTIAL REGIONAL DEVELOPMENT

In search of gold and silver, the conquistadores first concentrated their interest on the highlands, which were the source of these metals. The Spaniards stripped the country of the gold and silver artifacts that had been created over centuries, but they soon found that there were poor prospects for mining the ores of precious metals, which led them to lose interest in developing that large region. It was not until the end of the nineteenth century that the sierra's mineral wealth in copper began to be exploited.

Although the jungle to the east of the Andes constitutes more than half of the land mass of Peru, it was sparsely populated by scattered Indian tribes. The rubber boom, centered in Iquitos, attracted thousands of non-Indians, but the end of Peru's monopoly on natural rubber early in the twentieth century left the jungle economically stagnant and isolated.

The terrain, both in the jungle and in the highlands, has presented formidable obstacles for the development of transportation and communication in these regions. From Lima, to get into the valleys of the central highlands, the traveler has to go over a pass more than 3 miles high, and travel north to south in the sierra involves comparable obstacles.

The modern economic development of Peru, except for the enclaves of copper mining, has been concentrated on the coast. The coastal strip is exceedingly narrow and, except for the extreme north, is entirely desert, where rain hardly ever falls. While the tributaries to the Amazon flow eastward from the highlands, 57 small rivers cut through the desert to the Pacific. The land is fertile, and where the rivers provide irrigation water, crops are abundant. For many decades, coastal agriculture has been dominated by large and technologically modern commercial haciendas, devoted primarily to the export crops of sugar and cotton.

The industrial development of Peru began relatively late and slowly. By the early 1960s about three-quarters of the nation's industrial employment was concentrated in the Lima metropolitan area (including neighboring Callao, Peru's leading port). English investors and entre-preneurs played a major role in commerce and industry in the nineteenth century, and United States interests became increasingly dominant after World War I. By the mid-twentieth century, the largest industrial and mining firms were foreign owned. The Peruvian firms, with few excep-tions, had been founded by immigrants or sons of immigrants. Thus, the economic destiny of the country appeared to be in the hands of foreigners or of those who were still finding their places within Peruvian society.

The sierra has remained largely rural and agricultural. Traditionally, it has been dominated by owners of large haciendas, whose laborers have served under semifeudal conditions. It was not until 1908 that the Cen-tral Railway connected Lima with Huancayo in the Mantaro valley, and the same year the Southern Railway reached from coastal Mollendo to Cuzco in the southern highlands.

MODERNIZATION UNDER LEGUIA

The *oncenio* (11-year rule, 1919–1930) of Agusto B. Leguía was marked by a major effort to "modernize" Peru, with the aid of foreign invest-ments, loans, and advice. Two legislative programs of this era are par-ticularly important for our purposes.

In 1919, Leguía established a form of protection for indigenous, or Indian, communities. The law gave communities that had retained some traces of Indian culture the right to petition the government for official recognition as an indigenous community. Such recognition reestablished the principle of inalienability of lands for members of the community. It also established the community as a "juridical person," giving it certain rights in the legal system not otherwise accorded to villages. Most impor-tant, in case of disputes with neighboring villages or with large land-owners, the community gained the right to appeal directly to the Division of Indian Affairs in the government in Lima.

Peasants found the promise of protection and a channel of appeal sufficiently important to warrant the investment of considerable time, effort, and money to support delegations to Lima to push for legal recog-nition. As time went on, the requirement that the community exhibit some traces of Indian culture came to be very loosely interpreted so that villages where the speaking of an indigenous language and the wearing of

10

traditional Indian clothes had long since died out were able to get themselves recognized as indigenous communities. By the 1960s, the government had given such recognition to more than 1,500 communities, mainly in the highlands.

The law provided peasant communities with an important weapon for holding back further encroachments by large landholders. Although its effects were primarily defensive in the early years, the law provided a base from which peasants were able to take the offensive in the period of our study.

Leguía's *Ley Vial* provided for the building of "penetration roads" from the coast into the highlands. Peasants along the routes were forced to provide the manual labor. While this exploitation was bitterly resented by the men forced to bear the burden, the opening up of the countryside provided one of the essential conditions for peasant mobilization, which gained increasing strength in the following years.

BEGINNINGS OF POPULAR PARTICIPATION

Until well into the twentieth century, only a very small percentage of Peru's population was politically active or able to exercise any influence in economic affairs. Until 1930, the vote was limited to literate citizens who owned property.

Popular mobilization began with the labor movement on the coast. Although craft unions had been formed much earlier, it was the labor struggles in the industrial plants that first had an impact on the national scene. Labor won its first important victories with the unionization of the major textile mills and with the passage of the eight-hour-day law in 1919.

In these struggles, radical university students joined forces with workers, and it was here that Victor Raúl Haya de la Torre first became prominent. He was to remain a major political force in Peru and an influential figure throughout much of Latin America for the next half-century.

In exile from the Leguía dictatorship in Mexico in 1924, Haya founded Alianza Popular Revolucionaria Americana (APRA). The two principal planks in the party platform during this early period were "action against Yankee imperialism" and the "nationalization of land

11

and industry" (Haya de la Torre, 1936). Although the party was outlawed during several periods in the succeeding decades, APRA was the only Peruvian political party to survive and maintain itself as an important force for the half-century after its founding. The party was closely linked with the Confederación de Trabajadores Peruanos (CTP, Peruvian Confederation of Labor), and the unions provided the base for operations during periods when APRA was limited to clandestine political activities.

Shortly after overthrowing Leguía in 1930, General Sánchez Cerro removed the property qualification for the franchise, thus greatly extending the electorate and bringing rural communities especially into the national political arena for the first time. The 1931 contest between Sánchez Cerro and Haya stirred more widespread popular interest than any previous national election. While Haya had very strong support, especially among working people along the coast, Sánchez Cerro was a popular hero for ending the increasingly unpopular dictatorship, and he campaigned with populistic appeals similar to those of APRA.

In 1933, President Sánchez Cerro was assassinated by an *Aprista*, and APRA was again outlawed. The assassination did not alter the existing distribution of power; for the power elite, it simply dramatized the APRA menace of violent revolution. Balancing a vigorous repression of APRA with some concessions to urban workers, General Benavides managed to consolidate a military regime that lasted until 1939. In 1945, toward the end of the first six-year term of conservative President Manuel Prado, APRA was again legalized, but Haya himself was not allowed to run for president. APRA joined a coalition behind the successful candidacy of a progressive leader, Luis Bustamante y Rivero. The period 1945–48 marked the high point of APRA power and influence. CTP unions extended their membership rapidly in industry and in the coastal sugar plantations. APRA gained control of the student bodies in most of the universities. APRA mass meetings brought out large and enthusiastic crowds. The party organized the *bufalos* (its own shock troops) named after their founder, to protect APRA activities and to harrass the opposition.

Within a few months of the 1945 election, Haya withdrew APRA support from Bustamante, and that government gradually disintegrated into confusion, conflict, and paralysis. Some members of APRA conspired with military and naval officers to overthrow Bustamante, but the

12

plot was plagued by conflicting orders and communications, and finally only a few naval units participated in the abortive revolt.

The frustrated uprising prepared the scene for the intervention of General Manuel A. Odría and the beginning of the *ochenio*, his dictatorial rule from 1948 to 1956. Again APRA was outlawed and persecuted.

While the Odría repression kept the lid on politically, the regime could not turn back the changes already under way in the economy and in the society. The early 1950s were marked by rapidly increasing foreign demand for Peruvian raw materials, and the extended boom in the export sectors stimulated the growth of the national market. As industrial employment grew, migration to the cities accelerated. Industrialization contributed to the emergence of middle-class entrepreneurs and executives who were not in sympathy with the military oligarchical structure of power. The expansion of state activities was generating a growing number of bureaucrats and technicians, who, though not in sympathy with radical social changes, believed that the development of Peru required modernization of the political and administrative structure.

The urban masses were now too involved in political participation and union activities to be held back indefinitely, and the traditional dominance of the rural landlords was deteriorating. The expansion of demand for agricultural produce stimulated the growth of a new group of traders, merchants, and middlemen, who found it in their interests to bypass the traditional holders of power by establishing direct connections with the peasantry. Increasing numbers of peasants left the land to work in factories and mines; many returned to their native villages with new resources and new information and ideas derived from their urban labor and union experience.

In the 1940s, and particularly at the height of APRA power from 1945 to 1948, APRA political and union activities had spread rapidly in rural areas along the coast and into the highlands. Although open political activity was banned under Odría, APRA activists continued to spread APRA ideas and organization throughout the countryside in thinly disguised form.

1956 marked a major change in strategy for APRA. When Odría stepped aside for the election of that year, it was evident that the support of the large and well-disciplined APRA party would mean the difference between defeat and victory. At the last moment, Haya threw his support

13

to Manuel Prado. Out of this arrangement came six years of *la conviven-cia*, the living together of the once radical APRA leaders and the conser-vatives, led by a member of one of the most powerful families of the traditional oligarchy. APRA did not secure cabinet posts but was legal-ized once again and won freedom of action for union activities plus, perhaps, a promise by Prado to support the candidacy of Haya in the next election.

1956 also marked the rise to national prominence of Fernando Be-laúnde Terry, who came to be Prado's chief rival in that election. An architect and dean of the School of Architecture in the National Univer-sity of Engineering, Belaúnde organized his reformist Popular Action party while APRA was still outlawed and rallied around him members of the new middle class of professionals, bureaucrats, technicians, and intellectuals who were disaffected with the traditional order.

NATIONAL POLITICS IN THE 1960s

For the election of 1962, the Prado forces backed Haya de la Torre, but they were unable to carry with them many other influential conservative politicians, who supported the candidacy of Manuel A. Odría.

After his strong showing in 1956, Belaúnde had continued to work toward his 1962 candidacy in the intervening years, traveling to the far corners of the country and making special efforts in the central and southern sierra. Belaúnde and other leaders of the Popular Action party now claimed that theirs was the only major progressive reform party, since Haya had brought APRA into la convivencia with Prado. In fact, the anti-imperialism theme had dropped out of Haya's campaigning, and a banner across one of Lima's main streets proclaimed "Anti-Comunismo con Haya."

The election was the closest in history, with Haya running less than 1 percent above Belaúnde and with Odría coming in a strong third. Since the top candidate fell slightly short of one-third of the popular vote, the constitution required that the election be decided in the congress. The joint chiefs of staff put an end to the maneuvering among the parties, took over the government, and announced for the next year an election to be conducted under new legislation that would eliminate the vote frauds, which they claimed had marred the 1962 election.

The 1963 campaign was a rerun of 1962's, with one important difference. The new law made it impossible for small parties to get on the ballot, and this time the Christian Democrats joined with Belaúnde, while the parties of the extreme left gave him some tacit support. Belaúnde won in 1963, but APRA and Odría forces controlled both houses of congress between them.

Whereas during the Odría regime even the public mention of the desirability of agrarian reform was enough to put the "agitator" in jail, by the time of the 1962 and 1963 elections, all candidates endorsed some forms of agrarian reform, and Belaúnde campaigned exceptionally vigorously on this issue in the rural areas.

Belaúnde's victory in 1963 signaled to many peasants that at last agrarian reform was on its way. All over the sierra, peasants began to take reform into their own hands. Particularly in the central highlands, members of peasant communities "invaded" haciendas—or "recovered the land illegally taken from them"—depending upon the point of view of the observer. Particularly in the southern highlands, organization of hacienda serfs grew rapidly into a massive movement.

The peasant movement placed the new president in a difficult position. Belaúnde had hoped to relieve tensions by quick passage of an agrarian reform law and by a well-financed community-development program, but the opposition-dominated congress first delayed and then watered down the agrarian reform bill and provided scant support for *Cooperación Popular*, the new agency for community development.

Belaúnde was hoping for major financial support from the Agency for International Development (AID), and AID officials in Lima worked enthusiastically with their Peruvian counterparts to prepare proposals for Washington. However, during his campaign, Belaúnde had promised that within 90 days of his inauguration he would resolve the long festering problem of the International Petroleum Company, through direct negotiations with the company. The U.S. State Department decided to withhold AID funds until President Belaúnde made good on his promise. It took Belaúnde not 90 days but 5 years to reach that settlement—only to have it cancelled by the military coup of 1968. (Peru did receive a $20,000,000 loan for rural development from the Inter-American Development Bank in 1966, but by this time the momentum of reform and progress of the early months of his regime had long since been lost.)

In dealing with the rural crisis, Belaúnde was also confronted with an insoluble problem inherent in the Peruvian constitution. That instrument provided for *interpelación,* by which a cabinet minister could be called at any time, before either house of congress and required to answer questions put to him by the members. At the conclusion of such a session, the legislative body would take a vote of confidence. If the vote went against him, he was required to resign and the president was obliged to appoint a replacement. The president could have discouraged such challenges if, upon a vote of no confidence in a cabinet minister, he had been empowered to call a new national election, but the constitution made no such provision.

As the peasant movement spread, with demands for "law and order," the opposition majority aimed its fire at the prime minister and the minister of government, who was responsible for the police forces. In early 1964, Belaúnde submitted to these demands and appointed a minister of government who set in motion a drive to capture and imprison "political agitators" and peasant union leaders throughout the southern sierra. These actions halted the spread of peasant movements but did not reestablish the status quo of the 1950s.

POLITICAL POWER IN THE 1960s

Although property qualifications had been eliminated in 1930, literacy remained a requirement for voting into the period of our study. At the same time, the number of representatives allocated to each area was determined by total population. Particularly in the poorer rural areas of the highlands, where there were large concentrations of illiterate Indians, this meant that the large landowners and the mestizo elite held political power far out of proportion to their numbers.

The conservative Odría party naturally supported this mestizo elite, and the APRA politicians, in order to maintain their anti-Belaúnde coalition, fell in line with this position. While many United States intellectuals continued to think of APRA as a powerful party of the democratic left—as indeed it had been 20 to 40 years earlier—in Peru, APRA came to be seen increasingly as a conservative or even as a reactionary party.

In the 1960s, the struggle for control of student bodies of the universities was generally fought among Stalinist, Trotskyite, and Maoist factions, with APRA rarely showing much voting strength. Government support of collective bargaining and APRA influence in government helped APRA to maintain a strong base with workers in industry and in coastal commercial haciendas, but the CTP was increasingly challenged by the Communist-led Confederación General de Trabajadores Peruanos (CGTP), which had gained strongholds particularly in the areas of banking and mining. APRA efforts to organize unions of peasants in the highlands came late, in response to inroads made by parties of the extreme left, and were generally ineffective. APRA had traditionally concentrated its attention on citizens with the vote and was ill prepared to deal with peasant movements that grew up largely outside of electoral politics.

LONG-RUN INFLUENCES
FAVORING PEASANT MOBILIZATION

After centuries of subjugation, punctuated by sporadic movements and uprisings that were put down by the authorities, in the 1950s and 1960s the peasants began to win lasting victories. How do we account for this change?

The general answer is that conditions had become more conducive to successful peasant militance in the following respects.

1. *Population Growth*. The conquest had a catastrophic effect upon the Indian population, which dropped so sharply that the Spaniards had to establish *reducciones* to force Indians to move into areas where their labor could be exploited.

    The population of what is now Peru was estimated at 8,285,000 in 1548. The 1795 population of 1,232,122 was little more than one-seventh of that recorded in 1548, and most of the decline is thought to have occurred within the first century of the conquest. Through the nineteenth century the population was growing at a slowly increasing rate, the numbers reaching approximately 3 million at the end of that period. In the twentieth century, growth continued at a greatly accelerated rate, the population going over 7 million in 1940 and over 11 million in 1961. The trends are shown in Figure 1-1.

17

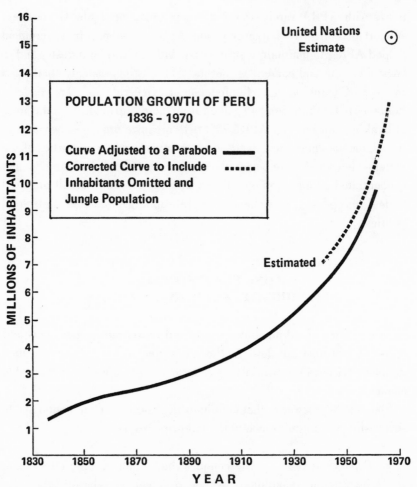

Source: David A. Robinson, *Peru in Four Dimensions*, Lima: American Studies Press S.A., 1964.

FIGURE 1-1

Through the nineteenth century, Peruvian rural areas remained underpopulated, which meant that in many areas land was available to anyone who would work it. As the twentieth century advanced, this situation steadily changed, and the pressures of man on land became especially severe as mid-century approached. Thousands of peasants in the 1950s and 1960s found themselves trying to support more people on less land than their fathers had utilized. Even if their input remained at the customary level, what they were getting out of the system had been reduced. The earlier exchange rate no longer prevailed.

2. *Education*. There has been a slow but steady trend toward increasing education in the highlands, and improved education is one of the first demands made by mobilizing peasants. Education tends to raise the individual's self-esteem. As he has learned Spanish, the Indian has become more capable of handling his relations with the outside world and therefore more able to escape from the monopoly of resources controlled by the *hacendados* (owners or renters of large haciendas). Education has also brought the peasant into closer touch with the "advantages" of modern urban life. All of these influences have tended to raise his level of aspirations and also his expectations as to what an acceptable exchange rate should be.

3. *Modern Communication*. Until recently, highland villages or haciendas without electricity were cut off from modern communications media. Although some newspapers might come in, few could read. The advent of the transistor radio produced a great leap in communications beyond the end of electric power lines. Even in the poorest villages, there was now likely to be at least one family with a transistor radio, and many other people in the community listened to it. Furthermore, programs were transmitted in the native languages of Quechua and Aymara, so that the monolingual Indian was included in the national system of communications. And Castro's Cuba transmitted its news and views by shortwave in Quechua. Thus, the Indian in the remote village became aware of events beyond his particular valley.

4. *Migration*. There are few highland communities without a significant number of inhabitants who have lived outside, not for brief visits but for months or even years. When migrants come home, they bring into the community the resources that can precipitate a shift in the distribution of power: money, information, and personal connections in urban centers.

5. *Occupational Differentiation*. The position of the hacendados was strongest when local society was made up predominantly of large landowners or renters and *colonos* (serfs) under their direct and enduring control and small farmers who had to hire themselves out to the hacendados from time to time in order to eke out a living for their families. As there came to be more merchants, traders, artisans, teachers, government officials, and even professional men,

19

the hacendados no longer had a monopoly on prestige and power. This did not mean that those practicing nonfarm occupations automatically allied themselves with the peasants. It did mean that the nonfarmers developed their own interests, which were different from those of hacendados or peasants. Thus, the peasants were at last in a position of competing with hacendados to win support beyond the ranks of those like themselves.

Although highland hacendados lost prestige and power in their local areas, their standing on the national scene may have suffered an even more serious decline. A 1960s study (Wils, 1975:157) found that industrial managers and entrepreneurs ranked hacendados from the sierra in 12th position in prestige, after bankers, industrialists, big traders, exporters, "modern professionals" (economists, engineers, scientists, business-administrators), "traditional professionals" (humanities, law), university professors, higher military, politicians, higher civil servants, and the clergy.

6. *Abdication of the Hacendados*. For generations, few hacendados had actually lived on their estates, but in earlier periods they had tended to make frequent visits to the land and to stay longer in the manor house. As communication and transportation between the countryside and the provincial cities and between those cities and Lima steadily improved, hacendados tended to lose interest in the land and to become more city-oriented. Their position on the countryside has been further undermined by the out-migration from the provincial towns of their natural allies, the leading mestizo families. In such towns, it is common to hear a mestizo say, "All the *gente decente* [respectable people] have moved away from here."

7. *Inflationary Pressures*. The traditional style of farm management did not yield increasing economic returns to keep pace with the rising cost of living. The hacendado did not spend much time on his hacienda, where the cost of living was relatively low. He and his family were committed to the "good things" of modern urban living, from education to entertainment to travel, and the price of those good things was constantly increasing.

When the hacienda no longer yielded the income necessary to maintain the status and style of life to which he had become accustomed, what could the hacendado do? He had just three alternatives:

1. He could try to squeeze more work out of the peasants.
2. He could sell the hacienda and invest the money in something else.
3. He could invest money in the hacienda to reorganize it in terms of "modern" scientific agriculture and farm-management methods.

The first strategy was likely to yield more increased peasant resistance than increased farm output. If he decided upon the second alternative, to whom could the hacendado sell? Long before the advent of the drastic agrarian reform program of the military government, the widespread increase of peasant pressures against landlords was making the purchase of haciendas a bad economic risk. Poor as they were, the peasants were emotionally attached to the land and were likely to be willing to pay the hacendado more for it than he could get from any other purchaser. If the hacendado sold to the peasants, the transformation of hacienda into community would thereby be accomplished.

We should note that the successful application of the modernizing strategy also brought about a drastic change in the social structure of the traditional hacienda. In other words, even before the government decreed the land reform of 1969, the large landowners or renters were encountering increasingly powerful forces that were making it impossible for them to maintain the hacienda in its traditional form.

cuzco II

Cuzco in the 3
Southern Highlands

We begin our exploration in a region where the pattern of dominance by the hacendado and the mestizo elite was firmly established, and yet even here we can see the beginnings of the breakdown of the monolithic power structure.

Cuzco is second only to the jungle department of Loreto in land area and remains a primarily rural region. The 1961 census showed that more than twice as many people lived in rural areas as in towns and cities.

The potato is the most important crop in Cuzco as a whole, followed by barley and corn, but the growing coffee production of the Convención valley has been an important factor in the social changes taking place there. Sheep have been the most important type of livestock, with the 1961 census recording 1,250,000 sheep, placing Cuzco in third position behind the department of Junín in the central highlands but far behind Puno to the immediate south, whose rural economy is dominated by sheep herding.

The capital city of Cuzco, with 87,750 people in 1961, had approximately 40 percent of the total urban population of the department. The areas or subregions with which we will be concerned vary greatly in their urban-rural population balance. In Paucartambo in 1961, the rural population outnumbered the urban by more than eight to one. In the province of La Convención, the proportion for that year was five to one. In the province of Calca, the proportion was somewhat less than four to one, and in the district of Sicuani in the province of Canchis, the proportion dropped to two to one. As we might expect, these proportions bore an important relationship to the position of the large landowners, who tended to be more dominant in areas of predominantly rural population. As we shall see in Chapter 9, even the psychological orientation of the mass of rural prople depended upon the distribution of rural population between haciendas and Indian communities. Where the hacienda population was close to 50 percent, as in Paucartambo, the large hacendados appeared to be all powerful; where the rural population was more evenly balanced between haciendas and small peasant villages, as in the district of Pisaq in the province of Calca, the system was somewhat more open; and where only 5 percent of the rural people lived on haciendas, as in the province of Canchis, the hacendados were in a much weaker position.

Although the hacendado might have appeared dominant during one time period, this did not necessarily mean that his position was impregnable. We will examine the shift of power away from the hacendado in all of these areas and will pay particular attention to the most striking change in La Convención, where a large area dominated by haciendas was transformed into peasant communities. We will follow three pathways of change: an evolutionary differentiation of the occupational structure (in Sicuani), peasant movements (particularly in the Convención valley but extending to other parts of the highlands), and an applied anthropology project (in Kuyo Chico in the district of Pisaq).

To study the rise of peasant power, we will need to establish a baseline from which to begin. From this baseline, we will describe the typical situation prevailing on haciendas and in peasant or Indian communities before the hacendados and their mestizo allies began losing their dominant position. No single description will be entirely accurate beyond the area on which it is based because there were local variations in the weight and types of peasant obligations and in the mechanisms of exploi-

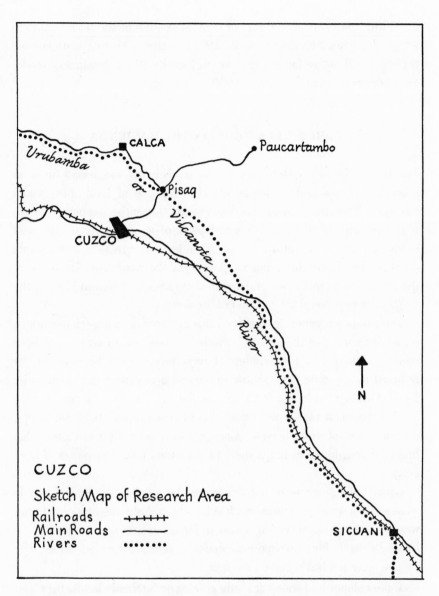

CUZCO

Sketch Map of Research Area
Railroads   +++++
Main Roads   ———
Rivers   ••••••••

tation, but the main features of the system were similar throughout Cuzco. The model of the extreme-dominance situation must also be placed in a time context. The model to be described applies to the 1950s for the Convención valley, the district of Pisaq, and the province of Paucartambo—in other words, for the period just before the beginning of peasant movements and of the applied anthropology project. Although we do not have the data to compare the Sicuani dominance model of

1900 with the 1950s model for our other areas, the historical information we do have on Sicuani (Orlove, 1975) suggests close parallels. We therefore will not go far wrong if we project the 1950s dominance model for other areas upon Sicuani in 1900.

LABOR RELATIONS ON THE HACIENDA

The labor-relations system of the typical hacienda was based upon an unwritten contractual exchange of labor for use of land, plus token payment. The hacendado owned or rented the entire property but allowed peasant families to use small parts of it, generally in the most unfavored areas, in return for labor under the direction of hacienda officials. The labor obligation was known as the *condición*: Those owing the condición were known under different terms in different parts of the sierra, but here we shall call them all *colonos*.

The condición generally involved at least three days a week of work by an adult member of the colono household, sometimes four days or even more. Furthermore, the number of days owed could be extended or reduced at any time through the unilateral decision of the hacendado. Beyond his right of land use for his own family, the colono received daily a token payment rarely more than 2 cents (in United States currency), plus a ration of coca leaves. (Coca chewing is a mild stimulant that highland people claim helps them to withstand cold and pangs of hunger.)

Labor obligations were not limited to the head of the household. In what was known as *ponguaje*, each colono household, on a rotating basis, was responsible for providing a woman for service for several days in the hacienda manor house or in the hacendado's home in the town or city. The women were fed but received no pay.

If the colonos had sheep or cattle grazing on hacienda lands, they were charged a fee per head and often were required to make a Christmas contribution of so much wool or other produce. If colono work involved cattle or sheep herding, colonos were required to make good the loss of any of the hacendado's animals from their own meager herds. If the colonos raised chickens or cattle, they were required to supply the hacendado's table with meat and eggs at a fraction of their market value.

There were a variety of other obligations that were imposed in some

28

places: for example, giving additional days of labor at harvest time for the whole family, delivering hacendado messages to distant points, or transporting the hacendado's produce on the colonos' own pack animals. For such services performed outside of the hacienda, the colono was given some corn and coca and a fraction of the money that the hacendado would have had to pay for labor not under his control.

The hacendado also controlled the marketing of the principal crops raised on colono plots and paid far below the market prices offered to peasants in communities. The hacendado also held a monopoly on the milling of the grain belonging to the colonos. Having little cash, the colonos generally had to buy where they could get credit—at the company store, with its inflated prices. The hacendado could also monopolize the growing of a crop that would give him a particular advantage over the colonos. For example, some Convención valley hacendados would not allow their colonos to grow sugar cane, so that the hacendados could maintain a monopoly on *aguardiente*, the flavored alcohol the hacendados sold in their company store.

Although according to law hacendados were required to provide schooling for the children of their laborers, few hacendados in the highlands did assume such a responsibility, and many took strenuous measures to discourage any peasant efforts to set up a school.

The hacendado rarely participated in the direction of the work. That responsibility was vested in an administrator who lived on the hacienda. Depending upon the size of the hacienda, there were several levels of authority below that of the administrator. For example, in Hacienda Chawaytirí in the district of Pisaq, the line of authority ran from administrator to *mayordomo* to *mandón* to *alcalde* to colonos. The mandón and alcalde were chosen by the colonos from among themselves—subject to the veto of the hacendado. As first line supervisor, the alcalde did not do manual labor himself but was responsible not only for directing the work and enforcing orders but also for collecting eggs, animals, and manure for the use of the hacendado. To help him maintain his authority, the administrator provided him each workday with two bottles of aguardiente to be apportioned among the colonos.

Poor as the colonos were, there were generally wide disparities from family to family in the amount of land in the family plots and the amount of cattle and sheep owned. These differences were not due simply to different degrees of diligence and efficiency among the colonos or their forefathers. Hacendados tended to play favorites, seeking to divide the work force by rewarding those who appeared to be particularly loyal to the hacendado.

At the height of hacendado domination, the dissatisfied colono had only one alternative: to leave the hacienda. But that meant giving up land, home, and animals without any compensation. If he and his fellow colonos sought to change conditions in the hacienda, and the hacienda officials could not overcome the protest, local political officials and the guardia civil (national police) were called in to put an end to the insubordination. Before a peasant leader could build much of a following, he was likely to meet with a mysterious and fatal accident.

Although the peasants in the villages and in the Indian communities were not subject to such direct and constant control as were the hacienda colonos, they were nevertheless at the bottom of a pervasive system of domination and exploitation. In the first place, few families in these communities had enough land to fully support themselves, so that they had to apply for work on the haciendas at harvest time and at other periods when the regular colono force could not get all the work done. For at least these days, they were subjected to the rigid discipline imposed on the colonos, although they did receive wages well above the colono token figure—and well below the legal minimum wage for the area.

As representative of the relationship between the mestizo elite and the Indian communities, we may summarize the description of the situation in the district of Pisaq (Núñez del Prado, 1973).

Although the large landowners of the area lived in the city of Cuzco, they worked with and through family relations and friendship ties with the political authorities in the district capital of Pisaq. Each Indian community elected its own *cabecilla* (head man), but the election was subject to the approval of the governor of the district, who could and did on occasion veto those cabecillas that he expected would not be properly submissive to the mestizo authorities. The cabecilla was responsible for carrying out the orders of the mestizo authorities. This involved particularly the once-a-week mobilization of all heads of households in a given community for the *faena* (donation of free labor) in and around Pisaq— including personal services in the homes of prominent mestizos. This obligation was rotated among the communities so that each community was responsible for one day of work a week and so that Pisaq was perpetually supplied with free labor.

The Pisaq justice of the peace and his assistants carried out judicial functions at the local level. The political authorities, such as the governor, the lieutenant governor, the police chief, and even the municipal officials, enforced the decisions of the local courts as well as those of the various superior courts. Núñez del Prado (1973:14–15) describes the local administration of justice in this way:

At the local level political officials went beyond the legal limits of their authority, as prescribed in the formal system of justice, and assumed a decision-making role as well as one of enforcement. Both they and the local judicial authorities displayed a great deal of favoritism in their decisions, which were influenced by the social class of the litigants, their economic situation, or their social ties with the authorities. Because these officials always expected to gain some benefit from a person involved or implicated in a case, it can be said that decisions were based on the way in which one supported economically those who made them. This attitude of expecting personal gain was due, in large part, to the fact that, with the exception of the police, the authorities in question were not paid by the state. The governor, lieutenant governor, mayor, and justices of the peace all had regular employment or professions in addition to their government posts. These posts provided sizable supplementary incomes. Since there was no regulation of the rates charged for their services, they charged in accord with the opportunities presented to them. When we arrived in the area, they were charging arbitrarily for personal inspections of problems, assessments, judicial dispositions which they received from higher courts, and so on. In strictly local cases involving concrete issues, the justices of the peace charged for contracts, records of transactions or agreements, and records of civil decisions, exacting money or personal services from the litigants. Even at the provincial level, a person who had been held in jail or needed some service would be required to do work in the homes of the authorities—if he was an Indian.

This system of arbitrary charges was supposed to be eliminated by a law requiring the giving of receipts, with the receipt books controlled by higher authorities. However, the law was not adhered to, and the arbitrary charges continued.

Beyond the centrally controlled system of forced labor, there were diffuse processes of exploitation. Many mestizos felt free to go to an Indian community, requisition a pig, a chicken, eggs, and other produce, and pay the Indian what they pleased, which was generally about

50 percent of what the Indian might receive in an open market. Vendors of kerosene, salt, sugar, and other staple necessities forced Indians to buy from them at inflated prices, often taking in return produce for which they paid cut-rate prices. Stores in Pisaq declined to accept money from Indians who came in to purchase such staples. This gave the storekeeper an opportunity to overprice his product and underprice the goods the Indian had to offer in exchange for it.

As Indians set out along the road to Pisaq to sell their produce in the Sunday market, they were often stopped by *alcanzadores,* who relieved them of the produce at about 50 percent of the market price.

There were also *enganchadores* who signed up Indian adults and even Indian children for work, particularly in the Convención valley, with contracts that greatly overstated the benefits to the Indians and understated their obligations. In any case, before the advent of the peasant movement, the Indian had no way of enforcing his contract. A number of public officials were involved in the *enganche* system, although such participation was prohibited by law, under threat of jail sentence and disqualification for public office.

The system of economic exploitation was supported by the ties of spiritual kinship in many cases. Many Indian families sought godparents for their children from among the mestizos or cholos of Pisaq. In his completely powerless position, the Indian felt that it was advantageous to have a relationship with a socially superior person, who might be called upon for help in time of need. In fact, this relationship tended to involve the Indian in further free services for a particular mestizo. It provided him little protection in the case of a major clash with political authorities, though it could provide some help in getting him out of jail on minor offenses. Mainly, the protection of the godfather was exercised against other Indians with whom the spiritual kinsman might have conflicts—thus further accentuating divisions among the Indians.

Finally, it should be noted that essential features of this system of exploitation, from the condición of the colonos to the forced faenas of the Indian communities, were illegal according to the laws and constitution of Peru. Under the old distribution of power, such laws were dead letters. In the following chapters, we shall see how the peasants changed the distribution of power so that they could breathe life into old laws and use them for their own liberation.

RACE AND SOCIAL CLASS

Although the original separation of Indians from Spaniards was determined along racial lines, now, more than 400 years after the conquest, there are few Peruvians who do not have some Indian blood. Stratification in mid-twentieth-century Peru must therefore be seen in social, cultural, and economic rather than in racial terms. Where class lines were most sharply drawn, as in Cuzco, we find at the top the mestizos who were the hacendados, business and professional men, and government employees who controlled or operated the machinery of government in rural areas. Generally, they had at least a high school education, and depending upon their wealth and contacts with the outside world, they wore more or less modern Western-style clothes. Where an indigenous language was widely spoken, they used it to communicate with the Indians.

At the bottom were the Indians: colonos on the haciendas, small farmers in the communities, unskilled laborers in the towns. If they had had any schooling, it had generally been only for a year or two—not enough to become literate in Spanish. Although they might know a few words of Spanish, they were essentially monolingual in the predominant indigenous language, Quechua or Aymara, which is spoken mainly in areas around Lake Titicaca in Puno. They wore hand woven fabrics in traditional styles.

In between the two extremes was a small but economically and culturally important segment known as cholos: people who had ceased being Indians but had not yet gained the status of mestizos. Generally, they had had three to a full six years of primary school. They were bilingual, though their written and spoken Spanish was not nearly as correct as that of the mestizos, and, within the hearing of mestizos, they tended to avoid speaking the indigenous language. (When a mestizo spoke to a cholo in an indigenous language, this was interpreted as a means of subordinating the cholo.) They farmed small to moderate-size plots, worked as small shopkeepers, artisans, truck or bus drivers, etc. If they held political office in the towns, their positions were at the bottom of the structure.

Generally, they sought to dress like the mestizos, but their clothes tended to be older and of less modern styles. If they wore any traditional Indian garb, it was the poncho worn when the weather was cold or rainy.

Although those classified as Indians, on the average, tended to have darker skins and more "Indian" features than did mestizos, there were many mestizos who, when appropriately clothed and put into an Indian setting, could pass for Indians. While individual social mobility for Indians in rural Peru was difficult, it was not impossible, and the rate of upward mobility has been increasing in recent years.

For the Indian, the main pathway to upward mobility has been education. If the child of an Indian family learned to speak, read, and write in Spanish, he had command of the most essential tool for social mobility; if he laid aside traditional clothing and found work in an occupation more prestigious and lucrative than subsistence farming, he came to be recognized as a cholo. If he went far enough in his education and in business or professional activities and dressed and acted in line with these achievements, he was recognized as a mestizo. But only a small minority were able to cross class lines in this way in the rural Peru of the mid-twentieth century.

While any generalizations of this sort are bound to be oversimplifications, it should be noted that our statements on culture and class apply particularly to the "classic" situation of sharply drawn social and cultural distinctions such as we found in Cuzco. For the same time period, the description holds for a large part of the southern highlands. For other areas in our studies—the Chancay valley on the western slopes of the Andes, the central highlands, and particularly the Mantaro valley—this description provides a poorer fit with economic and cultural realities. But in part this is what our book is all about: differences among areas in socioeconomic structure and cultural patterns and differences in stages of development. The classic situation is therefore an important point of departure, for it represents the most oppressive structure for the people at the bottom. We will be concerned with how they break out of this structure and also with the problems they encounter as they move into more open and fluid structures that offer them new possibilities but also new barriers to overcome.

The Opening Up of Sicuani 4

In 1876, the town of Sicuani was little different from several others in the province of Canchis. With an urban population of 2,299, it was only slightly larger than two other towns and a good deal smaller than Checacupe, with 3,175. In this era, the town itself was dominated by hacendados who lived in the rural areas surrounding it. The hacendados not only controlled their colonos on the land, but they also dominated the economic and political life of the town. The mestizo elite in the villages and towns got much of their work done through exploiting the peasants. Orlove (1975) reports that.

> Public work projects such as municipal buildings, roads, and irrigation canals were initiated and maintained with unpaid peasant labor, organized into faenas or public work groups by the village officials. The National government also delegated to the officials the responsibility of maintaining public order and apprehending criminals.

The local elite had a monopoly on grist mills located along the rivers and charged the peasants, who were either colonos or community members, for grinding their wheat, barley, and maize.

In 1897, the Southern Railway that extended from the coast through Arequipa and Puno reached Sicuani. The railroad was particularly important in opening up national and international markets for wool. Large buying and exporting firms began operating in Sicuani, and the number of local wool merchants grew.

The introduction of the wool traders reduced the peasants' dependence upon hacendados and provided them with potential political and economic allies.

Orlove (1975) analyzed the role of the traders in this way:

> In the first four decades of the century, the traders purchased nearly all the wool in the town of Sicuani itself. It was brought to them either by the producers themselves or by the traveling buyers in the punas. Peasant wool was somewhat more profitable, since the traders paid them lower prices than they paid the hacendados.
>
> The merchants had a stronger reason for favoring the peasants over the hacendados. The hacendados spent much of their money outside the area. The case of a member of the Aragón family, who sent his children to study in Paris, is extreme but not aberrant. Many hacendados took trips to Arequipa and Lima, where they purchased imported goods. They also maintained residences in those cities. By contrast, the peasant made purchases from the same merchants who received their wool; they bought sugar, aguardiente, tools, cloth, and many other small items. One reporter, concerned about a temporary scarcity of metal coins to which the peasants were still accustomed, stated [*La Verdad,* Sicuani newspaper, March 27, 1915]:
>
> > We know very well that . . . the Indians are those who sustained commercial activity, as in all the population of the interior, either as sellers of wool, leather and grain or as consumers of articles of primary necessity. . . . If the merchants don't come to an agreement to safeguard their own commercial life, within a short time . . . the people will suffer the most terrible consequences.

The hacienda system of forced unpaid labor was contrary to the interests of the traders in two respects. The traders needed some labor and had the cash to pay for it; they needed peasants in the market to buy their goods.

The reshaping of channels of commerce to the disadvantage of the hacendados was accompanied by the reshaping of social patterns, which

36

further favored the emerging power shift. Sicuani became the center of a number of clubs where traders from Arequipa mingled with local merchants, artisans, and government officials and schoolteachers. Men who moved around so actively needed places where they could meet each other, whereas the hacendados had no such day-to-day needs. Furthermore, their social relations were structured much more along family lines. Many of them were scattered geographically, so that it was not easy for them to come together at frequent intervals.

Although hacendados were, in the early stages of change, more numerous than traders, they were divided by suspicions based upon past conflicts over the boundaries of their estates.

The traders came to dominate local governments, so that local lawyers and politicians tended to side with them in conflicts with hacendados. Although the hacendados had been able to band together in the 1920s to get the military and political support to put down a peasant rebellion in a neighboring province, they were not organized so as to be able to stand in the way of the more gradual changes that steadily eroded their power.

The changes that we have followed through these decades transformed a stagnant rural village into a small but dynamic urban center. In fact, Sicuani became known as "the Huancayo of Cuzco." In the 1960s, Huancayo was a dynamic center of commerce in the central highlands, with a population many times larger than the approximately 11,000 population of Sicuani, but the little Cuzco city on the railroad and main Cuzco highway showed the same swarming activity up and down its main streets.

The Convención Valley 5
Movement

The peasant movement that swept through the department of Cuzco and into the department of Puno in the southern sierra had its origins in the Convención valley. It was a peasant movement led predominantly by peasants. Studies of other countries and other time periods have suggested the general conclusion that "peasant movements are not led by peasants." Although one of the most prominent leaders of the Convención valley movement, Hugo Blanco, did indeed come from a middle-class background, he did not enter the Convención valley scene until the movement was already well beyond the initial stages of its development.

THE SETTING

La Convención, together with the district of Lares of the province of Calca, lies on the eastern slopes of the Andes, in the valley beginning at the junction of Aobama and Urubamba rivers and ending in the northwest where the Urubamba flows into the Apurimac. The territory ranges in altitude from 17,000 feet down to about 1,600 feet. The terrain is highly uneven, with 82 percent of the land being located on slopes of 55 or more degrees. It is estimated that only slightly more than 8 percent of the land is fit for cultivation. The geographical area involved in the peasant movement was large: approximately 17,650 square miles, or roughly the combined sizes of Maryland and Delaware.

For most of its history, the Convención valley has been underpopulated in relation to its economic potential. Until 1881, the valley was made up entirely of haciendas. In that year, one hacendado gave away one-third of his property to be used to establish a town, which became Quillamba, the present provincial capital and now the most important city in the 60-mile-long valley. The creation of this independent town was an important step in the breaking up of the hacienda system, but the system was to survive for many decades more.

Indian migration into the valley from the highlands began early in the twentieth century, but a catastrophic malaria epidemic (1930–1934) left the valley largely stripped of its population. With the eradication of malaria in the 1940s, the population began to rise rapidly.

At the top of the structure were the hacendados, with land very unequally divided among them. Nine owners (4.3 percent of the total) each held lands of over 10,000 hectares. More than 57 percent of the territory was in their hands. One hacendado, Alfredo Romainville, owned 152,480 hectares. Sixty-six owners held lands of between 1,000 and 10,000 hectares, while eighty-eight owners held lands of from 50 to 10,000 hectares and twenty-five owners had plots small enough that they could work themselves.

The hacendados worked the land through colonos, called in the valley *arrendires*, who held plots that averaged 8.8 hectares, far larger than the plot available to the average colono in more thickly populated parts of the sierra. In fact, in order to meet his obligations to the hacendado and get his own work done, the arrendire turned over part of his land to *allegados*, who utilized plots averaging 1½ hectares. (One hectare = 2.47 acres.)

A government report for 1957 estimated per capita production in La Convención at 1,357 soles per year compared with an annual average for Cuzco as a whole of only 260 soles. The problem therefore was not a lack of resources but a highly unequal distribution of these resources.

39

The government also found that the development of the social infrastructure had fallen far behind economic expansion. In a report written in 1962 and published years later, then Lieutenant Colonel Enrique Gallegos Venero of the intelligence services of the army found that "78% of the population shows symptoms of nutritional deficiencies and anemia, which gives rise to a high incidence of tuberculosis" (Gallegos, 1973.)

The report found that 85 percent of the peasants were living in one- or two-room straw shacks without ventilation. Gallegos also found that less than 40 percent of the potential pupils were enrolled in primary schools and that high school education was available only to the relatively few young people who lived in Quillabamba.

THE STRUCTURE OF THE HACIENDA

The traditional Peruvian hacienda is often compared to the feudal manor. There are indeed important similarities with the social system of medieval Europe, but there are also important differences, as Fioravanti (1974) points out.

In medieval Europe, the lord of the manor owed allegiance to higher-ranking nobles, and they in turn owed allegiance to the king. No such unified chain of linkages existed in Peru. The important hacendados had almost absolute powers within their lands and owed allegiance to no one above them. They did indeed strive to build important political connections in the capitals of the department and of the nation, but they were not directly subordinate to any intermediate levels of nobles.

On the feudal manor, the lord acknowledged certain obligations to take care of his serfs and help them in time of need. The Peruvian hacienda system appears to have shown very little in the way of paternalistic obligations.

There was a further difference of considerable importance. The medieval manor was largely a self-sustaining unit that had little commerce with the outside world. Although the sierra haciendas in most cases were highly inefficient economic units, they provided crops that were sold in the market.

The hacienda system in the Convención valley was based upon a fixed-term contract between the hacendado and his arrendire. The contract was generally for five years, never for more than ten. Although it was customary to renew the contract at the end of each period, the arrendire had no legal claim on this renewal, nor did he have any right to compensation for improvements he had made on the property which would add to its value for another arrendire. He was thus kept in a position of insecurity and dependence.

The heavy labor obligations imposed upon the arrendire made it impossible for him to cultivate his own land without subcontracting parts of it to allegados, who thereby assumed part of the arrendire's labor obligations to the hacendado. For example, let us assume that the arrendire owed 200 days of work per year to the hacendado (which was somewhat less than the average). He would then offer parts of his plot to four allegados, receiving in return 100 days of work from each of them. In this way he could provide from the allegados his 200 days' obligation for the hacendado and retain 200 days for himself. When the allegado became too hard pressed to meet his work obligations, especially at harvest time, he could further subcontract, establishing a sub-allegado on a plot of his land.

Although this suggests the possibility of the arrendire fulfilling work obligations to the hacendado without himself doing any work, and in fact, some hacendados tried to depict the arrendire as the real exploiter of the peasants, Hugo Blanco (1972) argues that very few arrendires were in such advantageous positions. We should note that the possibilities of shifting obligations from arrendire to allegado were limited by the amount of land available to the arrendire. Unless he began with a plot a good deal larger than average, he could raise the amount of labor to meet his condición only through subcontracting out such large fractions of his own land as to drastically reduce his income.

The arrendires in many cases were not allowed to construct an adobe house or install a calamine roof, because this would seem to confirm their right to permanent possession of the land. In some cases, they were forbidden to use shoes or clothing purchased from stores, since doing this would give them the feeling that they were rising above their place in society. On some haciendas, the tenants were forbidden to use money, so they could make purchases only in the scrip used within the hacienda. There were also prohibitions against learning to read, write, or speak Spanish and against sending children to schools outside of the valley. The newspaper *El Sol* of Cuzco reported in April 1962 the case of an hacendado who had notified all of the peasants who could read and write that they would have to leave the hacienda. Ignorance was especially valued by the hacendados of the valley. Such requirements and restrictions varied somewhat from hacienda to hacienda, with Alfredo Romainville, the largest landowner, also having the reputation as being the toughest on his colonos.

THE VALLEY AGRICULTURAL ECONOMY

Fioravanti (1974:73) gives the figures for social characteristics and size of land holdings for arrendires and allegados shown in Table 5-1.

TABLE 5-1
Land Tenure of Colonos in 1975 (Averages)

	SIZE OF HOLDING, HA	YEARS IN VALLEY	AGE	NO. OF CHILDREN	PERCENT LITERATE
Arrendires	8.8	28	42	3.3	50
Allegados	1.5	20	35	2.2	45

Fioravanti estimates that the sub-allegados each cultivated an average of 0.30 hectares. The agricultural system of the valley required the use of hired agricultural labor in two categories: *habilitados* hired for just two to three months for the harvest and *tiapacocs,* year-round laborers, who received food and wages (below the legal minimum).

In 1961, there were in the Convención valley approximately 3,000 arrendires, 8,000 allegados, and a total of 7,000 of the two types of agricultural laborers.

The hacendados and arrendires gained their incomes in quite different ways. Fioravanti estimates that the hacendado depended less upon income from the sale of his own crops than he did upon income from the buying and selling of the crops grown on arrendire and allegado plots and the operation of the company store. The arrendires were almost entirely dependent upon income from their own crops. This situation naturally led the arrendires, compared with the hacendados, to make greater investments in their own land and to strive more for efficient production.

Fioravanti provides figures for only one hacienda, but these figures are based on a very intensive study, and the differences are so large as to suggest that the same trends would be found in other haciendas. In the hacienda he studied, Fioravanti estimated that the arrendire had invested almost three times as much money per hectare of usable land as had the hacendado. On an annual basis, the arrendires were investing more than six times as much as the hacendado per cultivated hectare. The greater efficiency in the arrendires' farm operations was reflected in a coffee crop per hectare 15 percent greater than that of the hacendado.

Although the arrendires were poor by United States standards, they were not operating largely outside of the money economy, as has often been said of highland peasants. They had a substantial stake in the Convención valley economy, and they directed their struggle toward protecting and improving this stake.

As the peasant movement got under way, the arrendires were less concerned over money income than over security. As coffee growing had expanded in the valley and as sharp price rises had made coffee much more profitable, hacendados had begun to reclaim lands they had contracted to arrendire.

CONTROL BY FORCE

Their political and judicial positions gave the hacendados a monopoly on the use of physical force either by their agents, the police, or by themselves. The largest landowner, Alfredo Romainville, was known among the peasants as "the monster of La Convención." Hugo Blanco (1972: 94–95) describes some of the atrocities in these words:

> The gamonal [exploitive landlord] Alfredo Romainville strung up a naked peasant to a mango tree and, among other things, flogged him all day in the presence of his own daughters and other peasants. Another peasant could not find the horse his master had told him to find. Romainville forced him down on all fours, ordered him to put on the horse's harness, and compelled him to haul six arrobas (150 pounds) of coffee; he made him travel in this fashion, on hands and knees, around the patio, where the coffee was dried, lashing him with a whip. He forced the women to shell peanuts without pay until their hands bled, and then with their mouths until those were bloody too. He had his own daughter, born of a peasant woman he had raped, jailed as a "communist." His brother was not satisfied with raping the peasant women himself—he forced a peasant at gunpoint to rape his own aunt.

The landlord Marquez took the children borne by the women he had raped and drowned them in the river. With a hot cattle branding iron, the landlord Barolomé Paz seared into the buttocks of a peasant the emblem of his hacienda. The landlord Anzel Miranda did likewise. . . .

These crimes were not punished by the authorities—who were very often the landlords themselves. The judges and the police participated in these crimes and protected the perpetrators. That is the real social context in which we agitators were "disturbing the peace" and "advocating violence."

For our purposes, it is not important to know whether these accounts by Blanco are accurate in every detail. There is abundant evidence regarding the widespread use of physical force by the hacendados, and the peasants themselves had enough experience so that they could well believe the reports they heard regarding the "monster of La Convención" and other cruel landlords. (It should be noted that Blanco worked and organized on an hacienda owned by Alfredo Romainville, so he was likely to have heard about the atrocities directly from people who had experienced or witnessed them.)

THE WEAKENING OF HACENDADO CONTROL

The weakening of hacendado control accompanied the increasing integration of La Convención into the economy of the nation through improvements in transportation and the growth of coffee production. Although the first commercial center, Quillabamba, was founded in 1881, the Convención valley was isolated from the rest of Peru until well into the twentieth century. The railroad from Cuzco reached Huadquina at the entrance to the Convención valley in 1951. A road connected Quillabamba with Huadquina.

This opening of transportation routes stimulated population growth and economic activities. The 1940 census showed a population of 27,243, and the 1961 population had more than doubled to a figure of 60,894.

Economic growth manifested itself particularly in coffee production. In earlier years, primarily coca, tea, and sugar cane had been grown. In most of Peru, the best agricultural land is relatively flat land along a river, so the hacendados naturally reserved this land for themselves and contracted out the slopes to the arrendires. Since coffee requires a combination of sunlight and shade, most readily supplied on hillsides, the hacendados discovered when the coffee boom began that they had turned over their most valuable lands to the peasants.

The peasants found that they could get into coffee production gradually, with small investments, and without taking any of their land out of production of other crops. They generally planted coffee between rows of corn or other more traditional crops, eliminating those crops only when the coffee bushes reached bearing age.

The peasants' shift of crops was carried out during a period of an extraordinary rise in coffee prices. Table 5-2 shows that between 1945 and 1954, the amount of coffee produced more than doubled while the price per kilo rose approximately twelvefold.

TABLE 5-2
Coffee Production and Prices, 1945–1954

	KILOGRAMS PRODUCED	PRICE PER KILOGRAM, S/.*	VALUE OF PRODUCTION, S/.*
1945	583,252	1.21	705,000
1954	1,308,349	14.77	19,300,000

*S/. is the abbreviation for "soles."
Source: Craig (1967:32–33).

As late as 1954, 36.1 percent of the cultivated land in the valley was devoted to coca as against only 13.8 percent devoted to coffee. By 1961, the coca area had grown only slightly, to 4,329 hectares, but the coffee area had experienced a sixfold increase, to 9,749 hectares.

While hacendados and colonos were rapidly expanding areas of coffee cultivation, coffee prices experienced a sharp and continuing decline in the world market. The export price of Peruvian coffee was $1,504.70 per ton (in United States currency) in 1954 and had dropped to $669.60 per ton in 1961 (see Figure 5-1). This drop of slightly over 55 percent from the peak year price meant that a sixfold increase in production from 1954 to 1961 yielded only about a 2.7-fold increase in income. But note that the sixfold coffee increase figure is for the valley as a whole. Probably, only a small proportion of this increase was accounted for by arrendires and allegados adding to the coffee acreage that they had cultivated

45

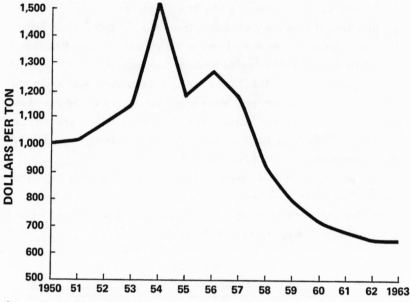

Sources: Cuentes Nacionales del Peru 1950–1967; Banco Central de la Reserva.

FIGURE 5-1

Peruvian Coffee Prices, 1950–1963

in 1954. The bulk of the increase was accounted for by the establishment of new arrendire and allegado plots and by the extension of the hacendados' coffee acreage. Thus, we can assume that most of the arrendires and allegados operating in the valley in 1954 experienced a substantial decline in their income in the succeeding years.

It seems significant that the rise of the peasant movement corresponded so closely with the decline of coffee prices from 1954 to 1961. By 1954, the peasants had gained an important stake in the economic system of the valley. Had prices continued to rise or had they remained at the same level, the peasants might have seen possibilities of maintaining and improving their position without changing their relationships with the hacendados. The large and continuing decline of prices from 1954 to 1961 made clear to them that they could hope to progress only through making basic changes in these relationships.

The rise in coffee production and prices made it impossible for the hacendados to retain their control over marketing. In the early 1940s, the first middlemen, known as *rescatistas*, began making clandestine contacts with peasants. The rescatistas lent money to the peasants against the crop and then purchased the crop from them, thus undermining the economic monopoly of the hacendados.

There was also a serious internal weakness of the hacendado position within the valley, as noted by Wesley Craig (1967:48):

Contributing to the inability to adjust to changes was the fact that many hacendados were over fifty-five years of age, including a number of widows who were still trying to run the hacienda. Few of the older children appeared to be staying on the farm. Most had been educated at better schools in the Cuzco area and were reluctant to return to agricultural work in the valley, although some were moving into Quillabamba, where they were active as professionals or in business.

Furthermore, when the showdown came there were 10,000 peasants on the voting lists, and few of them were any longer controlled by the hacendados.

UNION ORGANIZATION:
THE FIRST PHASE

The first union local was formed in 1947 at Maranura, an hacienda of 2,049 hectares with 100 arrendires each working 5.3 hectares and 200 allegados each with 1.2 hectares. A former teacher and small merchant, who had become an arrendire, was the first secretary-general of the first union. The union's first demands were as follows:

1. An eight-hour workday
2. The right to sell produce direct, bypassing the hacendado
3. Payment in cash rather than in scrip or credits at the company store
4. Exemption of women from heavy farm work
5. Construction of a school

In 1948, the colonos at Maranura gained the eight-hour day simply by stopping work after eight hours. This was the first example of successful collective resistance in the Convención valley. Also in 1948, the hacendado conceded the colonos right to sell their produce outside of the hacienda, and in 1949 they got the right to build a school. The record

47

does not show the hacendado making any contribution to the project, but presumably he made available the small plot of ground on which the peasants built the school. The union was dissolved in the 1950–1951 period, a casualty of the Odría repression. It was reestablished in 1957, shortly after the end of Odría's term of office.

Around 1950, some peasants sought help from outside the valley, approaching the Communist-led Federación de Trabajadores del Cuzco. At first the FTC leaders were reluctant to get involved, since their ideology did not allow for revolutions being promoted through peasant mobilization; and it is not clear what role they played in the organization of the second union local, at Mandor-Manawañunqha in 1951.

This was an hacienda of 4,224 hectares devoted primarily to coca. The total number of workers, in all categories, came to 258, with the arrendires each having between 3 and 5 hectares, the allegados each less than 1 hectare, and the suballegados each 1/3 hectare. On this hacienda, the peasants had been free to sell their produce in the market but had been denied, in their individual contracts, the right to organize so as "to avoid conflicts which would be harmful to both parties" (Fioravanti, 1975:153). In 1952, the Odría government officially recognized this union. The policy makers had not changed their ideas about unions in general but apparently saw some advantage in favoring one led by Communists so as to weaken the APRA-led CTP.

In 1952, the union demanded the eight-hour day, freedom of association, and a reduction in the number of work days. Mediation meetings were held in the office of the inspector of labor in Cuzco. The hacendado agreed to the eight-hour day, recognized the union, but refused to change the condición. In 1958, the hacendado granted land for school construction. A strike in 1960 eliminated the *palla* obligation of wives to work on the harvest and gained a first aid station but brought no increase in pay. Furthermore, the secretary-general of the union local was obliged to assume responsibility for the work obligations of the peasants.

In late 1954 or early 1955, the FTC established a Secretariat for Peasant Affairs to provide information and assistance on grievances, and in 1957 and 1958, the FTC sent in organizers to assist in establishing unions, which were soon to appear in eight or nine haciendas.

A breakthrough in this organization drive occurred on the hacienda Santa Rosa. This breakthrough was particularly important because it represented the first penetration into the territory of the hated Alfredo

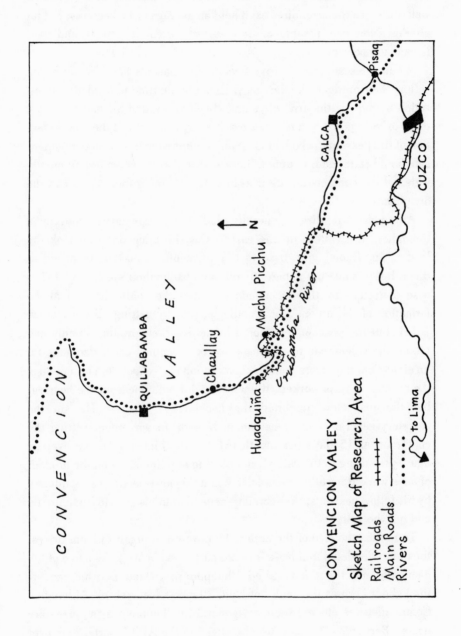

CONVENCION VALLEY

Sketch Map of Research Area

Railroads ┼┼┼┼┼┼
Main Roads ─────
Rivers ∙∙∙∙∙∙∙∙

to Lima

CONVENCION

VALLEY

QUILLABAMBA

Chaullay

Machu Picchu

Huadquiña

Urubamba River

CALCA

CUZCO

Pisaq

N

49

Romainville. Santa Rosa was an hacienda of 11,500 hectares producing coca, coffee, peanuts, and achiote. Here the peasants were relatively well off, since the arrendires each held an average of 17 hectares, but for all this economic advantage, they suffered great insecurity and tight hacendado control.

When the organization drive began, the peasants had already begun selling their produce clandestinely. Romainville tried to head off unionization by moving the arrendires and allegados around his hacienda, but this worked against him in two ways. It sharply increased the dissatisfaction of the peasants, who had to abandon improvements without compensation and start again in unfamiliar areas, and at the same time it greatly widened the contacts among peasants, thus helping them to spread the organization.

Although arrendires generally led the organization movement throughout the valley, in this case it was the allegados who took the leadership. Romainville tried to buy them off by making them arrendires, but this attempt apparently did not change their views. In 1957, a case of torture by the hacendado provided the spark that led to the formation of the union. Romainville reacted by getting all the leaders jailed, but the peasants countered by selling their produce openly and taking their demands to the inspector of labor in Cuzco: demands for an eight-hour day, more money, construction of a school, and reduction of the number of days worked. Romainville did not appear for the hearing, but the inspector supported the hacendado's wishes. He got the secretary-general of the local union to sign an agreement setting the condición at 15 days per month (which was higher than the average figure prevailing in the valley), not placing any limitation on the number of days worked for other programs. When this agreement was repudiated by his fellow peasants, the secretary-general sold his crop to Romainville and left the valley.

To reduce the size of the area to be covered in organizational drives, the union divided Santa Rosa into two parts, one bearing the name of the hacienda and the other called Chaupimayo (which became famous throughout Peru as the center of Hugo Blanco's leadership). Although a Communist was elected secretary-general in Chaupimayo, an arrendire named Bernardino Roman, who belonged to the APRA party, took over the leadership in Santa Rosa. Roman agreed with Romainville on new terms under which all members would sign *individual* contracts with the

50

hacendado under conditions that appeared harsh to the peasants. There followed a confrontation between groups of peasants from the locals of Santa Rosa and Chaupimayo, with heated debate that ended with the Santa Rosa peasants tearing up their individual contracts and declaring themselves on strike, along with their fellow peasants in Chaupimayo, on November 7, 1957. When this major stronghold was lost, the APRA effort to assume leadership of the peasant movement was on the wane, and by the time of the critical events of 1962, APRA was no longer important in the struggle.

In September of 1957, leaders of 15 locals, representing 1,500 peasants, met to form a labor federation (La Federación Provincial de Campesinos de la Convención y Lares). The federation also sent a plea to the government for expropriation of the haciendas in favor of the peasants. 1957 therefore marks the first public mention of expropriation, which became the chief peasant goal at the height of the movement. At this first federation meeting, five of the eight offices, including the three most important, were won by pro-Communists, the others being independents.

Peasant Victory and 6
Government Intervention

Although Hugo Blanco did not enter the Convención valley until 1958, he played a major role in the rapid expansion of the movement and was clearly the most prominent and influential leader at the height of the movement, during the 1960–1962 period. His name was the only one that became generally known in mass media reports on the Convención valley movement; and to thousands of peasants inside the valley and all through the department of Cuzco, Hugo Blanco became, in his lifetime, a legendary figure, endowed with supernatural powers.

Hugo Blanco was born in 1935 of middle-class parents in the province of Paruro in the department of Cuzco. His father was a lawyer, and his mother was of peasant origin. The young man went to high school in Cuzco and spent his school vacations in rural Paruro, where his father had become a judge. Blanco's father was a dedicated APRA party member with strong sympathies for the exploited Indian population. The father had become a close friend of Lorenzo Chamorro, who had led a peasant protest against the hacendado of San Jeronimo, about 10 kilometers from the city of Cuzco. In this abortive effort, Chamorro was shot and made an invalid for life. The disabled peasant leader had plenty of time to talk about peasant problems. Young Hugo became very close to him and later openly acknowledged Chamorro's influence upon him.

In 1954, Blanco went to Argentina to study agronomy at the University of La Plata, where he became a political activist and a Trotskyite. Blanco left the university to work in a factory and became an active unionist. At the end of 1956, he returned to Cuzco as a member of the Trotskyite party, Partido Obrero Revolucionario (POR). In his first organizing effort in Peru, he established a union among children eight to fifteen years old who sold newspapers in Cuzco. Then in Lima, he found work in the construction industry and was again active in union affairs. In 1958, POR sent Blanco back to Cuzco, where he immediately became involved in a general strike that paralyzed the city for four days.

The strike led to Blanco's first arrest and to a turning point in his career. During two months in jail, the young urban organizer had long discussions with peasant leaders from the Convención valley.

Upon his release, Blanco immediately went into the Convención valley to become an allegado to an arrendire from Chaupimayo. Blanco was soon elected to the top union position of secretary-general in Chaupimayo. From this base, he became active in the peasant federation and soon won support of local leaders, particularly in the haciendas where he led successful organization drives. As Blanco's influence grew in the federation, he became recognized as the leader of a Trotskyite faction opposed to the Communist leadership that he perceived as being too timid and too dedicated to social reform rather than revolution.

The 1959 election for federation leadership provided the first show of strength of the Blanco faction, with Andrés Gonzalez from Chaupimayo being elected to the key position of secretary-general. Now with 40 locals and 5,500 members, in a two-year period the federation had more than doubled its number of locals and almost quadrupled the organized peasant population.

Although from this point on there were contending factions within the federation, the reformists (Communists) and the radicals (supporters of Blanco), the movement continued to grow rapidly so that at its height in 1961–1962 it was composed of 122 locals with 12,500 members.

Who were the local union leaders? Although we have no figures for the movement as a whole, Fioravantí checked characteristics of these individuals for 11 haciendas that he studied in detail. Of the 50 local leaders, 80 percent were arrendires; 18 percent, allegados; and 2 percent (1 individual), a peón or laborer. Whereas Craig's earlier work (1967) suggested that a disproportionate number of the local union leaders were Protestants, in this 50-man sample Fioravanti found only three Protestants and one atheist (Hugo Blanco), the others being all at least nominal Catholics. Only 24 percent had been born in La Convención or Lares, but this figure is not significantly different from that for the peasant population as a whole.

As Table 6-1 indicates, Fioravanti found a strikingly consistent relationship between size of hacienda and percent of unionization: the union was markedly more successful in the larger properties.

Fioravanti also found a relationship between the size of arrendire parcels and the extent of unionization—but with one important exception. As Table 6-2 indicates, the union was more successful where the arrendires had smaller parcels and therefore were in an especially disadvantageous position, except in the extreme case of Santa Teresa, where the arrendires each had parcels averaging 17 hectares and yet the district was 100 percent organized. We should note that Santa Teresa was made up of four large haciendas, all owned by Alfredo Romainville, "the monster of La Convención." Furthermore, Hugo Blanco settled in this district, and he was instrumental in extending unionization throughout the four haciendas.

The meetings of union locals were carried out in an open and democratic manner. The general assembly was the final authority and was required to vote on any important decision. Attendance of all members was

TABLE 6-1
Size of Hacienda and Percent Unionized

SIZE, HA	PERCENT UNIONIZED
Over 5,000	100
500 to 5,000	80
100 to 500	61
50 to 100	25
Under 50	8

TABLE 6-2
Size of Arrendire Parcel and Percent Unionized

DISTRICT	SIZE, HA	PERCENT UNIONIZED
Maranura	3.3	100
Huayopata	4.7	86
Santa Ana	4.9	67
Lares	10.2	65
Echarete	8.0	65
Santa Teresa	17.0	100

obligatory, with a fine equal to one-half day's pay being levied for unjustified absence. At the opening of each meeting, the members elected a *director de debate* (moderator), who could be any member. The assembly then elected a secretary of discipline, who was responsible for seeing that everyone had a right to speak, that people paid attention, that nobody left the meeting without permission, and so on. The next step was to establish an agenda. Any peasant could propose any personal or collective problem. These items were listed on a blackboard, and members would vote to establish the order of importance of items, which determined the sequence to be followed. Next, officers would open the meeting with a general report on the situation and activities during the preceding week. When a peasant spoke from the floor, he was listened to in silence, being applauded or rebutted at the end of his remarks.

The weekly meetings lasted from five to eight hours. For the first time the peasant could speak openly and publicly and be listened to in respectful silence. After living through such a participatory experience, peasants could hardly relapse into passivity and timidity.

Local officers were elected annually in a meeting of the assembly but could be replaced at any meeting by a majority vote. In addition to secretary-general, there were secretaries for organization, defense, interior, recordkeeping, economy and finance, cooperatives, technical and statistical matters, the women's movement, and culture and sports and the treasurer. There were more officers than was strictly necessary, but it was union policy to spread leadership experience as much as possible. Nominations were made from the floor, and voting was done by raising of hands.

At the height of the movement, the local unions became, in effect, the local governments. Furthermore, the union developed such cohesion and strength as to block interventions from the national government.

During this period, Hugo Blanco quite explicitly planned and acted in terms of his theory of dual power: the state would support the hacendados, but the unions would establish their own control at the level of the hacienda and would even arm themselves for defense. Although this extreme militancy was rejected by the Communist leaders, who feared that it would provoke government repression, Blanco established a school for revolutionary unionism at Chaupimayo, where leaders supporting Blanco came from all over the valley for courses on unionism, agricultural problems, and military tactics. Chaupimayo formed the base for a peasant militia, which was a short of armament but full of enthusiasm. The peasant militia was linked with Frente de Izquierda Revolucionaria (leftist revolutionary front, FIR), which was an outgrowth of POR in a fusion with other radical splinter parties. However, these political linkages existed largely on paper. The heart of the FIR movement was the peasants in the Convención valley.

With Chaupimayo again in the vanguard, the peasant locals moved from collective bargaining to direct action to take over the land. Speaking for his federation, Hugo Blanco decreed an agrarian reform, whose principles were printed and widely circulated in Cuzco in pamphlet form. At Chaupimayo, the arrendires and allegados assumed direct ownership of their plots. The landlord's fields and buildings became collective property of the union. Uncultivated land was turned over to anyone who was prepared to work it.

Blanco (1972:59) further describes the political processes in this way:

> We formally named judges to replace the bourgeois authorities (their decisions were subject to appeal before the General Assembly).
>
> The police came very rarely, but communicated with the union with proper advance notice. For example: "We have an order to arrest so-and-so, we are going to come on such and such a day; to spare us embarrassment, kindly see that on that day the above-named persons are not at home." . . .
>
> We built our schools ourselves and paid the teachers hired by us and certified by the Ministry of Education. Public works were in the hands of the union, which determined their priority.
>
> All of this, of course, was backed by an embryonic armed force, the developing peasant militia.

On several occasions, the unions showed that they had the power to overrule the actions of the official authorities. A key instance occurred when an hacendado sought to evict Vega Caboy, a nonunionized arrendire on Hacienda Aranjuez. The hacendado won the case in court in Cuzco and again won when the decision was appealed in the Supreme Court. According to Blanco, the Communist leaders at this point assumed that nothing could be done and blamed Caboy for hiring APRA lawyers instead of lawyers representing the union federation. Since other evictions were in process, Blanco (1972:49) felt that this had to be made a test case. As he describes it,

> We issued a fairly good resolution—good enough to frighten the functionaries whose task it was to carry out the eviction, so that they all began to decline the job on various excuses. For the first time in a case like this the gamonal was heard muttering, "There is no justice for me!" The eviction was called off.

Blanco goes on to describe the union resistance to police power:

> Besides the pressure put on the court by the mass mobilizations, there were several occasions on which the masses actually freed prisoners. Chaupimayo by itself freed Comrade Fortunato Vargas on one occasion and me on another; these actions came as a consequence of night marches by the union members en masse to the police station where Vargas was held prisoner, in the first instance, and in the other, to the highway where they stopped and searched all passing vehicles including the one in which I was being transported.

In response to the work stoppage in the area controlled by the Chaupimayo union, Blanco (1972:64–65) describes the following events:

> The fury of one of the gamonales led him to set out armed to attack the peasants; after evading the landowner they decided to relieve him of his weapon. After the Chaupimayo people returned to their own locale, another incident occurred, this time with a policeman in the town of Santa Maria. The result was identical—the peasants took away the weapon.
>
> Their return was ecstatic, triumphal; the secretary of the women's front and a militant comrade, walked around with the policeman's cap on her head and his rifle slung over her shoulder. . . .
>
> The strength and pressure of the Stalinists in the Federation obliged us to return the weapon to the police, to avoid a severe repression. We have still not returned the weapon to the gamonal.

57

During this tense period, Blanco reports two attempts on his life by hacendados. The peasants protested to the police but were informed that the landlords had a right to bear arms in order to defend themselves. This response served to accelerate the growth of the peasant militia.

The peasant unions showed their militancy throughout the valley first in 24- and 48-hour work stoppages. As Blanco (1947:47) points out, work stoppages of this duration had no effect on work within the hacienda, which could simply be postponed:

> In view of this, the peasant work stoppage was a stoppage of transportation, of industrial and commercial activities, etc., throughout the province; the total paralysis imposed by the peasantry organized in picket lines. . . .
>
> It was on these occasions that the peasants felt their own power most forcefully. Even the office of the sub-prefect, the highest political authority in the province, had to shut down. Even personal travel from one place to another was carried out only with the permission of the peasants.

The next stage, in 1961, was a general strike that lasted for two months and, according to Blanco, was terminated only because the Communist leaders feared that a continuing strike would bring on severe political repression.

The peasants did not stop with strikes. There followed a general movement to occupy hacienda lands. At the height of this movement, most of the hacendados fled, seeking shelter and help in Cuzco. The Convención valley was effectively under the control of the Peasant Federation of Cuzco.

The peasant movement swept beyond the Convención valley and into the valleys of the department of Cuzco west of the Andes. The departmental Peasant Federation of Cuzco was formed in 1961, under supporters of Blanco. At the height of its activities, it had organized 600 unions throughout the department.

These organizing efforts throughout the department were accompanied by periodic mass meetings in the city of Cuzco, regarded by peasant leaders as the center for repression of the Indians and a location where humble and submissive behavior had been called for. Blanco (1972:47) describes the importance of these mass meetings in this way:

> The mass meeting put the Indian on top of the monster. A concentration of ponchos in the main plaza, the heart of the city. At the court on the cathedral

portico, which dominates the plaza like a rostrum. The odor of coca and quechua, permeating the air. Quechua, out loud from the throat; Quechua shouted, threatening, carrying away the centuries of oppression. A march down the main streets, before and after the meeting. Windows and doors of the powerful fearfully slammed shut at the advance of the multitudes, aggressive, insulting, threatening, shouting in Quechua truths silenced by centuries of Castilian Spanish. The Indian, master of plazas and streets, the entire street and the sidewalk. That's what peasant meetings meant, aside from the specific object for each gathering.

ATTEMPTS TO COUNTER PEASANT POWER

At the height of the peasant movement, the hacendados had completely lost their control over the marketing of peasant produce. They had also lost the battle to deprive peasant children of education. When the peasants built schools and even raised money to pay teachers, the Ministry of Education granted de facto recognition of the peasant unions by sending certified teachers to these schools. Even the then conservative government could not support the unconstitutional policy of denying education to peasant children. The hacendados continued to win court cases against peasants, but the unions had demonstrated their power to prevent court-ordered evictions.

The hacendados appealed to their elected representatives and the national administration to provide them with police and military forces. The government responded instead by sending a fact-finding mission to the valley. The fact finder submitted to the Ministry of Labor and Indigenous Affairs an extensive report that ended with recommendations that the government institute a land reform program to expropriate hacendado properties in favor of the peasants. The report was never publicly released, but the peasants did not fail to note that the hacendados had appealed for the use of force and the government had failed to respond.

During this period, the military had its own channels for gathering information in the Convención valley. This is well documented by the report of then Lieutenant Colonel Enrique Gallegos Venero (1973), who headed a military-intelligence group in the area. The report is noteworthy for two reasons. In the first place, it demonstrates that the military-intelligence officials had accurate and detailed knowledge regarding social and economic conditions in the valley and regarding the structure of relations between hacendados and peasants. In the second place, the Gallegos report is written with obvious sympathy for the peasants, depicting them as an oppressed people exploited by the hacendados. Military-intelligence officers were seeking a solution that would favor the peasants against the hacendados but would win them away from revolutionary leaders such as Hugo Blanco.

Also in this 1961–1962 period, General Winkelreid (personal conversation), then head of the joint chiefs of staff, presented to Prime Minister Pedro Beltrán a report based on military sources which argued that, in a number of cases, hacendados were illegally occupying land that belonged to the state. The report recommended that such hacendados be dispossessed so that the government could work out arrangements to turn the land over to the peasants. Although the prime minister showed no sympathy with these recommendations at the time, this report by the most important military man made clear the reluctance of military leaders to act against the peasants.

An indication that the hacendados of the Convención valley had lost the support of conservative political leaders is found on the editorial pages of *La Prensa*, a conservative newspaper owned by Prime Minister Beltrán. Editorially, *La Prensa* had been advocating agrarian reform in terms of colonization. The colonization idea was particularly attractive to conservatives since it involved settling peasants on previously unoccupied land and therefore did not present any threat to the existing distribution of power. But at last *La Prensa* itself endorsed more meaningful land reform in the specific case of the Convención valley. On November 11, 1962, under the heading "The Events in Cuzco," the newspaper printed an editorial that read in part:

> Out of the inconceivable exploitation to which the peasants of La Convención have been subjected by a cruel and inhuman gamonalismo, there has arisen an exploitation by agents of Communism who utilized the legitimate aspirations of the peasants, not in order to satisfy them, but rather in order to use them as instruments of power. . . .
> What is the solution? Nothing can be done except through the development of an energetic program on two fronts. Carry out agrarian reform and take measures against the Communist exploiters. Police action without agrarian reform would be as unsound as agrarian reform without police action to pursue the agitators.
> Peru faces a possibility of converting La Convención into an example of

60

agrarian reform. The peasants who have never yet experienced it must be shown what it is like to work within a regime of liberty and justice. And that is the task of agrarian reform.

FROM PEASANT MOVEMENT TO ARMED STRUGGLE

The level of violence rose in the Convención valley with two major developments: the shift from collective bargaining to peasant occupation of hacienda lands and the split in the peasant federation. Although some of the union leaders had been worrying that Blanco's militancy would provoke a repression, until 1962 they had refrained from taking any open action against him. The split became irrevocable in April 1962, when Hugo Blanco ran for secretary-general. When he won a majority in a hotly contested election, leaders of the opposing faction claimed fraud and pulled out of the federation the locals that they controlled—almost as many as the number of locals that Blanco led. At this time, they also protested what they called the "politicization" of the movement.

One important factor that precipitated government intervention was the FIR-organized program of "bank expropriations" in Lima. The plan called for appropriating bank funds to carry out the revolution led by the Trotskyites, with the initial aim being support for the peasant movement in the Convención valley.

The Gallegos (1973:7) report describes the first and most spectacular of the politically motivated bank robberies:

Public opinion is shocked by the audacious assault on the bank of the capital executed in the daylight hours and according to a plan that was ably prepared; but the public is still more surprised when it learns that the perpetrators are not confirmed criminals, but rather university students that have been won over to the red ideology.

Only chance made it possible in Cuzco on April 28 [1962] to capture part of a band that assaulted the bank and recover part of the stolen money. This proves the connections of this group with the leaders of La Convención. Money from this assault and of others that followed, is destined to finance the revolution.

Blanco reports that these spectacular events proved a disservice to the revolutionary cause for they brought on a severe repression in Lima and

Cuzco, which destroyed the small party apparatus in those cities. At the same time, orders went out for Blanco's arrest and he found it necessary to go underground in the Chaupimayo area. For some months, he moved about from place to place, managing to keep in touch with his chief lieutenants but unable to come out in the open.

COUNTERINSURGENCY

When a military government took power in July 1962, counterinsurgency became the responsibility of intelligence officers. The then Lieutenant Colonel Gallegos reports a meeting held in October 1962 in Investigación y Desarrollo (the Department of Research and Development) of the general headquarters of the army. The meeting was attended by representatives of all the ministries and the Institute of Agrarian Reform and Colonization (IRAC). Its purpose was to develop an "emergency plan" for La Convención.

The representative of IRAC reported that the general serving as minister of agriculture was working with great enthusiasm toward a new agrarian reform law and had decided that this should be applied first in La Convención. The delegates from the other ministries agreed to budget extra amounts for development projects for the improvement of the hospital in Quillabamba, for the construction of schools, and for a new project connecting La Convención with a road running from Cuzco to Ollantaytambo.

The minister of war pushed the program energetically, arguing that the government should act with the same sense of mission and dedication as in time of war. On December 27, 1962, Lieutenant Colonel Gallegos was named general coordinator for the Convención valley and given government backing to go there and personally direct the campaign.

Meanwhile, the level of violence was escalating. Fioravanti estimates that a total of 500 peasants were killed throughout the years of the peasant movement. Since Fioravanti gives no documentation for this figure, it may be exaggerated, but there is no doubt that many peasants lost their lives.

At the same time, lives were lost among the forces opposing the union .

leadership. Gallegos (1973:7) reports that on October 18, 1962, in hacienda Echarete, a local union leader who dared to oppose the policies of the Blanco-controlled federation was brutally murdered.

Gallegos (1973:7) also reports two attacks on the police, one on November 14 in Pucyura in the neighboring valley of Vilcabamba and one on December 18 on the road from Chaullay to Chaupimayo. He claims that in the first attack, the police officer in charge was killed and in the roadside ambush, two policemen were killed. In both cases police weapons fell into the hands of the guerrilla leaders.

It was one thing for the local police to adapt themselves to de facto control of the valley by the peasant leaders, but it was quite another to have police officers killed by peasants. This situation led to demands for major reinforcements in the Convención valley and an energetic campaign to put down the uprising. The director general of the guardia civil personally surveyed the valley from a helicopter and directed the campaign to capture Hugo Blanco and his associates.

The government created 12 new police posts in the valley, and the police forces were raised to 160 men and were reinforced by two sections of the *guardia de asalto*, an organization noted for toughness and discipline. As the reinforcements combed the valley, they picked up caches of dynamite and arms and ample supplies of propaganda.

These activities led to open conflict on December 25, when a police patrol in Chaupimayo zone came upon several peasants carrying rifles and picked them up for interrogation at the nearest police post. Word spread rapidly, and the police patrol was met farther down the road by a militant band armed with rocks, clubs, and shotguns. The crowd forced the vehicle holding prisoners to stop and, after throwing a barrage of rocks, sought to rush the police to release the prisoners. The lieutenant in command gave the order to fire, and eight police officers discharged their automatic pistols into the advancing crowd. When the bullets had dispersed the crowd, the police were able to proceed with their prisoners. (Although Gallegos gives no figures for dead and wounded, eight automatic pistols fired into a crowd at point-blank range must have produced substantial bloodshed.)

On January 4, 1963, acting on extensive information gathered by government intelligence, the police struck simultaneously throughout the country, and particularly in the Convención valley, to round up those

63

suspected of revolutionary activities. These included a number of union leaders associated with Hugo Blanco, although he escaped capture for several more months.

THE GOVERNMENT'S SOCIAL REFORM PROGRAM

January 5, 1963, marks the turning point in the government's Convención valley program. On the same day as the countrywide roundup of "extremists" occurred, Lieutenant Colonel Gallegos and his assistant went to Cuzco in a plane carrying two amphibious jeeps, radio equipment, and other packages of equipment and supplies for the establishment of the coordination office in Quillabamba. On January 9, the officers established their headquarters in the valley.

Lieutenant Colonel Gallegos (1973:46) reports his first steps to shift the government program from repression to social reform:

> The captain of the Guardia Civil . . . tells me that he is responsible for my safety and that he is going to provide me immediately with bodyguards from the Guardia de Asalto and that I should not come to Quillabamba alone and unarmed. Naturally I reject this suggestion and no one ever saw me in the Valley carrying a pistol or any other weapon.

Gallegos's assumption was that the military and the police were in the valley not to fight the peasants but to protect the social reform program that was just then getting under way. He reports that at first, no one came to his offices except other government officials:

> The office of coordination is approached only by official authorities, public functionaries and police officials. It is necessary to attract the peasants; if they do not come, we must go out and seek them and the two jeeps are beginning to crisscross the valley in all directions.
>
> We carry only a bag of candy for the children, a notebook and a pen, that is our equipment for the campaign.
>
> We talk with the peasants in the haciendas, in the small towns, they do not trust us, they look at us with indifference, so many "commissions" have passed through La Convención, promising roads, reforms, schools, and nothing has ever materialized. We invited all of them to come to the office to express their problems, their complaints, "we are going to help you, that is why we have come" (1973:46).

Gallegos reports that gradually the suspicions and hesitations subsided, and the peasants began to come in:

An avalanche of peasants comes to the office, it is impossible to find enough time, but no one fails to get a hearing nor promise that his problems are going to be resolved. The telephone rings a thousand times a day, the police, the sub-prefect, the judge, the mayor all receive suggestions and recommendations; the typewriter is constantly turning out announcements, reports, telegrams, the pace is feverish; but the exhausting labor is producing its fruits, the people have put their faith in us and we must not disillusion them (1973: 46–47).

The field activity continued also:

Daily the jeeps of the coordination office go out over the dusty roads; the two officials visit schools, coordinate the transportation of school supplies, aid in the creation and organization of more than a hundred centers for literacy education, attend meetings of peasants in the haciendas, accompany the inspector of labor as he inspects the haciendas. Fines from a thousand to ten thousand soles are imposed for infractions of social and labor legislation. There are visits to field health clinics, there is aid to the plan for school breakfasts, and thousands of complaints and petitions are resolved (1973:47).

The government made no moves directly against the unions. The strategy was one of recognizing the unions, cooperating with them in school construction and other activities, but seeking to split them off from "extremist" leadership.

The announcement on March 28, 1963, of the new Agrarian Reform Law for La Convención and Lares enabled the coordination office to gain the support even of most union leaders. Although the law called for the peasants to pay for land expropriated from the hacendados—a point that is still in dispute—the essential point of the law was that it recognized and confirmed peasant ownership of the land.

Gallegos reports that the manifestations of public support for the reform program reached a climax on May 1, 1963, at a meeting at which 7,000 peasants who came to hear speeches and join in cheers for the reform were "perfectly lined up by their [local] unions, carrying flags and posters" (1973:47).

Some weeks later, betrayed by a young peasant who was tortured by the police, Hugo Blanco was captured. He was convicted of subversion and sentenced to 25 years in prison. In late 1970, a new military government released him in a general amnesty of political prisoners.

Hugo Blanco had contributed enormously to the spread of the peasant movement, but he had also led it into open conflict with the state. In a sense Blanco failed, for he lost his own freedom and saw his attempted revolution aborted by skillful government countermeasures. But if the government won so, in a very real sense, did the peasants. The hacendados did not return; the Convención valley began a new stage of development based upon peasant communities. Perhaps even the extremely militant tactics that led to Blanco's defeat contributed to the thoroughgoing nature of the reforms carried out in the valley. It was the alarm caused in high government circles by the militancy of the Blanco faction which persuaded key government leaders that piecemeal measures would not solve the problem. And it may well be that the military government's success in counterinsurgency and pacification in the Convención valley in 1963 served to encourage and guide the framers of the new military government's Agrarian Reform Law of 1969, which called for expropriation in favor of the peasants of all of the large haciendas of Peru.

EPILOGUE: THE RETURN OF HUGO BLANCO

After being released from jail and spending long periods abroad, at this writing Hugo Blanco is back in Peru and once again active in the Convención valley. This time, he is seeking to organize small peasants and landless laborers against the larger peasant farmers, who have turned out to be the chief beneficiaries of the peasant movement and government reform programs of the 1960s. However, this incipient new peasant movement belongs to another chapter of history that cannot yet be written.

Peasant Progress and 7
Government Reaction

The Convención valley movement set the pattern. First came a struggle to organize the union and get it recognized as the bargaining agent for its members. Then followed a struggle for better contractual terms with the hacendados. The final stage was the struggle for peasant land ownership through which the traditional hacienda system would be transformed into a series of communities of small peasant farmers.

The peasants of the Convención valley had eliminated the hacendados. Peasants in other areas had not reached that point when their advance was cut short by national political developments to be described later, but they were following the same line of march, as we can see by examining cases in the provinces of Paucartambo and Calca.

PROGRESS IN PAUCARTAMBO

According to Julio Cotler (1967), early in the 1960s a representative of the Peasant Federation of Cuzco was sent out from the capital city to organize the colonos of the haciendas along the Paucartambo River. The movement gained momentum during the early period of Belaúnde's presidency, and from October into December of 1963 the Indians were on strike, refusing to meet their traditional obligations to the hacendados.

Although the organizer aimed at having the Indians take possession of the hacienda lands and turn them into communities, they were not ready to go so far so fast. As were other farm labor conflicts in the region during the same period, this one was settled in a "statement of conciliation" signed by the union and hacendado representatives in the Cuzco offices of the Ministry of Labor and Indian Communities. Although some hacendados violated some of the provisions of this agreement, the strike clearly brought about a major improvement in the position of the Indians.

Julio Cotler (1967) describes three different types of adaptation of the hacienda system to the new balance of forces in Paucartambo. The colonos of Sunchumbamba had become particularly militant and were threatening to take over the lands. The hacienda was located at a strategic point between the city of Cuzco and the advance bases of the military for road construction in the jungle to the east of the Andes. The army purchased the land from the hacendado and converted it into a training center for its recruits. The military base offered certain social services to the rural people and organized an ambitious program to train colonos as carpenters, electricians, masons, etc.

The explicit purpose of the program was to develop a trained labor force for military public works programs, but the program may also have been designed to relieve pressures toward a regional uprising. The program served to provide employment and to teach skills that would give Indians more attractive alternatives than serfdom on the haciendas. Of course, such programs also reduce the supply of free labor available to the hacendados and thus tend to drive up the wage rates of rural labor.

In one of the largest haciendas, Cusipata (25,000 hectares, of which 500 to 1,200 were in active cultivation), the hacendado began selling off lots to colonos and to members of surrounding communities. At the same time, the hacendado shifted toward more intensive and highly mechanized farming on his remaining land. He was hoping in this way to maintain good relations with the colonos and the members of neighboring communities so that he could recruit the labor needed in periods during which a large work force was necessary.

Another modernization strategy was put into effect by the hacendado of Mollomarca, who differed markedly from the average occupant of this role in the sierra. He had lived in Bolivia, Argentina, and Paraguay and had visited in the United States and Venezuela, where one of his brothers held a high post in the Ministry of Agriculture. This hacendado had had some university education and was a man of active intellectual interests. He was one of the few hacendados who lived full time on his property. He interrupted our interview to pick up a walkie-talkie and call his foreman out in the fields. The foreman reported on the work accomplished up to that point, and the hacendado then gave him further instructions.

Recognizing both the inefficiency of the old system and the increasing pressures to change it, the hacendado first proposed to convert the colonos into wage workers. If they would agree to give up their own plots of land, he would employ them at the legal minimum wage for the area. Since the colono plots were scattered throughout the hacienda, this arrangement would enable the hacendado to consolidate his holdings and would open up the way for the introduction of more efficient farming methods. At the same time, the wage workers would receive substantially larger incomes than had been theirs as serfs.

The colonos rejected this proposal. They were not prepared to give up the land and the relationships they knew in favor of an unknown wage relationship.

The hacendado then made a new proposal, which the Indians accepted. They retained their work obligations to the hacendado and received from him full ownership of 1,000 of the 1,400 hectares of the hacienda. Those living and having their family plots on the remaining 400 hectares agreed to resettle within the 1,000 hectares allocated to the colonos.

By this arrangement, the hacendado resolved his dispute with the colonos (at least temporarily), consolidated his holdings, brought to bear more modern and intensive methods upon the reduced acreage—and, with the aid of unpaid labor now more willingly provided, found himself making more money than every before. (This unorthodox strategy led other hacendados to denounce him as a Communist.)

THE UNIONIZATION OF CHAWAYTIRI

We have a more detailed record of events on Hacienda Chawaytirí in the neighboring province of Calca. Chawaytirí was the only hacienda in the highlands above the valley, where the land reaches an altitude of 12,000 feet. It was a large hacienda, extending over 14,000 hectares. Chawaytirí had been dedicated primarily to the raising of cattle, horses, sheep, and alpacas, supplemented by some cultivation of potatoes. In 1965, the population was about 405 inhabitants living in 84 family groups scattered over the hacienda.

There was a direct link between Hugo Blanco and Chawaytirí. When one Chawaytirían was sixteen years old, he went to work in the Convención valley. On one occasion, he described to Blanco the exploitation in Chawaytirí. Blanco gave him travel money and advised him to return home to spread the news about the Convención movement and get his relatives talking about the need to form a union. The young man discharged his responsibility effectively. His uncle became one of the chief local organizers of the union.

The potato harvest early in 1962 precipitated the unionization of Chawaytirí. The work was especially hard, and the colonos were required to work day after day until 6:30 in the evening. By this time, representatives of the Peasant Federation of Cuzco had passed through the area several times, stopping to make contacts at Chawaytirí. Four men traveled to Cuzco to talk with the union organizers. Returning to the hacienda, they worked out plans for a strike.

The hacendado was so feared that it was difficult to hold a meeting for organizing purposes. In person-to-person contacts with the colonos, the organizers announced a strike. Since the men at work were scattered throughout a large area, it was not possible for the authorities to keep track of all of them all of the time. By prearranged plan, one by one, the men left the fields. By the time the administrator and the mayordomo recognized what was happening and began shouting orders, it was too late.

70

That night, the men of the hacienda gathered for their first union meeting in the delapidated schoolhouse. The administrator and the mayordomo discovered them and tried to break up the meeting, but the colonos defied them. After this meeting and every union meeting for some months, they emerged from the building shouting: "Long live the union! Death to the gamonal [exploitive landlord]!"

Unionization brought immediate symbolic changes in interpersonal relations. No longer did the alcalde and other colonos bow in the presence of superior authorities.

After beginning their strike, the colonos set up their organization, establishing categories of officials taken over from Indian communities. They elected three *personeros* (representatives) and three *tenientes escolares* (lieutenants for education) to go to Cuzco and get their union officially registered. On May 28, 1962, they submitted a written complaint to the Ministry of Labor and Indian Affairs office in Cuzco. The strike continued until June 15, and negotiations to end it were conducted before the Ministry representative on June 13 through 15.

With the aid of representatives of the Peasant Federation of Cuzco, the colonos of Chawaytirí signed their first contract with the man whose serfs they had been. Although two of the following contractual points confirmed certain rights of the hacendado, the others represented clear gains for the now unionized Indians.

1. The colonos recognize the property rights of the hacendado.
2. The hacendado confirms the colono rights to the land they currently occupy.
3. The condición is limited to 10 days per month, and the workday is limited to 8 hours. The hacendado is required to keep books to avoid his exacting more work than is his due.
4. The jurka [payment] is one sol per day. The hacendado now agrees to provide lunch as well as the usual ration of coca.
5. Women and minors are exempt from work obligations. When the son gets the family land, he assumes the family obligations.
6. The ponguaje is eliminated as extra service. If such work is required of anyone, it counts as part of his 10 days per month of condición.
7. No other contributions from the Indians nor forced sales are to be required.

71

8. The hacendado agrees to provide land and materials for a new school. The colonos agree to contribute their labor to building the school.
9. The administrator is declared *persona non grata* by the colonos and is to be fired within 60 days.
10. The colonos are not to be held responsible for loss of cattle.
11. The colonos recognize the hacendado's authority.

If we look at the condition of the colonos following the agreement, we can certainly say that they were still "exploited" by the landlord, but that judgment obscures the magnitude of the gains they had won. If we compare the condition of the workers before and after the signing of the first contract, rarely will we find such a dramatic improvement.

The struggle was not over with the signing of the first contract. There followed a period of months in which the union applied pressure to secure compliance. The hacendado did not always pay the daily sol, and union leaders had to keep after him to make good. He kept putting off the discharge of the administrator, and it finally became apparent that he was not going to carry out this part of the agreement.

From the time of the signing of the first contract, on June 15, until early August, the colonos sought to gain compliance with the contract through direct dealings with the hacendado. From that time on, they sought to bring outside pressures into play. The record shows a series of written appeals to the judge of the labor court in Cuzco and to the prefect himself.

The judge sought to mediate the dispute, but, as often as not, the hacendado failed to appear for the officially scheduled meetings. Apparently, he found it difficult to accept the idea that he could be required by any authority to meet with his colonos. It may be that informal and unofficial pressures were brought to bear upon him, since, on occasion, he did appear for a meeting or present written answers to charges made against him.

In a communication (October 15) to the labor court in Cuzco, the personero concluded with the following statement:

In the store of the hacienda, the hacendado has fired into the air, threatening me, and shouting that he will liquidate me, the personero of the colonos, and that he will also send me to jail.

I ask of the Prefectural office that a guarantee of safety be provided and that arrangements be made so that the Guardia Civil of Pisaq and Calca are not surprised by labor complaints on the part of the hacendado, and THAT THEY DO NOT IMPRISON ME IN ANY JAIL, because it is the custom that, when a hacendado formulates a complaint, immediately the peasants are imprisoned for at least 24 hours. [Emphasis as in the original document.]

While the hacendado was threatening to use force against the colonos, he himself was becoming a victim of escalation. His approach to Chawaytirí from Cuzco brought him into view of the colonos long before he reached the relative safety of his hacienda home. As he came in, he was greeted by a volley of rocks and boulders rolling down the mountain. After one or two such greetings, the hacendado found it prudent to remain in Cuzco.

In this period, the colonos were especially concerned about getting land on which to build their school. They appealed to Oscar Núñez del Prado, who was conducting an applied anthropology project in neighboring Kuyo Chico (Núñez del Prado, 1973). The anthropologist did not find it easy to approach the hacendado, who considered him a Communist and his project a threat to law and order in the district. Núñez del Prado arranged a meeting through a relative of the hacendado who was friendly to his project. The anthropologist suggested that if the hacendado would make land available for the school, the colonos might be persuaded to grant him free passage to his hacienda. The issue was resolved on this basis.

Although other contract issues remained unresolved, we now note an important change in the content and style of the documents sent by the union leaders to the hacendado or to the labor authorities. In the early weeks following the signing of the contract, the statements were phrased in the style of polite requests. For example, in a September 1 letter to the hacendado signed (in fingerprints) by three colonos, after an enumeration of the points on which the hacendado had failed to comply, we find this paragraph:

We do not want to bother you, and we are not going to appeal to the authorities until we have exhausted friendly and peaceful means. Therefore, we appeal to you to be good enough to comply with the labor contract in all respects.

When this direct approach failed, the union leaders wrote their protests in stronger terms to Ministry of Labor and departmental political officials, as illustrated by the October 15 statement (already cited) in which the personero complained about the threats against him.

The following months revealed a shift from efforts to get contract enforcement to claims for outright land ownership. The record also shows a shift from local contractual matters toward statements on human rights, backed by citations from the constitution and laws of Peru.

On December 1, 1962, we find the first claim for the right to purchase the land. The union leaders followed up, on December 12, by calling the colonos out on strike, notifying the labor court judge that they were withdrawing all personal services from the hacendado for a period of 60 days. The strike seems to have continued beyond that point, for on August 23, 1963, the union leaders presented to the regional labor inspector a statement that, after repeating the familiar charges of hacendado violation of the contract, continued with the following words:

> The Constitution of the Nation requires that personal labor must not be obligatory but voluntary; the basic law of Agrarian Reform requires the absolute abolition of personal service by the colonos, a provision which agrees with the Supreme Decree of April 24, 1962, for the provinces of La Convención, Urubamba, and Calca; therefore we communicate to you that we are not going to resume the offering of personal services to the hacienda because such arrangements are prohibited.

As the strike continued, and the colonos continued to press for land ownership, it was now the hacendado who appealed to the regional labor inspector to get the men back to work—on the basis of the June 1962 labor agreement that he himself had repeatedly violated. And now it was the colonos who turned against the agreement. In their reply (September 23, 1963) to the inspector, they argued that the contract was invalid for the following reasons:

1. It was not honored by him [the hacendado].
2. It was only valid for a year and therefore had lapsed.
3. No pact has any validity when its contents are contrary to law.

They concluded with this admonition:

[The hacendado] should understand that rights of property have their limitations and that the proprietors are not all inclusive owners of the colonos as well as the land. That epoch has been historically left behind us, and the parties are obliged to accept the social and agricultural laws now in effect.

The strike came to an end only when the parties signed a new contract, in early 1964, embodying two principal changes: reduction of the work obligation from 10 to 6 days per month and raising the daily jurka payment from 1 to 3 soles. The hacendado died shortly after signing the new contract, and since political conditions made it impossible to interview the peasant federation advisers to the colonos, we can only speculate upon the motivation that led to this agreement.

Since the peasant movement was spreading rapidly throughout the southern sierra and many hacendados were losing control of their lands, the proprietor of Chawaytiri probably concluded that there was no hope of getting the colonos back to work under the traditional arrangements or even under the 1962 contract, so he was forced to offer something better. Why did the colonos accept an agreement that they knew to be in violation of the constitution? Presumably, they recognized that they could still denounce the new contract as illegal when it suited their purposes. Their land claims were not getting any government encouragement, and a contract representing a 40 percent decrease in hours of work and a 200 percent increase in daily pay was a striking improvement in their condición. In any case, this proved to be a wise decision, since early 1964 marked the high water mark of the peasant movement in this region, and conditions for effective peasant mobilization were sharply reduced by government repression shortly thereafter.

THE CONSERVATIVE REACTION

The peasant movement in the southern sierra precipitated a severe crisis for President Belaúnde. Throughout 1963 and early 1964, the opposition majority aimed its attacks at the minister of the interior, who was responsible for maintaining law and order. At last, Belaúnde gave in to these pressures and appointed a new minister, who began his term of office by directing a large-scale roundup of "political agitators" who allegedly had been inciting the peasants. All the top leaders of the Peasant Federation of Cuzco were thrown in jail.

The intervention of the national government served as a cease-fire-in-place. The impact of the repression may be illustrated by developments on Hacienda Chawaytirí.

When the ties of the colonos at Chawaytirí to the federation were severed by this decapitation of the top leadership, the local union at Chawaytirí withered away; but this change did not bring back the preunion status quo. The ties the colonos had forged among themselves could still be reactivated in a crisis. Over a period of months, the hacendado had been able to extend the work obligations, but when he announced that he could no longer afford to pay 3 soles per day and would cut back to the 1 sol payment in force before the 1964 contract, the colonos went on strike. Shortly the hacendado capitulated and reestablished the 3 soles payment. Informants report that he thought he had found some mining opportunities on his land and was especially concerned about the possible loss of an available labor force. Whatever his reasons, colono solidarity caused him to reestablish the higher level of payment.

The disappearance of the union did not restore the tensions that had prevailed in the preorganization period. The colonos reported that the administrator did not resume use of physical force or shouting at them.

The unionization also brought about marked changes in the relations of the mandón and the alcalde to the workers and to the administration. Before unionization, these lowest-level officials necessarily had to carry out the orders of their superiors regardless of their own feelings or of the feelings of their fellow colonos. Now they were balancing the orders they received against peasant rights. The changed situation is illustrated by an incident that occurred one day during a rainstorm. The administrator encountered the mandón with the other colonos seeking shelter under a large tree. He ordered the mandón to send the men back to work. The mandón simply shook his head and commented, "Times have changed." The administrator did not press the issue.

Intervention for Social Change 8

Although the peasant movements were the most important force for social change in the southern highlands, they were not the only force operating to undermine the economic and political power of the hacendados. Whenever the government undertook a public works project, its entry into the labor market tended to weaken the hold of the hacendados over their serfs. On occasion, the government also backed direct intervention in limited areas.

The first such intervention occured in the early 1950s, on the basis of an agreement between Dr. Carlos Monge, president of the Indian Institute, and Allan R. Holmberg, professor of anthropology at Cornell University. (Dobyns et al. 1971). The research and development project at Hacienda Vicos, in the highlands somewhat north of Lima, was financed almost entirely by the university, on the basis of Carnegie Corporation grants. The conservative governments of that era took pride in Vicos as a symbol of their humanitarian concerns, without making any general commitment to social reform. When urged to honor their implied commitment to transfer hacienda ownership to Vicosinos at the end of the project, Prime Minister Beltrán was much concerned lest this move form a precedent for widespread expropriations; and it seems likely that Vicosino ownership would have been postponed indefinitely if the government leaders of that era had not been so concerned about maintaining good relations with the United States.

In 1959, another anthropological intervention project was launched by Oscar Núñez del Prado in the department of Cuzco. This project differed from the one at Vicos in four important respects:

1. It was planned and carried out entirely by Peruvians.
2. It was financed (at times quite precariously) by the Peruvian government, as part of the National Plan for the Integration of the Aboriginal Population (PNIPA).
3. The project was carried out at a later time and in a region of widespread peasant mobilization, which tended to support the change being introduced.
4. Intervention at Vicos was on an hacienda; the focal point of intervention in Cuzco was the Indian community of Kuyo Chico.

THE SETTING FOR INTERVENTION

The tourist who travels from Cuzco into the Sacred Valley of the Incas for the well-known Sunday fair at Pisaq has the impression that he is visiting a traditional Indian community. As he crosses the Vilcanota River and arrives at the central plaza, he is impressed by the colorful Indian textiles and other handicrafts and by the traditional costumes worn by the vendors and their families.

Although some of the vendors do indeed come from neighboring Indian communities and wear clothing customary for a Sunday in their villages, many are residents of Cuzco who put on their costumes and hustle out to Pisaq ahead of the tourists to set out their wares. When the Sunday fair is over and Pisaq emerges from its disguise, it becomes evident that the town is not an Indian community in any traditional sense. In fact, only 16 percent of the respondents in Pisaq in our 1969 survey classified themselves as Indians—with 27 percent being so classified by the interviewers.

Over 50 percent of the Indian community respondents reported themselves as Indian, and 78 to 90 percent were judged Indians by the interviewers. The difference between self-identification and interviewer identification seem to stem from two sources. The interviewers, being university students, themselves were mestizos and perhaps were inclined to underestimate the status of respondents below them. There also seems to be a rather common tendency for respondents to claim a social class higher than that to which they would have been classified by observers. In any case, there is a clear and marked contrast in ethnic composition separating Pisaq from the Indian communities.

The differences between Pisaq and the Indian communities are most simply indicated by occupational comparisons. In 1969, the percentages of male respondents identifying themselves as farmers ran from 91 to 100 percent in our three Indian communities, whereas only 39 percent of Pisaq respondents were farmers, with 43 percent being in commerce and 10 percent being white-collar workers—a category unrepresented outside of Pisaq in this area. (The Hacienda Chawaytirí population was made up almost exclusively of colonos.)

Kuyo Chico, Maska, and Qotobamba were typical of small Indian villages of the region. They were made up of the families of small farmers who worked plots of land that were too small and too unfavorably situated to provide full support for the families, so that the head of the family and any children old enough to work had to work sporadically as farm laborers in the neighboring haciendas or on jobs in Pisaq or elsewhere.

The land ownership situation for Kuyo Chico, given in detail below, was probably quite similar in the other Indian communities. Although the farmers of Kuyo Chico owned approximately 100 hectares, little more than 35 of these were cultivable without extension of the irrigation system. This meant that the 62 families each had slightly more than ½ hectare (1.4 acres) of cultivable land on an average. Of the land under cultivation, less than 10 percent was irrigated. The remainder depended upon uncertain and often inadequate rainfall. The lands were divided as shown in Table 8-1.

The 62 families owned among them 154 head of cattle—

TABLE 8-1
Land Owned per Family in Kuyo Chico

SIZE, HA	PERCENTAGE OF FAMILIES
1.3–2	7.5
0.8–1.2	24.5
0.5–0.7	32.1
0.1–0.4	34.0
Without land	2.0

approximately 2½ per family. They also owned 377 guinea pigs, 160 chickens, 74 sheep, 36 hogs, 22 goats, 9 burros, 2 mules, 2 ducks, as well as 46 dogs and 4 cats.

About 50 percent of the cultivated areas was devoted to corn, with all families cultivating this traditional crop. Twenty-eight percent was devoted to wheat and 16 percent to barley.

Kuyo Chico used no farm machinery. Power was provided by men and oxen. The Indians purchased no commercial fertilizer: they depended upon manure from cattle and other animals.

INTERVENTION OF THE
APPLIED ANTHROPOLOGIST

Oscar Núñez del Prado, professor of anthropology of the University of Cuzco, had persuaded officials of the Indian Institute of the Ministry of Labor and Indian Affairs to establish an Applied Anthropology Program in the Department of Cuzco. One day, on the road from Pisaq to the neighboring Indian communities, the anthropologist and his associates encountered Tomás Diaz, cabecilla for Kuyo Chico. Núñez del Prado was impressed by him. On the basis of his wide experience in rural Cuzco, the anthropologist expected that a cabecilla would be a submissive tool in the hands of the mestizo authorities. This cabecilla at first did speak hesitantly and with obvious apprehension, but he gave a full and vivid account of the exploitation suffered by his people. The anthropologist found that the cabecilla had carried out his duties to the mestizo authorities in as humane a fashion as possible and that, on occasion, he had risked his own interests to protect the community. For example, he had sought to press a suit in court for the recovery of Kuyo Chico lands from the neighboring hacienda of Chongos and had met the expenses of the proceedings by selling some of his farm animals.

Núñez del Prado's first associates on his project were a schoolteacher and an agricultural engineer. When they had chosen Kuyo Chico as the central location for their program, they devoted several months to a study of the culture, social organization, and economic activities of Kuyo Chico.

When the change agents were ready to act, they chose first to challenge the power structure of the area. Such a decision is highly unusual in the annals of applied anthropology. The literature gives the impression that the applied anthropologist brings about change through developing an understanding of the local culture and working cooperatively with all of the local groups involved. The same point of view is implicit in most of the literature of community development. It is assumed that the change agent brings about change through developing processes of communication, involvement, and participation. In effect, the change agent helps the people to organize themselves to bring about the changes they desire. Núñez del Prado reasoned that it would be impossible to help the Indians to develop their potential unless they were first freed from the mestizo system of exploitation, which absorbed much of their time and energy and sapped their self-confidence.

A university graduate in law as well as the possessor of a doctorate in anthropology, Núñez del Prado decided to base his challenge to the mestizos upon the constitution and laws of Peru. Although he was not at all confident that he could count on backing from Lima in case of a showdown between his project and the local power structure, Núñez del Prado decided to act as if he had behind him all the powers of the national government. He informed the mestizo authorities that the Kuyo Chico project was part of the National Plan for the Integration of the Aboriginal Population, which was supported by the Ministries of Defense, Education, Health, Agriculture, Labor and Indian Affairs, the Institute of Agrarian Reform, and the Agricultural Development Bank. Núñez del Prado and his associates then distributed to all of the authorities a circular describing the project, listing the organizations backing it, and detailing the legal penalties to be imposed upon anyone violating the rights of the Indians.

Núñez del Prado called a public meeting in Kuyo Chico which was attended also by many Indians from neighboring communities. As the meeting was about to begin, there arrived a group of mestizo authorities: the justice of the peace, the governor of the district, the mayor of Pisaq, and the commander of the guardia civil. Presumably, they came to look after their own interests and intimidate the Indians, but their presence provided an opportunity for the dramatization of the change in the structure of power which was now in progress.

After describing the purposes of the project, Núñez del Prado concentrated on explaining to the Indians, in their native Quechua, their rights as citizens, the various laws designed to protect those rights, and the penalties that could be invoked against those who violated them. He then turned to the mestizos and asked them either to vouch for the correctness of the information or else to explain to him and to the Indians any errors he had committed. Thus, the Indians were treated to a spectacle of the mestizo authorities acknowledging that some of the timehonored practices in which they themselves had participated were illegal and subject to drastic penalties.

Impressed by this dramatic beginning, the Indians of Kuyo Chico agreed that they would no longer respond to any calls for faena labor from Pisaq. This strike was immediately effective in Kuyo Chico. When Indians in other communities observed that the men of Kuyo Chico had not suffered any reprisals, they came to consult the Kuyo Chico leaders and project members. Núñez del Prado explained to each delegation that forced labor was against the law and that should they be pressed into faena service, he would see to it that legal action was taken against the local authorities. Suddenly the mestizos of Pisaq lost the free labor they had depended upon for public works and personal service and comfort.

Such a drastic change was bound to provoke opposition from the mestizo elite. They spread the word that the anthropologist was a Communist, and they looked for ways of getting rid of him and his program. The anthropologist decided that the best defense would be to continue his offensive. He describes a series of events that enabled him to secure a solid political shield for his program.

> From then on it was necessary to use all the resources at our disposal to counter the pressure exerted on the Indians. We made charges before the criminal courts, presented cases to the ministerial authorities, and, in some cases, went so far as to use physical force. On one such occasion I was on my way into the town of Pisaq with the agricultural engineer when we saw a crowd

of Indians gathered at the entrance to the town and stopped to see what was happening. We were told that the lieutenant governor was seizing their products and paying them extremely low prices for them. The lieutenant governor was there, and when we asked him what he was doing, he replied, "These Indians are monopolizers and speculators," whereupon he produced a Lima newspaper in which there appeared an article describing measures being used to crack down on the monopolies and speculation which were raising the cost of living. He was using this argument to rob the Indians of their goods, which he was placing in a house by the side of the road. We told him that what he was doing was illegal, because these Indians were neither monopolizers nor speculators but were carrying their products on their backs to the market in Pisaq. I said that he should return the articles he had taken and made an attempt to enter the house, whereupon he placed himself in the doorway to impede me. I found myself obliged to hit him, and he fell down inside the house. At this point the governor arrived, and, hearing of the incident, came toward me. However, it was his bad luck that the engineer was standing nearby and moved in quickly to halt him. I immediately ordered the Indians who were present to take their things back and leave. They did so and in a few minutes were gone.

The next day I received a summons to appear before the prefect of Cuzco for resisting the authorities. I was also charged with trespassing, for having ordered the Indians to go into the house to retrieve their possessions. After being rebuked by the prefect, I replied that what I had done was to impede an individual who was committing a crime, namely, assaulting the Indians. I asserted that although this individual was the lieutenant governor, he had abused his authority by committing this crime and thus, at the point of my intervention, this authority had been nullified.

Before leaving Kuyo Chico, I had formulated a plan to take advantage of this occasion to produce a break in the chain of authority from the prefect to the governor. For this purpose I brought along a photostatic copy of a document which had come into our possession some months earlier, concerning the enganchadores working in the Pisaq area for the prefect's own hacienda. During the course of our conversation, I made it clear that the governor and lieutenant governor were putting the prefect's reputation in jeopardy, to the point that they could get him into serious trouble concerning their enganchador activities. I handed him the photostat, and he became visibly startled upon reading it. It seemed that the prefect owned an hacienda in the jungle region of Q'osñopata, and that the governor was the person in charge of the enganchador activities in Pisaq. It was a communication to this effect, written by the governor himself, that had fallen into our hands. I suggested that the prefect dismiss these authorities, and permitted myself to propose as a replacement for the governor a man over whom we had some influence. About a week later, the governor and lieutenant governor were removed from their posts. (Núñez del Prado, 1973:49–51).

THE DEVELOPMENT PROCESS

Núñez del Prado and his associates proceeded to fit their program into the local culture and social organization and at the same time to introduce changes that would permit Kuyo Chico to improve its economic position. He worked with the community and federal authorities to get Kuyo Chico recognized as an Indian community under the protection of the Division of Indian Communities of the Ministry of Labor and Indian Affairs. This meant that the position of cabecilla, subordinate to the local mestizo authorities, was abolished, and Tomás Diaz was elected personero, representative of the community to the national government.

The anthropologist introduced into the traditional monthly assembly community discussion of improvement projects. He worked not only on the development and acceptance of new ideas but also on the social process of discussion and decision making. No project was proposed in the community assembly until it had been informally discussed with a number of the *comuneros* (community members) and had been adopted at least tentatively by the *junta comunal* (community council). In the assembly itself, the anthropologist found that members were not accustomed to the confrontation of opposing points of view, the general pattern being that what was proposed by a highly prestigious person was passed without debate. The anthropologist took the initiative in asking various members for their views on a particular proposal, until it became normal for people to speak up freely. The program also brought women more openly into assembly participation.

In education, the changes began with an adult literacy program, on the assumption that parents would more likely support education for their children if they themselves had made some progress toward reading and writing in Spanish. The adult program also resulted in approximately 18 percent of the adults of Kuyo Chico demonstrating their literacy sufficiently to gain a voting card (compared with 12 percent for Qotobamba and 4 percent for Maska—both communities having been affected, but less intensively, by the education program in Kuyo Chico). Thirty-three percent of the respondents in Pisaq reported that they held voting cards, reflecting the higher level of education in the mestizo town.

84

As the adult education program moved ahead, the community built a new school and secured teachers to man it. When the program started, 50 pupils were enrolled in the Kuyo Chico school but average daily attendance was only 17. With the building of the new school and the strengthening of the educational program, the enrollment rose steadily from 1960 through 1966, going from 50 to 134, and attendance became much more regular. There was also a notable increase in the proportion of female pupils, from 24 percent in 1960 to 42 percent in 1966, indicating that the change agents were overcoming the traditional belief that education was of no value to females.

The most important needs of the community were more land and an extended irrigation system, but both of these projects promised only long-run payoffs, the first depending upon the winning of the court case against the hacienda and the second involving several years of hard communal labor. The change agents decided to encourage projects that would provide more immediate rewards. They got the community involved in home improvements and then in building a kiln to fire tiles for roofing which they could use themselves and sell in neighboring communities. They also introduced improvements in agricultural methods and brought in a new crop, malting barley, which was in demand by the Cuzco brewery. Only as these projects were beginning to show payoffs did they encourage the community to begin the irrigation project and to plant eucalyptus trees, which would hold the soil and in about 15 years would provide wood for use and sale.

EXTERNAL RELATIONS

The most important and dramatic change in external relations was that which occurred at the outset: a cessation of faena forced labor for Pisaq. Gradually, the Indians, supported by the change agents, brought to an end the mestizo requisitioning of farm produce at cut prices and the forced sale of staple products to the Indians at inflated prices. When the Kuyo Chicans had made plans for establishing a community cooperative to sell kerosene, salt, and sugar at market prices, the Pisaq storeowners abruptly abandoned their practice of selling to the Indians only on a barter basis. When the change agents had prosecuted charges against

85

enganchadores and had brought back children who had been pressed into labor service, the enganchadores went elsewhere.

In 1969, shortly before our resurvey, Kuyo Chico won its supreme court case to recover land usurped decades earlier by the hacendado of Chongos. This unprecedented victory increased Kuyo Chico's agricultural land by 50 percent.

Before the beginning of the Applied Anthropology Program, Kuyo Chico's relations with the outside world had been channeled through mestizo political authorities and businessmen. With the changes brought about by the intervention program, supported by other changes precipitated by the peasant movement, Kuyo Chico established its own links upward, independent of the local mestizos.

RESTRUCTURING OF INDIAN-MESTIZO RELATIONS

Until the early 1950s, Pisaq had been dominated by one extended family. Backed up by strong ties in Cuzco, the department capital, the mestizo elite had held firm political and economic control over the area. This was a period of mestizo intransigence. By the time of the peasant challenges to this elite, in the 1960s, a number of the younger members of the dominant family had left Pisaq, and positions of political leadership and social prestige were in a state of flux.

The emergent new leadership of Pisaq recognized that changes were inevitable. Instead of waiting for changes to be imposed on them, they sought to take the initiative in shaping that future.

Some of the remaining mestizos and rising mozos (a local term for cholos) of Pisaq recognized that community development was the theme of modern rural man, and they set about forming the Junta de Promoción Socio-Económico de Pisaq (Committee for the Socio-Economic Development of Pisaq) to bring together (on paper) all the organizations of Pisaq—including the Peace Corps. The full list of organizations is given below.

Governorship of the District	Public Health Office
District Municipal Council	Women's Committee
Office of Justice of the Peace	Junta de Regantes (Irrigation-Control Committee)
Parish of Pisaq	Artisanship Center

Nuclear School of Pisaq	Applied Anthropology Program
Post and Telegraph Office	Patronato Escolar (Parent-Teachers Association)
Schoolteachers' Union	Peace Corps
Agricultural Society of the District of Pisaq	Personeros of Indian Communities
Tambohuacso Social and Sports Club	

Although the records of the junta list the applied anthropology program as a member, Núñez del Prado reports that he was simply informed of the inclusion of his organization. He attended only one meeting. Since the chairman of the junta was also administrator of Hacienda Chongos, the anthropologist suspected that the junta would be used to back the plan to sell to Qotobamba the parts of Chongos that were being claimed by Kuyo Chico. To avoid being placed in a minority of one, Núñez del Prado resigned from the junta.

There is no record of any of the personeros from the indigenous communities of the Sacred Valley having ever attended a junta meeting.

The strategy of the junta was to demonstrate to the national government that the community was prepared to work to better its own condition and was therefore worthy of outside technical assistance and financial support. Junta leaders developed plans for agricultural modernization, for public works, and for social services.

After a short period of activity accompanied by much publicity, the junta fell apart. It appears to have been defeated by the discrepancy between its rhetoric and the pattern of distribution of its resources. The junta did negotiate a loan of a farm tractor from SIPA (the agricultural extension agency), and SIPA also provided some improved seeds and fertilizer, but some former members of the junta claimed that it was only the leaders of the organization who really benefited from these new resources.

If the junta had been able to bring in large outside resources, the "trickle-down" strategy might have worked. Then the leaders could have retained a disproportionate share for themselves and still have had some "goodies" available for poorer people. However, when the few resources were monopolized by the leaders, the other members lost interest.

87

During this same period, a mestizo who could be described as a "modernizing conservative" came to political power as the mayor of Pisaq. Serving also as administrator of Hacienda Chongos, he had a strong base for action in rural areas.

On the hacienda, the administrator abolished the old serfdom system and substituted wage payments—the first such transformation in the valley. He also reorganized the hacienda administration and introduced mechanization, fertilizers, and insecticides.

As mayor, beginning in 1956, he inaugurated a campaign to recover Pisaq communal lands that had been "usurped" by influential individuals. He raised town income by imposing a small tax on tourist cars and by collecting license fees from local merchants, which previous administrations had neglected to do.

With increasing local income and energetic efforts to gain national government support, the mayor sought to develop public works projects such as a potable-water system, a sewage system, electric power, improved irrigation, and improved roads to the major tourist attractions. The mayor found himself with strong support only from the mozo or cholo segment of Pisaq, and he came under heavy attack from several mestizos, who denounced him as a Communist. Here he faced the same opposition, expressed in the same symbols, which confronted the members of the Applied Anthropology Program. With most of his improvement program still unrealized, in 1963 he lost the mayorality campaign to a hacendado of the Popular Action party of President Belaúnde.

EMERGENCE OF NEW LEADERSHIP

While the power of the mestizo landholding elite was declining, during the 1960s a new leadership group of young schoolteachers arose in the province of Calca. Generally, the rural schoolteacher had been a person working where he did not want to be. In many cases, he had lived in the provincial or departmental capital, arrived at his classroom on Monday afternoon or Tuesday morning, and abandoned it on Thursday afternoon or Friday noon. Typically, he had regarded his pupils as too stupid to learn and had looked upon the customs and beliefs of their parents as barriers to progress. Often the teacher himself had fallen into the pattern of mestizo exploitation of the Indians, sending the children on personal errands, requiring birthday gifts of fowl or farm produce, and so on.

By 1970, the educational scene in the Sacred Valley around the town of Pisaq had undergone a marked change. The teachers were young, with an average age of twenty-eight, and the most senior teachers had only eight years of service. (We would expect to find beginning teachers in the Indian communities, but the teachers in the district capital of Pisaq might well be older and have more seniority.)

The new schoolteachers came from families of similar background to those they replaced. They tended to be children of mestizos and cholos, but they had studied education at the University of Cuzco or in a normal school in the department during a period when the Ministry of Education was emphasizing the role of the teacher as change agent and community developer.

At least of equal importance was the process of political radicalization that was taking place among university students during the late 1950s and through the 1960s. University students held meetings and demonstrated in support of agrarian reform and peasant mobilization in the Convención valley and elsewhere. Many university students became involved with the Peasant Federation of Cuzco.

The young teachers had more of a social change orientation than did their predecessors. They showed their commitment to change by forming their own professional association devoted to discussion and self-education on agrarian reform and rural development. They extended the program to adult meetings in the Indian communities.

In the past, Peruvian learning had consisted largely of memorizing what the teacher set forth. Although we have no information regarding the methods of the new teachers, we do have reports that their approach to adults in the Indian community was drastically different from the traditional authoritarian approach. For example, one meeting was devoted to the question, Are men smarter then women? The traditional answer would have been a resounding affirmative, but the teacher led the men and women through an extended discussion to reach a consensus that women were as intelligent as men. At a subsequent meeting, the Indians discussed the question, Are mestizos smarter than Indians? In the past, the Indian had been inclined to accept the inferiority imposed upon him by the mestizos. Again, after extended discussion, the Indians arrived at the consensus that "the Mestizo is the fruit of the educational opportunities he has enjoyed."* With equal educational opportunities, the Indian would be as smart as the mestizo.

Some of the schoolteachers also constituted themselves communication links from the community to government agencies. Long before the military government's drastic Agrarian Reform Act of 1969 was officially put into effect in the department of Cuzco, teachers in the Pisaq area were informing the Indians about their rights under the law. In some cases, the schoolteachers encouraged the Indians to take actions anticipating the application of the law to their area. For example, in the community of Viacha, the teacher encouraged sharecroppers to retain control of the land but to cease sharing the income from their crops with the hacendado. The schoolteacher pledged that if the Indians were subjected to any reprisals for this action, he himself would assume responsibility for the decision.

In another community, whose irrigation system had been largely taken over by neighboring owners of medium-size properties, the schoolteacher intervened to help the Indians to establish more equitable distribution of water. The teachers played major roles in helping a number of communities to reorganize themselves in accord with the new laws on Indian communities promulgated by the military government. This activity also provided the teachers with an opportunity to encourage younger people to become candidates for community office, thus assuring leadership that was more modern—and more receptive to the influence of the teachers.

By the beginning of the 1970s, schoolteachers had emerged as political leaders in the area. Three of them had won positions on the Pisaq municipal council. The old mestizo landowning elite had lost control to the schoolteachers and the rising cholos.

MESTIZO ADAPTATIONS TO INDIAN PRESSURES

The peasant movement and the Applied Anthropology Program brought about a restructuring of ethnic and social class relations in much of the department of Cuzco. In the Convención valley, the hacendados were completely eliminated as haciendas were transformed into peasant communities. In the province of Calca, the changes were far-reaching but less drastic.

*Unless otherwise indicated, all quoted passages are from program field reports or notes.

There was a sharp rise in the wages for farm labor as the free labor supply was drastically reduced. When hacienda colonos were on strike, the hacendados had to bring in wage labor from outside or else abandon their crops. Furthermore, the mestizo elite in the town of Pisaq and in a large part of the province of Calca had lost the forced labor that had been traditionally exacted from the Indian communities.

Even for those Indians who remained on haciendas, relations with mestizos were softening. The obligatory gestures of deference from Indian to master were passing into history. Hacendados and administrators were less likely to shout and curse at the Indians, and they were moderating the severity of penalties for noncompliance with orders.

Mestizo recognition that major changes had taken place is illustrated by the following statements of two Pisaq hacendados who still had Indian labor:

> Now they no longer pay any attention to orders if they are not paid first. If we did not have godparent relationships and acquaintances among them, it would be impossible to get their collaboration for work on the haciendas.

> Now they don't want to pay any attention to orders unless we pay them first. They have become very rebellious, and therefore it is necessary to use much tact in dealing with them. In relation to the colonos, the hacendado must be a father, mother, or brother. He must take an interest in all of their family problems in order to win their trust. Nevertheless, the Indian thinks one thing, says another, and does something else again. Therefore it is difficult to understand them fully. Always we have to be very close to their problems, to practically live with them in order to know all their plans and thus keep them from leaving the hacienda, since it is getting more difficult to get the labor we need.

In the old days, the mestizo could simply force the Indian to do his bidding. Now the mestizo had to cultivate the Indian's good will. But note that the mestizo was not talking about a relationship of equals. He was thinking in terms of a parent-child relationship. The father must take good care of his children and even humor them at times, if he wants them to be loyal and obedient. Even so, the movement from ruthless despotism to more or less benevolent paternalism represented an enormous gain for the Indian.

In the 1960s, the remaining members of the mestizo elite in Pisaq came to the conclusion that the day of the large hacienda was passing.

Only through subdivision might it be possible to escape the impact of government—imposed agrarian reform or peasant militancy.

The largest subdivision project was undertaken by the Dominican order, which owned 7,000 acres that had been rented to a Pisaq mestizo who had operated the farm under the traditional condition system. When the religious order announced that it was prepared to undertake its own land reform, the landless peasants had high hopes. The Organización de Lotizantes de la Hacienda Sañahuasi included the Indians who worked as serfs, some cholos, and some mestizos. According to the rhetoric of the organizers, those now entirely without land would be favored in the distribution.

When it finally became apparent that the poorer members of the organization were not going to be able to pay the prices set, the Dominicans began selling off parts of the hacienda to the highest bidders. Thus, the chief beneficiaries turned out to be mestizos from Cuzco. Several Indian families did get small pieces, but only in the highest and least desirable areas of the hacienda.

In the other haciendas, the owners subdivided among family members. In several cases, this led to bitter disputes and legal conflicts that further weakened the position of the mestizos.

Finally, there was a possibility of selling parts of an hacienda to the Indians who were working on it. The owners of Chongos tried this maneuver unsuccessfully when they offered the land in dispute with Kuyo Chico to the community of Qotobamba. In other cases, owners sought to come to terms with Indians on their land for the sale of the most unproductive parts of the hacienda. They would work out an agreement for a series of annual payments so that the Indian was not required to provide a large amount of capital at the outset. One of the hacendados describes the process in these words:

> We, the hacendados, had to face up to this worsening situation in various ways. For example, I am selling land to the colonos on time payments. I keep accounts in a notebook so that the peasants who want to buy land can make annual or semi-annual payments, with money from the sale of their animals, which they often sell to the hacienda. In that case, we discuss the price, and when it suits me, I buy the animal to sell it later myself. Sometimes they make payment in cash. According to the arrangement we reach at the beginning, the Indian gets to occupy the land under a promise to purchase it. Under this system, nearly all the colonos already have their individual properties.

Structure, Process, and Personality 9

Up to this point, we have been focusing our attention on structure and processes of social change. Where we have referred to attitudes and beliefs, we have presented illustrative material rather than statistics. In a later chapter, we will deal with the question of causation. Here we present data to illustrate the striking relationships between structure and process on the one hand and psychological orientation on the other.

We begin with a comparative study carried out in 1968 under the direction of Julio Cotler and Lawrence K. Williams in the provinces of Paucartambo and Canchis, the province in which Sicuani is located. The original aim of the project was to compare haciendas and Indian communities across two provinces with sharply different demographic characteristics. As Table 9-1 indicates, the population of Paucartambo was heavily concentrated on haciendas, whereas the population of Canchis was largely divided between Indian or peasant communities and towns, with only 5 percent living on haciendas.

TABLE 9-1

Percentage Distribution of Population by Province According to the 1961 Census (%)

	PAUCARTAMBO	CANCHIS
Population on haciendas	48	5
Population in peasant communities	29	54
Population in towns of over 2,500 inhabitants	26	45
Seven- to Fourteen-year-old children in school	26	45

We found that we lacked the resources to carry out the hacienda surveys in Canchis because the haciendas there, devoted largely to sheep and cattle, had an average of about only 10 families in each, so that to get an adequate sample, our student interviewers would have had to roam all over the province. Other problems prevented us from carrying out surveys in peasant or Indian communities in Paucartambo, so the study leaves us with a comparison in which both structure and demographic characteristics are operating together to produce the extreme differences we see. (In dealing with our studies within the district of Pisaq, we will have an opportunity to compare an hacienda with Indian communities in the same area.)

Table 9-2 gives the number and sex of respondents in this survey.

TABLE 9-2

Number and Sex of Survey Respondents

	MALE	FEMALE	TOTAL
Paucartambo haciendas	45	38	83
Canchis communities	78	64	142

As Table 9-3 indicates, the inhabitants of the Canchis communities were far more closely linked with the past and present of the nation through radio listening, reading and writing, knowledge of history, and command of the national language than were the inhabitants of Paucartambo. They participated more actively in politics. They had more relatives outside of the community, traveled to the provincial capital far

94

TABLE 9-3

Communication and Psychological Orientation
of Population (%)

	PAUCARTAMBO	SICUANI (CANCHIS)
Owns radio	6	84
Listens to radio daily	11	49
Never listens to radio	40	13
Can read and write	6	39
Knows name of president of Peru	26	51
Knows who Incas were	8	42
Knows how old he/she is	34	88
Is bilingual (Spanish and Quechua)	16	62
Has relatives elsewhere	24	53
Goes to provincial capital at least once a week	6	74
Has thought of emigrating	19	35
Has voting card	5	39
Identifies self as Indian	81	37

more often, and also had thought more often of moving away from where they lived. Most of the inhabitants of Paucartambo haciendas identified themselves as Indians, whereas a minority of the Canchis population did so.

As Tables 9-4 and 9-5 indicate, the colonos of Paucartambo were far more fatalistic and the comuneros of Sicuani were much more inclined to

TABLE 9-4
Fatalism (%)

AGREEMENT WITH THE FOLLOWING STATEMENTS	PAUCARTAMBO	SICUANI (CANCHIS)
The Indian was born to obey.	86	40
One cannot change one's fate.	84	62
Some have been born to lead and others to follow.	90	66
It is not worth the trouble to make plans for the future.	70	46

TABLE 9-5
Progress and Opportunities (%)

AGREEMENT WITH THE FOLLOWING STATEMENTS	PAUCARTAMBO	SICUANI (CANCHIS)
This place is making progress.	35	73
Opportunities for poor people are increasing.	47	62

feel that their communities were progressing and their opportunities were increasing.

However, an activistic orientation and a sense of progress and increasing opportunities seem to go along with perception of a higher degree of conflict within the community and between Indians and mestizos in the area, as Table 9-6 indicates.

Having shown how social structure tends to shape attitudes, values, and perceptions, we take a further step in noting how these structural influences are transmitted from one generation to the next. Williams (1973) found a marked relationship between social structure and expressed preferences for child-training practices. In both settings, interviewers asked respondents what the parent should do if a child lost the money given to him when he was sent out to buy sugar. Sixty-nine percent of the hacienda respondents, compared with 37 percent of the community respondents, recommended whipping (a difference significant at the .001 level). Only one of the hacienda respondents thought to ask whether this

TABLE 9-6
Conflict and Cooperation (%)

AGREEMENT WITH THE FOLLOWING STATEMENTS	PAUCARTAMBO	SICUANI (CANCHIS)
There is a high degree of internal collaboration here.	81	30
We do have internal conflicts here.	39	60
Here the relations between Indians and mestizos are good.	70	39

was the first time such irresponsible behavior had occurred; the community respondents were much more inclined to ask questions putting a given item of behavior in a broader context.

Although authoritarian values were markedly more prevalent within the authoritarian structure of the hacienda, when he pooled the responses from both settings and divided them along the lines of the type of punishment recommended, Williams found strong relationships between this attitude and fatalism and future orientation, as Table 9-7 indicates.

We now turn to the district of Pisaq, where we are able to make a broader range of comparisons, including a mestizo town, an hacienda, and three Indian communities with the same area. Since we do not have detailed ethnographic studies of the adjoining Indian communities of Maska and Qotobamba, and since the responses of their populations were quite similar, we have combined those two communities so as to simplify the comparisons.

Before the applied anthropology project began, in 1959, we can assume that Kuyo Chico was very similar to Maska and Qotobamba. We have already noted that the program had major impacts in many other Indian communities, particularly in breaking the dominance of the Pisaq mestizo elite, but we would expect its effects to show up particularly in Kuyo Chico.

TABLE 9-7
Comparison of Values of Parents and
Preferred Mode of Punishment

AGREEMENT WITH FOLLOWING STATEMENTS	PREFERRED WHIPPING, % (N=113)	PREFERRED RESTRICTION, % (N=61)
Man cannot change his fate.	80	56
One's chances in life depend upon luck.	88	70
Most important in bringing up a child is that he		
Obey	73	59
Show initiative	23	33
The Indian was born to obey the mestizo.	74	36
It is important to have plans for the future.	31	45

97

TABLE 9-8

Number and Sex of Survey Respondents

	MALE		FEMALE		TOTAL	
	1964	1969	1964	1969	1964	1969
Pisaq	70	52	30	60	100	112
Chawaytirí	32	29	28	32	60	61
Maska-Qotobamba	43	51	29	51	72	102
Kuyo Chico	38	22	11	29	49	51

The survey responses reported below are based upon the numbers of respondents indicated in Table 9-8.

If we look at evaluations of Indian-mestizo relations, we find that as in the reported comparison between Paucartambo and Canchis, Kuyo Chico—the community that has experienced the greatest progress—found interethnic relations most unsatisfactory. Pisaq, the local center of the declining mestizo elite, was second to Kuyo Chico in its negative evaluations. (See Núñez del Prado, 1973:136-137.)

Unfortunately, we did not have the same item that asked about mestizo-Indian relations in the 1969 questionnaire, so we are unable to determine a trend directly. However, responses to the question. What effect do you think the Applied Anthropology Program has had on this area? indicated a marked shift, at least in Pisaq. In 1964, 100 percent of Kuyo Chico's responses regarding the program fell into the "very favorable" or "somewhat favorable" categories, with the favorable responses in Chawaytirí and Maska-Qotobamba all over 90 percent. Also in 1964, only slightly above 20 percent of the Pisaq respondents gave favorable evaluations, more than double that number gave neutral or unfavorable ones, and the rest declined to express opinions. In 1969, the responses were slightly more negative, but still overhwelmingly favorable, in the Indian communities and on the hacienda, whereas the favorable responses now ran substantially ahead of the neutral and unfavorable combined in Pisaq. The figures suggest that in the course of 10 years, the opposition to the applied anthropology project had faded and it had become more or less accepted. The countinuing emigration of the members of the mestizo elite may also have served to reduce the opposition to the program.

The figures for perceived cooperation and conflict in all communities are reported later, but we should note here that compared with the Indian

communities, Pisaq was much higher in conflict and lower in cooperation. The mestizo town was going through a difficult period of transition.

The figures for Chawaytirí give evidence of a colono settlement in
frustration. In 1964, only 2 percent of the people perceived "much
conflict" in their community; in 1969, that percentage had risen to 15.
At the other end of the scale, 60 percent of the respondents reported
"hardly any or no conflict" in 1964, and that percentage had dropped to
36 in 1969. There was little change in those perceiving "much cooperation" (50 percent in 1964; 47 percent in 1969), but there was a major
change in those perceiving "poor or no cooperation" (8 percent in 1964;
27 percent in 1969). In its evaluation of progress and future prospects of
the community, Chawaytirí was little different from the other communities in 1964 and was far more pessimistic by 1969.

Although the union no longer existed officially in Chawaytirí in 1964,
its impact was fresh in the minds of the inhabitants, and they perceived
the impact of labor unions much more favorably than did the inhabitants
of other communities, as Table 9-9 indicates.

TABLE 9-9
Attitudes toward Labor Unions (1964) (%)

WHAT IMPACT DO YOU THINK UNIONS HAVE ON LIFE OF THE COMMON PEOPLE?	PISAQ	CHAWAYTIRI	KUYO CHICO	MASKA- QOTOBAMBA
Generally beneficial	15	42	16*	23*
Sometimes beneficial, sometimes not	29	33	24	18
Generally harmful	46	18	53	25
NA	10	7	6	33

*Percentages that do not total 100 percent have been rounded off.

Unfortunately, our item on labor unions was worded differently in the
1969 questionnaire, so that an exact comparison between the two surveys is not possible, but as Table 9-10 indicates, the people of
Chawaytirí still showed far more faith than respondents in other communities in the importance of labor unions for improving lives of the
workers.

TABLE 9-10
Attitudes toward Labor Unions (1969) (%)

WHAT IMPORTANCE DO YOU THINK LABOR UNIONS HAVE IN IMPROVING THE WORKERS' LIFE?	PISAQ	CHAWAYTIRI	KUYO CHICO	MASKA-QOTOBAMBA
Much importance	16*	51	35*	43*
Fair importance	16	13	22	17
No importance	18	5	12	21
NA or does not know	49	31	32	20

*Percentages that do not total 100 percent have been rounded off.

In 1964, Kuyo Chico was most negative toward labor unions and Pisaq was only slight less opposed. In response to this somewhat different 1969 item, Pisaq is most negative, and the fact that about 1 of every 2 persons surveyed failed to answer (compared with 1 of 10 in 1964) suggests that unions were becoming a more sensitive issue in Pisaq. Here we see Kuyo Chico responding about as favorably as Maska-Qotobamba, which suggests that following the abrupt withdrawal of the Applied Anthropology Program, the Kuyo Chicans were more inclined than before to consider the value of linking themselves with such an outside power base as a labor union.

As we focus on the Indian communities, we see Kuyo Chico resembling Maska-Qotobamba in some respects but differing in others. All three communities were perceived by respondents as high in cooperation and low in conflict. All of the communities we surveyed in the Pisaq district were more pessimistic in 1969 than in 1964 regarding the future progress of their communities, but we find Kuyo Chico's negative shift very small in comparison with the shift in the other communities.

The 1969 survey was carried out in Kuyo Chico shortly after the abrupt closing of the applied anthropology project by the government. This event seems clearly reflected in our 1964 and 1969 responses to items measuring confidence in the national government. In 1964, Kuyo Chicans expressed much more confidence in the national government than did the other Cuzco communities. For example, in 1964 55 percent of the men and 64 percent of the women rejected the statement that "the government takes no interest in the problems of the people," and in 1969 this rate of rejection had dropped to 18 percent and 28 percent, respectively. On this particular item, Kuyo Chico was more negative toward government than was any of the 11 other communities and 5 haciendas of the 1969 survey.

Did this government action sap the confidence of Kuyo Chicans in their ability to solve the problems of their community? Apparently not, as Table 9-11 indicates that Kuyo Chicans also have a higher degree of civic awareness and concern for problems at the community level.

Regarding correct identification of the president, there is a marked difference by sex. Not a single female respondent in Chawaytirí or Maska-Qotobamba could identify the president. Thirteen percent of the women of Pisaq, compared with 7 percent of the Kuyo Chico women gave the right answer. More than half (54 percent) of the Kuyo Chico male respondents knew who the president was. (On this question, we cannot make a valid comparison between the Pisaq and the Paucartambo-Canchis studies because the latter study was carried out more than four

TABLE 9-11
Civic Awareness, Concern, and Confidence (1969) (%)

	PISAQ	CHAWAYTIRI	KUYO CHICO	MASKA-QOTOBAMBA
Remembers the president's name.	30	8	28	15
Have you ever worried about some problems of (village) so as to be willing to do something to solve them?				
Yes, many times	18	8	28	23
Have you ever worried about any Peruvian problem so as to be willing to do something to solve it?				
Yes, many times	12	2	8	6
What chance do you and others like you have to solve the problems of this community?				
Very good	30	30	57	54
Fair	38	25	29	29
Poor	25	34	10	12
NA	8	12	4	4

years after President Belaúnde had taken office, and he had gained that position after extraordinarily extensive campaigning in 1962 and 1963. The 1969 survey in the Pisaq district was carried out approximately eight months after the military government had taken office—and President Velasco had not done any campaigning in this area or anywhere else.)

The best measure of economic progress is provided by our survey items regarding possession of modern artifacts, reported in Table 9-12.

TABLE 9-12

Posession of Modern Artifacts (%)

	CHAWAYTIRI 1969	1964	PISAQ 1969	1964	KUYO CHICO 1969	1964	MASKA-QOTOBAMBA 1969	1964
Radio	0	2	33	45	10	26	0	14
Sewing machine	0	7	40	45	12	24	4	4
Kerosene stove or Primus stove	0	5	17	39	16	24	0	11
Watch or clock	0	0	29	33	10	14	0	4
Bicycle	0	0	9	18	4	8	0	2
Truck, tractor, or automobile	0	0	3	0	0	2	0	1
Record player	0	2	3	17	2	12	0	3
Typewriter	0	0	13	17	0	8	0	2

The table suggests the following four conclusions:

1. Pisaq ranks first in possession of modern artifacts, in 1969 as in 1964.
2. The rate of increase in possession of these objects has been much greater in Kuyo Chico than in Pisaq.
3. In 1964, only Pisaq and Kuyo Chico participated in the market economy of manufactured goods.
4. In 1969, Maska-Qotobamba and Chawaytirí had also entered into the market economy. The economic growth in Maska-Qotobamba is particularly impressive.

CONCLUSIONS

Chawaytirí stands out from the other communities in its favorable attitudes toward unions. The period 1964–1969 seems to have been one of stagnation and frustration, which was reflected in increased perception of conflict, decreased perception of cooperation, a sharp decline in interpersonal trust, increasing pessimism regarding community progress, and reduced confidence in ability to solve community problems. And the colonos did not look to the hacendado or administrator to improve conditions; only 8 percent of the respondents thought the activities of these individuals tended to improve conditions. Having lost the outside support of the union, Chawaytirí was waiting impatiently for the government's promised agrarian reform.

Pisaq was a more affluent community than the others in both years and had made some small economic gains during the five-year period between surveys, but its social organization showed the strains accompanying changes in the distribution of power. In this valley, Pisaq was the highest community in perceived conflict and the lowest community in perceived cooperation in both surveys; and the 1969 figures show a drop in cooperation and an increase in conflict there. During the five-year period, the people of Pisaq came to be less optimistic about the progress of their community; at the same time, they came to be more favorable to the Applied Anthropology Program.

Kuyo Chico, Maska, and Qotobamba resemble each other in being high in perceived cooperation and low in perceived conflict. Kuyo Chico stands out in its confidence in its future and its orientation towards collective action. Although the structural changes flowing from the Applied Anthropology Program had important impacts upon Maska and Qotobamba also, the more intensive work of the program in Kuyo Chico may account for the difference in favor of that community on a series of items designed to measure modernism. The structural and attitudinal changes in these Indian communities have been marked by accelerated economic progress. (For more detailed treatment of these changes, with emphasis on Kuyo Chico, see Núñez del Prado, 1973.)

JUNIN III

Junín in the Central Highlands 10

Within the department of Junín, we will focus our attention on two adjoining valleys that followed markedly different but converging lines of development. The two are linked together through geography and history by the Mantaro River and two cities along its banks, Jauja and Huancayo. The Yanamarca valley rises from Jauja to the north; the Mantaro valley follows the river from Jauja southeast to Huancayo and beyond.

The Mantaro valley has long been noted for its independent and dynamic rural communities. Until midcentury, the Yanamarca valley was dominated by haciendas. As we follow the development of the peasant movement in the Yanamarca, we will see the emerging peasant communities fitting into the pattern of the neighboring valley villages. Through examining the distribution of power and the processes of conflict and cooperation in three peasant communities in the Mantaro valley, we shall also be illustrating some of the problems and processes we would expect to find in the Yanamarca valley a few years later.

Although there is as yet no air service into these valleys, otherwise this part of the central highlands is more readily accessible to Lima than is almost any other part of the highlands. The Central Railroad makes the run in eight hours. On a road that is well paved most of the way, in three hours drive from Lima we reach the altitude of a little over 3 miles, at the pass of Ticlio. Another hour brings us down to La Oroya, a great mining center at about 12,500 feet; and in a little more than five hours from the coast, we find ourselves in Jauja, at about 10,500 feet. On one of the level, paved roads that run along either side of the Mantaro River, we reach Huancayo by the end of the sixth hour.

The central highway is heavily traveled from Lima to Huancayo, which is not only the end of the Central Railroad but is also the connecting point for highways to other parts of the highlands. As we drive through the Mantaro valley, we see some buses that go to and from Lima and others that provide frequent service through the valley. Along with busses, there are a number of lines of *colectivos* (six-passenger cars) that make daily runs between Huancayo and Lima or between Huancayo and other sierra cities.

The two cities along the river differ markedly. Jauja (population 15,000 in 1972) has the charm of colonial architecture and the slow pace of a provincial town, whereas Huancayo (population 46,000 in 1961 and growing explosively during the next decade) looks like an unfinished frontier city, buzzing with industrial and commercial activities. Huancayo is famous for its Sunday market, where stalls sell everything from plastic ware to native handicrafts, on the main street and spreading into some of the side streets.

Between these two cities, along both sides of the river, are the Mantaro valley villages we were studying. In general, they are not located on main roads but have easy access to them, with frequent bus service to Huancayo or Jauja. Most of the villages are built around a central square, the Plaza de Armas, which has a church, often without a resident priest, and usually a municipal office on one side. Houses are generally built of adobe brick, locally produced, and many are whitewashed or painted.

Houses and public buildings and squares in the Yanamarca valley resemble those of the Mantaro valley and yet, within a given village, present marked contrasts, between poor, deteriorating structures and new buildings. In the Yanamarca valley, the peasants have only recently emerged from serfdom and are still building their communities.

Although Junín and Cuzco are similar in altitude, with most of their areas being 10,000 feet or over, and in 1960 had similar per capita incomes ($82 for Cuzco; $76 for Junín), and two departments differ in important respects. Junín has only about two-fiths the land area of Cuzco but is much more densely populated: in 1961, the populations were 14.10 per square kilometer for Junín versus 8.27 per square kilometer for Cuzco. The Junín population is concentrated particularly heavily in the Mantaro valley.

In the context of our study, the per capita income figures for the two departments are misleading. In Junín, and particularly in the valleys of our study, the farm income was much more evenly distributed than in most parts of Cuzco. Furthermore, although we do not have detailed figures for area comparisons, where we have the most comprehensive community study data, average income was much higher in our Mantaro valley villages than in those in the district of Pisaq in Cuzco.

We were studying only a small part of Junín, but we were at a central point in the commercial and transportation network of the department. The road north from Jauja up the Yanamarca valley goes over the mountains and then drops steadily through Tarma and into the tropical lowlands, where fruits and coffee are raised. Huancayo is the major road-transportation center to the neighboring departments of Pasco, Huancavelica, Ayacucho, and Cuzo and, besides being the rail terminal of the line from the coast, through Jauja has rail connections into the mining areas to the northwest.

PIZARRO MEETS THE HUANCAS

The differences in social structure between the Mantaro and Yanamarca valleys in the early 1900s had their origins four centuries earlier. The Huancas, who occupied the Mantaro valley at the time of the conquest by Pizarro, had been defeated and incorporated into the Incan empire only about 1460 and had not ceased to regard the Incas as their enemies. When Pizarro and his men reached Jauja, they were given a warm welcome by a large crowd. Five days of feasting, drinking, and dancing led to the signing of a treaty whereby, in return for their military support of the Spaniards, the Huancas were guaranteed continued possession of their lands and local autonomy.

After the death of Pizarro, the treaty was disregarded with the establishment of the first *encomiendas* in the valley and with the requirement that the Indians pay tribute, in silver and gold, to the *encomendero*. Huanca delegations went in vain to complain to the government at Lima.

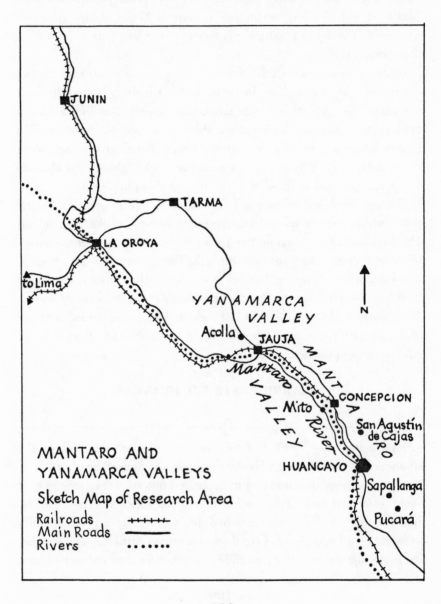

MANTARO AND
YANAMARCA VALLEYS

Sketch Map of Research Area

Railroads ++++++
Main Roads ———
Rivers ••••••

In 1560, two Huanca leaders made their way to the court in Spain and secured an audience with King Philip II. The king was surprised and impressed with the petitioners' letters and documents, signed by Pizarro. He granted all their requests, the most important one being that the Spanish haciendas already established in the valley should be eliminated and that, in the future, no Spaniards should be permitted to own large estates in that area (Espinosa, 1973). This decision did not apply to the Yanamarca valley, which continued to be dominated by large landholders.

If we jumped directly from this early history to the present time, we might assume that the absence of haciendas in the Mantaro valley provided the basic explanation for the growth of independent democratic communities and that transportation linkages to the coast and to the mines simply served to speed up the pace of development within a society already receptive to change. However, as we dig into the history of the last century, we recognize the absence of haciendas as a necessary, but not sufficient, explanation of rural independence and dynamism. In fact, our studies reveal a clear-cut dominance— submission system based upon the distribution of political power. The breakdown of that pattern must be seen in the context of the changing positions of Jauja and Huancayo.

HUANCAYO VERSUS JAUJA

Jauja had been the capitol of the Huanca tribe, and it was here that the Spaniards established their first administrative center in the region. Jauja was important in the struggle for independence in the central highlands, and its importance was not challenged by Huancayo until early in the independence period. The immediate post-independence years saw a struggle of military *caudillos* for the control of Peru. General Gamarra camped in Huancayo and called a constituent assembly there to produce the Constitution of 1829, but the general then moved on to Jauja.

In 1854, Ramón Castilla, one of Peru's great presidents, established his military headquarters in Huancayo to wage the struggle against General Echenique. Echenique had the solid support of the important landowners of the valley, who resided in Jauja, so Castilla had to seek support in the southern part of the valley, among the Indians who were struggling against the mestizo elite. The Indians rallied around Castilla, and he responded with two measures, one economic and the other political. He abrogated the tribute law through which the national government had levied a head tax on Indians, and he rewarded the villages that had favored his cause by creating new political districts, including that of Huancayo. Huancayo was made the capital of its political district in 1857, and in 1864 it was elevated to the status of capitol of a province, thus freeing the entire southern part of the valley from the control of Jauja.

In this process, Huancayo had become a political rallying point and a growing commercial center for the indigenous population. By 1876, Huancayo had grown well beyond Jauja in population as well: it had 5,848 inhatibants, whereas Jauja had 2,773.

In the latter part of the nineteenth century, small mining enterprises developed at Cercapuquio in the southern part of the valley and in the neighboring department of Huancavelica. Generally, the proprietors of the mines took up residence in Huancayo, which had become a transportation center, with at least six roads fanning out from it into the departments of Ayacucho and Huancavelica as well as back to Jauja.

The War of the Pacific (1879–1883) had a disastrous effect upon the Peruvian economy in general, and Jauja was much more adversely affected than Huancayo. All of the finances for General Caceres's army were raised by the leading citizens of Jauja. The wives of the leading citizens even turned over their jewels to support the military campaign.

Jauja did enjoy economic recovery toward the end of the nineteenth century because of two new factors. By 1893, the Central Railroad had reached La Oroya, making it possible for a group of European immigrants to establish residence and headquarters in Jauja and to import merchandise from Europe and Lima by railroad to La Oroya and from there by mule team down into the Mantaro valley. In this same period, the market for luxury items in Jauja was expanding because of the establishment of a tuberculosis sanitarium. Only the rich could afford sanitarium treatment; and when one family member was hospitalized in Jauja, relatives resided there for long periods. Immigration from Europe and commercial activities greatly increased again around 1908, when the Central Railroad was completed through to Jauja and Huancayo.

Until close to the turn of the century, there was little commercial

112

traffic from Lima into the Mantaro valley. Commerce from the outside consisted largely of coca and aguardiente, both products coming from the eastern lowland areas. Otherwise, centered in Huancayo, there was an internal market for farm products and native handicrafts.

In the first years of the twentieth century, with the completion of the railroad and the new wave of immigration, the growing commercial import traffic from the coast came to be entirely controlled by eight Jauja families, all originally immigrants from Europe or migrants from the coast. They also monopolized the export of valley products, particularly wool, to the coast.

Although, before 1890, the larger landholders had controlled political and economic power and had dominated the social life of the area, by 1910 the leaders of commerce with Lima had become accepted into the social elite of Jauja and also were sharing in political power. Even some members of the local landholding elite were sufficiently stimulated by the success of the businessmen from outside as themselves to enter commerce, particularly trade with the mining areas, which expanded rapidly after the founding of the Cerro de Pasco Corporation, in 1902.

The first decades of the twentieth century also marked the expansion and modernization of cattle-raising operations in the Mantaro valley, with the formation of the Sociedad Ganadera Junín (1906) and the Sociedad Ganadera del Centro (1910). The latter was of particular importance, because it was a joint venture of the valley elite and members of the so-called oligarchy in Lima. The Cerro de Pasco Corporation was involved first as a minor stockholder and, in 1926, assumed full ownership of the Sociedad Ganadero del Centro. A United States–owned company, the Cerro de Pasco Corporation had a major influence in developing the cattle and wool enterprises in the area.

The Junín society was important because the Jaujan landholder members who had put their estates into the new enterprise now found it possible to move to Lima and leave their interests in the hands of local administrators. Only owners of medium-size lands remained in Jauja.

In the decade of the 1930s, the importance of Jauja again declined sharply, and Huancayo increasingly dominated the valley. The worldwide depression drastically reduced local demand for manufactured products from Europe and the coast and reduced the sale of local products outside the valley. This led some of the most prominent commercial families to abandon Jauja for the coast.

This economic change was accompanied by a political shift of major importance. The capitol of the department of Junín was transferred in 1931 from Cerro de Pasco to Huancayo. This move has been attributed to the desires of leading departmental officials to escape the rigorous climate of Cerro de Pasco, almost 15,000 above sea level. But why the transfer to Huancayo rather than Jauja? Along with the commercial growth of Huancayo there were important political considerations.

The Jauja elite, which stood to gain commercial advantages through the government road-building program, had been strongly allied with Leguía. Since the major burden of road building fell upon peasants of the region, they were hostile to Leguía and welcomed his overthrow by Sánchez Cerro. The new president and his prefect were naturally unwilling to locate the department capital in the heart of Leguía country.

The completion of the central highway to Huancayo, in the early 1930s, also marked a gain for Huancayo over Jauja. Before 1908, it had been a day's journey from Huancayo to Jauja, so travelers from Huancayo to the coast had been obliged to stay overnight in Jauja. The railroad, and later the highway, minimized Jauja's advantage in relation to the coast, while Huancayo continued to grow in importance as a highlands transportation center.

ECONOMIC ACTIVITIES

Around the mid-twentieth century, the agricultural production patterns of Junín and Cuzco were similar. In the highlands of both departments, the potato was the most important crop, followed by corn or barley. In the eastern lowland areas of both departments, there was substantial coffee production. In livestock, the pattern was also similar in 1961, with Junín having somewhat more sheep (1,500,000) and somewhat fewer cattle (215,000) than Cuzco.

The major difference between departments was found in mining. Cuzco's mines were small, scattered, and generally unproductive, whereas Cerro de Pasco's mines in Junín produced large amounts of copper, lead, zinc, and other metals.

Outside of the city of Cuzco, only the Sicuani area could be compared with the Mantaro valley in the pace of commerce, the development of artisan and industrial shops, and the growth of occupational differentiation. The Yanamarca valley resembled the hacienda-dominated areas of Pisaq and Paucartambo in Cuzco before the rise of peasant movements.

THE STRUCTURE OF LOCAL GOVERNMENT

The formal structue of local government in Junín is no different from that of other departments of Peru, but we have deferred a detailed description of formal local governmental structure up to this point because it is not until we discuss Junín that the problems we studied require such background information.

Peru is divided into 23 departments (plus the constitutional province of Callao) and subdivided into 149 provinces. At the lower levels in the rural areas, we find political districts or municipalities and, within them, villages or Indian communities.

At the time our studies began, the minister of government (now called the minister of the interior) appointed a prefect for each department (roughly equivalent to a state in the United States). The prefect appointed subprefects for each province. Below the subprefects, there were governors, one for each district. At the bottom of this official hierarchy was the lieutenant governor, who had jurisdiction over one or more small villages. Unofficially, in the past, the lieutenant governor appointed or approved the election of a mayor or a head man (*alcalde envarado* or cabecilla) from among the villagers.

A town important enough to be classified as the capitol of a district or municipality had its own mayor (alcalde) and council, directly responsible to the prefect, as shown in Figure 10-1.

The police were also under the control of the minister of government. (The hierarchy of the police force is not shown in Figure 10-1). The subprefect had considerable influence over the activities of the police in his province.

The municipal council derived its revenues primarily from the national government. Since in recent years, this subsidy has amounted to a flat 50,000 soles (which has varied from $1,800 to $1,200 at prevailing rates of exchange) for each municipality, regardless of population, level of economic activity, or needs, and since, traditionally, the subsidy has

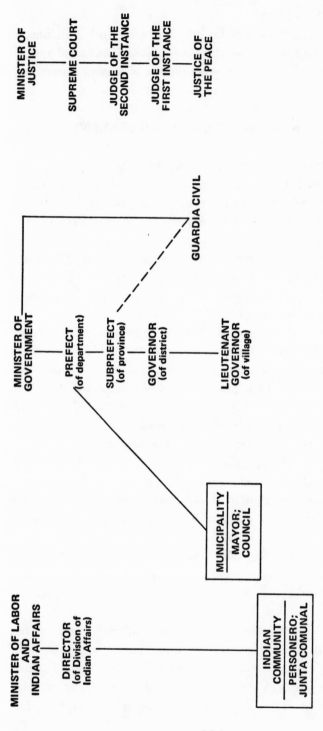

FIGURE 10-1

Local Government in Rural Peru in the 1960s

116

been used entirely or very largely within the district capitol, there were obvious incentives for people in a village to try to establish a new municipality, with its own subsidy, under its own control.

The municipality derived some small revenue from the paper work so important to life in Peru: certificates of birth, death, matrimony, and other papers. The municipality also got fees from vendors who had places in its local market and from licenses for other small businessmen. It maintained a cemetery, charging the families who made use of it. Finally, small amounts were raised from fines against violators of local ordinances.

Official government recognition of an Indian community established a dual system of local government at the bottom level. Such a community was under the general jurisdiction of the municipal authorities, but the community also had a direct link with the national government through the Division of Indian Affairs (now called the Division of Peasant Communities) in the Ministry of Labor (now in the Ministry of Agriculture). According to the regulations established in national legislation, each officially recognized Indian community elected a personero for a two-year term to represent its interests before the national government. It also annually elected a junta comunal, presided over by a president elected by the members of the junta, as its local governing body. All adults were eligible to vote for these local officials, and there was no literacy requirement, although the personero had to be literate. This junta presided over asembleas (meetings of the whole community) held monthly for the discussion of community problems.

In theory, the land was owned in common and none of it could be sold to nonmembers of the community. In fact, most recognized Indian communities involved family ownership of property; but in any case, the legal provision of inalienability of the property from members of the community did provide important protection. The Indian community has traditionally been based upon agriculture, with the grazing lands, at least, being held in common, providing for a base of common interests.

The Indian community could receive revenue from renting communally owned land to some of its members and for granting grazing rights on these lands, with each member paying according to the number of animals owned. The community generally had less financial income than did the municipality, but it was *not* primarily dependent upon higher authorities for its income.

The Peasant Movement 11
in the Yanamarca Valley

Although the peasant movements in the Convención valley and throughout the southern sierra received wide coverage in the media, the movement in the Yanamarca valley was unreported in the Lima press. The
Convención valley movement and related movements built a regional
labor organization, promoted radical political ideologies, and produced a
charismatic leader, Hugo Blanco. The Yanamarca valley movement had
no central coordinating organization. The colonos on each hacienda were
strongly influenced by what they heard of developments elsewhere, but
they carried out their struggle against the hacendados on an hacienda-to-
hacienda basis. Although there may have been individual peasant leaders
who believed in revolutionary ideologies, no one among them gained much
more than local attention. Nevertheless, the history of the Yanamarca
valley movement will show important similarities with those described
earlier. In Part V, we shall use these several cases to build a theoretical
model of peasant movements in Peru.

Outside of Jauja, the only town of importance in our story is Acolla, next to the hacienda of Yanamarca. Most of the land in the valley was in the form of six haciendas whose owners or renters lived in Jauja and were important members of its power elite.

The mines of Cerro de Pasco provided the most important impetus to change in the valley. While their fathers stayed on the hacienda to retain the claim to family lands, sons left to spend months, and sometimes years, in the mines. They earned money to bring back to their families. They not only were exposed to the discipline of industrial life, but they also gained experience in union activities. Although the company did not formally recognize the union until 1944, union activities predated this event by many years.

HACIENDA YANAMARCA

Yanamarca had maintained closer contacts with the outside world than other haciendas had because it bordered on Acolla and was only a few miles away from Jauja. During the last years of the colonial period, the hacienda had belonged to a Spanish captain. With the establishment of the republic, it passed to the control of the state, which rented it to private individuals. Yanamarca consisted of 3,269 hectares of which only 540 were cultivable. Its main products were barley, potatoes, quinua, and more recently, onions.

The traditional hacienda regime continued with insignificant changes up to the 1930s. Early organizing efforts centered on education. The colonos invited a teacher from Acolla to give classes to their children. Then they established connections with the Ministry of Education, which beginning in 1940, provided the local teacher. After their first years of instruction in the hacienda, the children of the more affluent colonos continued their schooling in Acolla.

In 1945, national events speeded up the process of change. With the direct participation of APRA members in positions of regional and national power, unionization spread not only among the urban proletariat but also in the rural areas of the coast.

A group of young ex-miners, under the leadership of an Aprista schoolteacher of Acolla, mobilized a large segment of the colono population. After a series of general meetings, held at night to avoid discovery,

119

the colonos presented their first series of complaints to the hacendado. At first, their aim was to improve their relationship with the hacendado. In the presence of an official of the Ministry of Labor and Indian Affairs, representatives of the colonos and the hacendado agreed that the *patrón* (hacendado) should abolish some of the labor obligations and the colonos should comply regularly with their work responsibilities. Soon afterward, the colonos filed a complaint with the Ministry of Justice, accusing the patrón of breaking the agreement. Later, they sent a statement of their grievances to the Ministry of Labor and Indian Affairs.

This was the beginning of a long legal struggle in Lima and Huancayo. At one point, the prefect of Huancayo intervened when the patrón accused the leaders of the movement of being Communists and social agitators. The colonos reacted with a written statement to the minister of the interior, but in spite of their relentless efforts, the ministry ordered expulsion of the peasant leaders. The order was not carried out because the leaders signed an agreement with the hacendado not to participate in any subversive activities, to obey orders, and to drop all of their demands. But this was not the end. In a general meeting, the peasants repudiated these leaders, and a new leadership emerged.

At this point, the colonos decided to get in touch with the member of parliament for the province of Jauja. After many trips to Lima, they obtained an audience with this important figure, to whom they presented the details of their long conflict with the hacendado. Before the deputy could help, national events blocked peasant progress. With the establishment, in 1948, of the Odría dictatorship and the closing of the national parliament, connections with the deputy became irrelevant. Thus, Yanamarca temporarily returned to the style of life and work that had existed earlier.

In 1950, an important change occurred at the top of the hacienda organization. The previous patrón did not renew his lease and was replaced by the ex-deputy who had earlier established contacts with the colonos. The new hacendado introduced a more rational system that clearly specified, in a written contract, the rights and obligations of both parties. He accorded the colonos a few concessions and, in exchange, received a written statement in which they fully accepted responsibility for their work obligations. For several years no overt conflict occurred. Meanwhile, the organizational activity that had been directed against the patrón was now turned toward other endeavors. It was at this time that the parent-teacher association became important. This organization went beyond educational matters into many aspects of life on the hacienda. Under its auspices, a school building was constructed, after the leaders of the parent-teacher association persuaded the hacendado to provide the school with a small plot of land whose production would go toward expenses of the school.

One of the most prominent figures of the next stage of the struggle after completing primary education in the hacienda school had continued his education in a secondary school of Acolla. Afterwards, he worked as a miner in La Oroya, where he was active in the union. When his father died, he came back to the hacienda to take over the family land and obligations. As was the case with other ex-miners, he was anxious to share what he learned in the mines with those who had never left the hacienda.

While ferment was continuing among the peasants, the hacendado changed the production process, introducing new machinery, insecticides, and new crops, such as onions. After a few profitable years, the hacendado faced a serious economic crisis when bad weather caused severe losses to two consecutive harvests. The first reaction of the hacendado was to offer more land and higher wages to the mayordomo and the foreman to make them get more work out of the colonos.

Increased work pressure provoked a peasant reaction. On the night of April 20, 1961, the peasants all gathered to form a union. Then they contacted a lawyer from Huancayo for help in gaining legal recognition of their union. Their first effort failed because the hacendado was an active member of APRA, with which the CTP was closely linked. This did not discourage the peasants, who sought and won support by local leaders of the Communist-led CGTP. Two years after the founding of the union, the colonos of Yanamarca gained official recognition from the subregional office of the Ministry of Labor in Huancayo.

In its new legal position, the union renewed and expanded the 1945 demands. When the hacendado rejected the demands, the union called a strike. The hacendado reacted by calling for the intervention of the prefect of Junín.

When the situation had reached a standstill, national events once again had a direct impact on the local situation. After the election of

1963, the peasants, feeling that President Belaúnde was now behind them, decided to radicalize their goals. They sent the president a statement asking for the right to rent the hacienda, thus eliminating the patrón. After a long delay, the peasants were notified that their request had been taken into consideration but that they should wait for the impending promulgation of an agrarian reform law.

Meanwhile, the two years of union struggle were disastrous for the hacendado. When he could no longer pay the rent, the peasants negotiated the transfer of the lease to a cooperative they formed for the purpose of taking over the land.

HACIENDA TINGO

The liberation of Tingo began in 1952. The initiative came from a young highlands man who had gone to Lima for a medical education and had become involved in APRA activities. When Odría took over the government in 1948, the student had to go underground. He turned up in Tingo, settled down to work the land, and married a Tingo girl.

The first organizational step centered on a project for establishing a school. The hacendado sought to discourage the project, arguing that education would be of no value to peasant children. However, the peasants won support from the Ministry of Education, so that schooling began in Tingo even against the landlord's opposition.

Now the hacendado ran into further difficulties. His father had divided several haciendas and a power plant in Jauja among the children, with Tingo going to one of the sisters. At great expense to himself, the hacendado had carried through litigation that won him Tingo in exchange for other properties. He thus started his operation of Tingo in tight financial straits. From 1942 to 1952, he secured large loans from the Agricultural Development Bank, but he had spent most of the money on international travel and gracious living in Jauja and Lima.

Until 1952, the hacendado spent very little time in Tingo. When the bank began to press for repayment, the hacendado turned his attention to Tingo and sought to squeeze more work out of the people. When some failed to respond, he expelled them from the land. On this occasion, there was no overt response from the other colonos. Some time later, when he found two of the community leaders not applying themselves diligently, the hacendado ordered them and their families to leave the property at once. At this point, all the colonos vowed that if these two men were to be thrown out, the hacendado would have to throw them all out, and they flatly refused to do any further work for him. He appealed to the authorities in Jauja, but this did not break the unity of the community.

When the peasant challenge came, the hacendado found himself in a deteriorating position. The legal struggle against his brothers and sisters for Tingo had been expensive and had destroyed family solidarity. The family had held unquestioned social and political preeminence in Jauja in the days of his father, but the hacendado now found himself in acrimonious competition for prestige and influence with a rising businessman-farmer who actually worked in his various enterprises. Furthermore, the hacendado's arrogant manner had made him unpopular with both his peers and his social inferiors.

He responded to the colono challenge in a traditional manner. In Jauja and Huancayo, he lavishly entertained members of the local and national elite—thus further depleting his resources. As the bank pressed for repayment, he sought to cultivate Huancayo bank officials, two recent graduates of the National Agrarian University. He urged on them the following arguments: "We are friends." "We are gentlemen." "We are fellow white men."

When the officials persisted in their unfriendly, ungentlemanly, and unwhite demands, the hacendado went to Lima to call on the president of the bank, whom he considered a friend of the family. The president telephoned Huancayo to ask for information on the case. When the Huancayo officials submitted a written report that documented in detail the incompetent and irresponsible management of Tingo, the president took no further action, and the Huancayo office renewed its pressures on the landlord.

By the time of the strike, the community leaders had already been in touch with lawyers in Jauja and with union leaders in Jauja and Huancayo. Through these contacts, they learned that another family claimed to own the property. On the advice of their lawyer, they made a deal to buy Tingo from the other claimant. At the same time, they arranged with the Agricultural Development Bank to take over the mortgage on which the hacendado had defaulted. While the hacendado continued to press his case in the courts, the peasants had won their struggle, with the support of local politicians and the bank's recognition of de facto ownership.

ELSEWHERE IN THE YANAMARCA VALLEY

We have less detailed accounts on the three other communities that arose out of haciendas, but we can fill in the main outlines. What is now Armonía was a cattle hacienda. Beginning in 1946, in response to the expulsion of peasants from a neighboring hacienda, the colonos formed a union. When Armonía was sold to a new proprietor, he established a system requiring fewer cowhands and expelled 44 families.

The peasant leaders got help from the miners' union in La Oroya and from lawyers in Jauja. They pursued a two-pronged strategy: on the one hand, they sued the hacendado for the pay that they had not received for many years of work; on the other hand, they offered to buy the hacienda. In 1949, with the help of their lawyer, they arranged the purchase. They named their new community Armonía, in recognition of the solidarity displayed by the peasants.

The liberation of Chuquishuari was influenced by earlier developments in Tingo, although Chuquishuari achieved legal recognition of its independence long before Tingo did. Mobilization began in 1955, when the peasants were under the domination of a very tough owner who was seeking to exact six days a week of work from each family. The peasants organized, and their leaders went to the Jauja office of the Ministry of Labor with their protests. The owner retaliated by getting some of the leaders arrested and getting the authorities to pursue those who left the hacienda as "fugitives from justice." The unrest continued into 1957, when the owner died. His widow, tired of the apparently endless problems and having no wish herself to assume the responsibilities, agreed to sell the land to the peasants. The transaction was carried out with the assistance of lawyers in Jauja.

The Sacas case differs from the others in that the change in ownership took place there through a long process of evolution and without any legal confrontations or physical conflicts. The change took several decades, and it began when the owner of the property left it in equal parts

124

to four sons. The plots were too small for any of the sons to make a living as an absentee owner. The sons met this problem by living and working in Sacas alongside the peasants. By 1940, the descendents of the owner had intermarried with nonowning peasants, so that owners and nonowners were now linked in family ties.

By the 1960s, another generation of owners had moved to Jauja, leaving the land in the control of their sons. The owners' sons and the sons of nonowners worked the land together and worked out an agreement so that all the families in the community would own land. The transaction was completed in 1967.

The Evolution of Peasant 12
Communities

The political and economic competition between the traditional city Jauja) and the rising commercial center (Huancayo) is paralleled by the evolution of the peasant communities of the Mantaro valley. Mito represents the breaking up of the traditional control pattern, whereas Pucará and San Agustín de Cajas represent former *anexos* (satellite villages) of other political districts which gained their independence as they grew in population and political influence.

Even today's casual visitor to these three villages is impressed by their contrast in the pace of economic and political activities. Mito is a village living in its past. Many of the homes have been abandoned. Villagers speak nostalgically about the good old days when Mito was an active center of economic and political activity. The inhabitants talk vaguely about possible future improvements, yet mainly one hears laments about how the town has gone downhill.

In Cajas and Pucará, we find a spirit of dynamism and political activism. People talk confidently about future improvements, and the villages are alive with diverse economic activities.

It would be impossible to explain this contrast in terms of the natural resources available to these villages. Only as we examine their political history do we find clues to the present state of decadence in Mito and dynamism in Cajas and Pucár.

Up to 1854, there were just five political districts in the rural area of the valley, each one with a village as its capitol. Mito was the capitol of its district, whereas Pucará and Cajas were anexos of other district capitols. History shows Mito losing population and influence as its anexos gained political freedom, while Pucará and Cajas grew and gained the status of municipalities and district capitols.

In the late nineteenth and early twentieth centuries, the Indians in the anexos were subject to exploitation by the mestizo elite in the district capitols. The system was particularly onerous in Mito, where the local elite was closely allied with the dominant mestizos in Jauja. There the system of exploitation of the anexos included the following features:

1. The people in the anexos were obliged to carry out public works for the exclusive benefit of Mito. This involved cleaning the streets, building new roads, and providing labor for other types of public works.
2. The people of the anexos were required to provide construction materials for public works in Mito.
3. Jauja levied tolls on all roads and bridges leading into the city. Half of the income went to Jauja and the other half to Mito.
4. The leading citizens of Mito owned large tracts of land. Since it was not fitting for mestizos to work with their hands, they exploited the labor of the Indians in the anexos.
5. Until 1931, the people of the anexos were excluded from the electoral process, since voting was limited to those who were literate, owned moderate-size property, and paid taxes to the municipal council of Mito.
6. Jauja controlled the educational system of the region. It was customary to establish schools in the district capitols, and although children in the anexos were not legally excluded, they had to walk long distances, and social discrimination by the children of Mito

127

further discouraged attendance. Thus literacy tended to be concentrated in the district capitols until well into the twentieth century.

7. Jauja held a monopoly on the judicial system. The judges, notary publics, and scribes, who drew up legal documents for fees, were all located in Jauja, along with lawyers and nonprofessional "fixers." The Mestizo elite of Jauja controlled this system and worked closely with its counterpart in Mito in any matter involving conflicts between Mito and people in the anexos.

This system of political domination came under increasing pressure from migration to and from the mines and from the growing population. The census of 1876 reported 119,933 in the valley, and the figure had risen to 226,862 by 1940 and to 339,948 by 1961.

Work in the mines stimulated rural change in several ways. People in the anexos within the same political district had not known each other. As they lived and worked together, they came to see that they shared common interests as people exploited by the district capitol. Union activity encouraged them to look to union leaders for help on all sorts of problems. Finally, as mine workers returned to their home communities, they brought back savings to be used for political activities.

The mobilization of people in the anexos brought about their separation from Mito in three stages (1917, 1929, and 1941). We do not have figures for Mito before 1917; but in 1929, Mito possessed 1,348 hectares of cultivable land, devoted largely to potatoes, barley, and wheat. Mito also controlled 17,227 hectares of grazing lands, which provided pasturage for 3,370 sheep and 3,180 cattle. By 1941, the cultivated lands had dropped to 522 hectares and the pasture land to 1,348 hectares.

These reductions in territory were accompanied by sharp decreases in population in both the political district as a whole and the town of Mito. The figures are given in Table 12-1.

As they lost control of lands and cheap labor, the mestizos in Mito faced a dilemma. Many of them could still have made a living by farming but only if they had been prepared to work the lands themselves. The other alternative was to migrate to the city, selling the land, renting it out, or working out a sharecropper arrangement. Increasing numbers of the mestizos of Mito chose to leave the town.

The villages of Pucará and Cajas did not seem to be as tightly controlled as the anexos of Mito, which was much closer to Jauja.

TABLE 12-1
Population Trends for Mito

YEAR	DISTRICT	TOWN
1876	5,065	1,775
1940	3,090	797
1961	1,470	627
1964	—	432

Note: Figures from the national censuses, except for the 1964 count in Mito done by a Cornell project reported in Castillo (1964).

Nevertheless their social and economic development also depended upon gaining control over their own affairs.

Pucará had been an anexo of Sapallanga. In the early years of the twentieth century, there was increasing friction between Pucará and Sapallanga, centering particularly upon the positions of municipal agent and lieutenant governor. These officials were supposed to look after the interests of Pucará, but they were named by the mayor and the governor in the district capital. In 1916, the people of Pucará launched a campaign to choose their own municipal council representative. The struggle became bitter and led to physical violence. The conflict built solidarity within Pucará and also stimulated political activities to gain support of higher-level government officials. In 1918, Pucará was granted its freedom from Sapallanga and became a political district. In 1925, a road from Pucará to Huancayo was completed, and mounting bus and truck traffic tied Pucará more closely into the commercial activities of the city.

Cajas had been part of the political district of Huancayo. Since Huancayo itself had been the center of Indian resistance to the mestizo elite in Jauja, Cajas did not suffer the tight controls of the anexos of Mito. In fact, Cajas was in conflict not with Huancayo but rather with the neighboring communities of Hualyas, San Geronimo, Paccha, and Cochas and with the Sociedad Ganadera del Centro. In 1940, through politicians in Huancayo, Cajas won designation as capital of its own district.

Occupational Differentiation, 13
Politics, and Community Development

In his inaugural address on July 28, 1963, President Belaúnde announced that municipal elections would take place as soon as the necessary arrangements could be made. Although comuneros in Indian communities had been electing their personero and junta communal, this extension of popular democracy was greeted with universal enthusiasm.

Our 1964 surveys were carried out less than a year later, while high expectations still prevailed. The 1969 surveys showed a marked decline in faith in local government. This general trend will be discussed in more detail later; however, our studies of Yanamarca and Mantaro valley communities provide illustrations of the kinds of events and problems that led to increasing frustration and disillusionment.

The key to explaining this trend is found in the existence of dual power structures at both national and local levels. At the national level, Belaúnde's Popular Action administration was opposed by the APRA—Odriá—controlled congress. At the local level, there were two organs of government, the municipal council and the junta comunal. Problems became particularly acute when different factions won control of these two centers of local power.

YANAMARCA

The problems can be most simply illustrated by the case of the community of Yanamarca in the valley of that name. In their struggle against the hacendado, the colonos had been united. The elimination of their common enemy precipitated a chronic community cleavage centering upon the distribution of the land formerly owned and controlled by the hacendado.

As was commonly the case under the hacienda system, there had been wide differences in amount of land alloted among colono families. After victory over the hacendado, the former colonos with the smallest holdings wanted to distribute the hacendado's land so as to equalize the total amount held by each family, whereas those who had been favored under the previous regime naturally wanted to maintain their superior situation.

During the Belaúnde regime, one faction won the support of the executive branch and another faction gained the backing of power figures in the APRA-Odría congressional coalition. The struggle seesawed back and forth, with the apparent victory of one faction in the community always being appealed by the opposing faction to its allies in Lima. No stable solution was possible in Yanamarca until the military junta took power in 1968, dissolved congress, and imposed a unified national power structure.

MANTARO VALLEY COMMUNITIES

In the district of Pisaq, social cleavages and conflicts fell along ethnic lines. In the Mantaro valley, respondents did indeed recognize ethnic differences, as Table 13-1 indicates, but these social distinctions did not fit cleavages and conflicts nearly as closely as they did in the Sacred valley of the Incas. There we found the mestizos concentrated in Pisaq and the Indians concentrated in the Indian communities and on the

131

hacienda. In the Mantaro valley, there was, at the time of our study, no mestizo town dominating the peasant communities, and mestizos, cholos, and Indians—as identified by themselves—were found in large numbers in each community. In fact, outsiders tend to disregard these distinctions altogether; some anthropologists see the Mantaro valley as being made up entirely of mestizo communities.

The decrease in mestizos and the increase in Indians in Mito may reflect a continuing emigration of high-status mestizos during the 1964–1969 period. Nevertheless, in 1969 the Miteños still regarded themselves as more mestizo than did respondents in our other two villages. This finding fits with the small percentage claiming ability to speak Quechua: less than 20 percent for Mito compared with about 60 percent for Cajas and close to 95 percent for Pucará.

In accordance with its mestizo heritage, Mito showed the highest level of education of the three communities (see Table 13-2). All three were far above the average of Pisaq district communities and above average for the highlands in general.

Our data do not allow us to say that ethnic differences played no role in conflicts within a given community, but we need to look for other

TABLE 13-1
Ethnic Self-Identification

| | PUCARA, % | | MITO, % | | CAJAS, % | |
	M	F	M	F	M	F
Mestizo						
1964	48.1	41.6	65.3	69.1	49.9	32.5
1969	53.3	33.8	60.0	55.3	45.3	28.6
Cholo						
1964	19.2	18.5	22.4	21.8	6.8	10.4
1969	16.8	10.4	20.0	28.9	14.1	30.2
Indian						
1964	32.7	39.8	12.2	9.1	51.4	57.1
1969	29.0	50.6	20.0	10.5	34.4	39.7
Others						
1964	0	0	0	0	0	0
1969	0	5.0	0	5.2	6.2	1.5
1964 N =	163	111	49	55	74	80
1969 N =	110	86	25	41	68	77

Note: Mestizo includes those few who responded "white" or "criollo." Cholo includes those few who in 1969 responded "Misti."

TABLE 13-2
Educational Level Reached

	PUCARA, %		MITO, %		CAJAS, %	
	M	F	M	F	M	F
0–1 yr						
1964	21.5	54.9	10.2	30.9	14.9	63.8
1969	10.9	43.1	4.0	36.6	10.3	48.1
2–4 yrs						
1964	29.4	18.9	22.4	34.5	37.8	23.8
1969	21.8	17.4	20.0	31.7	39.7	26.0
Elementary complete						
1964	27.6	22.5	44.9	29.1	27.0	8.8
1969	29.1	22.1	48.0	7.3	20.6	14.3
More than elementary						
1964	15.3	2.7	16.3	5.4	12.2	1.3
1969	29.1	12.8	12.0	17.1	22.1	9.1
Secondary complete and beyond						
1964	6.1	.9	6.1	0	8.2	2.6
1969	9.1	4.7	16.1	7.3	7.4	2.6
1964 N =	163	111	49	55	74	80
1969 N =	110	86	25	41	68	77

factors in order to understand the cleavages we found in Pucará and Cajas. Since Mito showed a low level of conflict and an absence of projects around which conflict might have arisen during the period of our study, we shall concentrate our analysis on the other two communities.

PUCARA

Agriculturally, Pucará was more prosperous than the average Mantaro valley community, and it had also been experiencing a growing occupational differentiation. Land holdings were relatively equal among farm families, with the largest landholder having 6 hectares.

In the 1940s, the agricultural growth of Pucará was stimulated by technical assistance in crops, animal husbandry, and organization by officials of the Division of Indian Communities, the Agricultural Development Bank, the SCIPA (the agricultural extension agency). Out of these projects grew a small elite: the Sociedad Agrícola Pucará (SAP), a cooperative, formed in 1945, of 11 members who pledged their personal property in order to get a bank loan so that they could rent community-owned land and expand their own farming activities.

In 1946, joined by a twelfth member, SAP used its profits to buy a 700-hectare hacienda in the province of Tacacaja in the department of Huancavelica. As they became involved in this major expansion, SAP members relinquished the Pucará lands they had rented. By removing themselves from competition with other Pucará farmers, SAP members increased their popularity and influence.

While SAP continued raising the traditional crops of potatoes, wheat, barley, beans, and corn, a new group went into truck gardening. Six men had migrated to the coast in the 1930s and had worked under Asiatic immigrants who were raising vegetables for the Lima market. (One of them had also gained extensive union experience under APRA leadership.) Returning to Pucará in 1946, the innovators went beyond the onions and cabbages traditional to the area to introduce a wide range of green vegetables. On moderate-size plots in the lower part of Pucará, with ample irrigation water, and using the methods they had learned on the coast, the returned migrants were able to raise three crops a year.

Although the percentage of families concentrating on truck gardening and achieving substantial production for Huancayo and Lima markets rose to less than 15 percent of the families of Pucará in the 1960s, our field researchers estimated that more than half of the remaining families had adopted some of the methods and crops of the returned migrants.

During the 1960s, over half of the heads of families continued to work full time as farmers, with many others farming part time. With a good road giving Pucará access to Huancayo and with transport of agricultural produce steadily growing, the community showed increasing occupational differentiation.

A 1970 census of the occupations of the 397 heads of the family carried out by our group shows 23 (5.8 percent) proprietors of cars or trucks used in commercial service, 23 (5.8 percent) drivers or mechanics, 22 (5.5 percent), local store operators or traveling salesmen, and 22 (5.5 percent) teachers and office workers. The office workers were employed mainly in government agencies in Huancayo. The teachers were working largely in the Pucará schools. A significant new group, not shown in the occupational distribution, was the university students, who have played increasingly important political roles in recent years.

During the 1950s and 1960s, Pucará carried out two projects that contributed to community solidarity. The first was a successful struggle to recover the church-owned lands, which had been rented to citizens of the once dominant town of Sapallanga.

The second was an electric light plant. Stimulated by the example of Muquiyauyo (Adams, 1959), a Mantaro valley community that had won national fame for developing such a community project, the Pucareños secured government money and technical assistance. With members of the community providing the labor, Pucará started construction in 1958 and opened the plant in 1961 amid a great burst of national publicity.

The first fissure in solidarity arose over a fare increase by the bus company operating between Pucará and Huancayo. The founder and head of this company was a member of a family involved in SAP. Although several truck gardening families now shared in ownership of the firm, other truck gardeners took the lead in organizing the community to protest the fare increase. When Huancayo officials rejected their protest, in 1957 the dissidents persuaded their local government to form a cooperative bus line. The owners of the private company, supported by their large-farmer friends, countered by getting Huancayo officials to rule that the cooperative must provide free rides to its members. To keep their enterprise afloat, drivers surreptitiously collected fares, but this violation of regulations provoked heavy fines.

In 1959, through the intercession of a Huancayo politician, the cooperative got permission from the National Transportation Office in Lima to charge fares. By this time, its second-hand busses had seriously deteriorated, and the enterprise could be salvaged only by having several individual members join together to purchase new vehicles. In this way, the cooperative became simply a second private bus company. Although the cooperative failed, its leaders gained political experience and APRA contacts in Huancayo and Lima. The effort also tended to rally popular support around the group that was challenging the leadership of the large farmers.

By means of these growing APRA contacts, in the early 1960s the truck gardeners, supported by some local merchants and professional people, secured control of the municipality. With their allies, the truck gardeners had shown sufficient voting strength to take over control of the Indian community. With the announcement of the municipal elections for November of 1963, the leading members of this emergent group declared in favor of the APRA party. At the time popular elections were announced, the large farmers lacked contacts with any national party, but since their rivals had opted for APRA, they declared for Belaúnde's party. The electorate was further divided by the organization of a leftist party spearheaded by the schoolteachers and the young university students.

As the independent ticket showed surprising strength, with 137 votes (26.8 percent), the Popular Action–Democratic Christian coalition led by the large traditional farmers won over the APRA-Odría alliance by the narrow margin of 191 (37.3 percent) to 184 (35.9 percent). At the same time, the AP-DC alliance regained control of the Indian community.

The first issue before the new administration was the construction of a reservoir to provide potable water for Pucará. The project was proposed by leaders of the emergent group, but at first the officials of municipality and community agreed to go along. When Health Ministry officials designated a stream in the high area above the community as a source for the water supply, the large farmers lost interest in a project that promised to reduce their irrigation water. They delayed calling faenas to provide the necessary labor. Leaders of the emergent faction used this issue in the annual election of officials to take over leadership of the Indian community.

The next issue splitting Pucará involved the reconstruction of the church, which had fallen into disrepair. Through representatives in Congress, in 1964 the municipality secured 65,000 soles from the national government for the project. The Indian community was committed to building a secondary school, and members of the emergent group felt it was preferable to spend whatever money was available on the school. Furthermore, some prominent members of the emergent group were Protestants and naturally had no interest in contributing labor to a Catholic church project.

When the municipal officials called upon the Indian community to provide the faena labor to rebuild the church, the request was voted down. Within the memory of the Pucareños, this was the first split between the two organs of governments.

Members of the emergent group utilized their APRA contacts to get through Congress a school-construction subsidy of 100,000 soles. This strengthened the position of the emergent faction, but interest in advanced schooling was so general that the project initially had almost

136

unanimous popular support. Conflict arose when decisions had to be made regarding the location of the school. The leaders of the municipality had understood that the school was to be constructed on municipally owned land above the village. The university students, the schoolteachers, and the leaders of the emergent faction favored a level area below the village, next to the road to Huancayo.

Before the 1966 municipal elections, the students and young professionals who had organized the independent ticket in 1963 found themselves under attack by the traditional community leaders for their leftist tendencies. This led the independents to throw in their lot with the APRA-Odría faction and assured their victory with 286 votes (54.1 percent). At the same time, the APRA-Odría faction retained control of the Indian community.

The new municipal leaders now proposed a new location for the high school: the soccer field of the community. The leaders of the Indian community promised to provide the voluntary labor necessary. This provoked a split along age lines within the APRA-Odría faction. Members of an athletic league organized a protest meeting and burned the new mayor in effigy. In early 1968, the impasse was broken when the APRA-Odría leaders arranged to provide other land for a new sports field.

The new municipal administration entered in 1966 with big promises of community improvement, but the school-construction project was the only project that it was able to carry out. The community was now so sharply divided as to render any cooperation difficult. This was particularly apparent in the Indian community, where young men had taken over the leadership but were unable to mobilize the support of their elders.

The attitudes of the deposed leadership of the large farmers are well expressed in this statement of the man who served as mayor from 1963 to 1966:

> The [Indian] community has been divided since 1966. The personero did not want the community people to work in the faenas for the church. . . . He would call the delegates and tell them that they should not work, that the project should be done by the government with the money that it had sent. . . . The community has poor leadership. . . .
>
> Before my election the community and the municipal council were equal. The community had its delegate before the council. The council would propose that the people be called in to carry out a project. In that way, we did the

school for girls and the St. Martin Park. The council provided money, the community provided work. After me, a group of youngsters came to power and they don't do anything.

The military coup of October 1968 deprived the APRA-Odría local officials of national support. Leaders of the new government claimed that the old political parties had failed Peru and promised to transform the country without them. In early 1969, the national government installed in Pucará a new municipal council, drawn from several factions, with preference for those who had not been active before in any party. Thus ended Pucará's six years of experience with the locally elected municipal council.

SAN AGUSTIN DE CAJAS

Since colonial times, Cajas had been known as a town of hat makers, but competition of factory-made hats had steadily reduced this craft so that few hat makers were left in the 1960s.

Although the land owned per family averaged about one hectare in Cajas, only slightly less than in Pucará, the Cajinos did not have the quantities of irrigation water available in Pucará, and they also lack Pucara's extensive pasture lands.

In 1940, Cajas was a relatively poor agricultural village, with only a few of the larger landholders making a good living off the land. At that time, the barrios of Yaulí and Awako had the least desirable land for agriculture, and the poorest people lived there.

This situation changed as families in these barrios discovered that their land was rich in clay that could be fired into bricks. By 1970, 65 out of the 275 Cajas heads of families (23.6 percent) had become involved in brickmaking. This produced a great stimulus to commercial activities. By 1965, there were 25 trucks in Cajas; by 1970, the number had risen to 41, most of them used in brickmaking and marketing.

We find a growing number of men (11, or 4 percent, in 1970) occupied as truck drivers and mechanics as the business expanded. There was also a growing need for full-time wage workers in brickmaking (13, or 4.7 percent, in 1970).

The 1970 occupational census showed 36.7 percent farmers and 4.7 percent farm laborers. When we combine those involved in brick making and brick selling, we arrive at a total of 32.2 percent, indicating that brickmaking was competing with farming in numbers employed and no doubt surpassing farming in income. At this time, the number of hat-making families had dropped to 8.4 percent, 9.8 percent had gone into other artisanship (carpentry, masonry, shoemaking, etc.), and 8 percent were listed as local merchants or traveling salesmen.

The political development of Cajas revolved around the rise of the brickmakers and their struggle for control against the farmers and the traditional hat makers, who were also part-time farmers. One of the main political issues involved ownership by the church of approximately 40 percent of the cultivable land. According to charges made before the junta communal, these lands had been ceded to the church through a "fraudulent contract." Signers of the 1929 contract testified that they had been pressured into signing by the police and the priests.

These church lands were farmed by Cajinos, but on a rental basis. The church lands were especially extensive in the barrios of Awako and Yaulí. Those families that did not rent the parish lands (somewhat more than 50 percent of the population) carried on a sporadic campaign to recover the property for the community. In 1954, the church offered to sell the lands and use the money to build a new church to replace one that had been destroyed in the earthquake of 1947.

The great majority of former renters now made purchase arrangements with the church. All of these new owners were residents of the barrios of Awako and Yaulí who were already well on their way from poverty to relative affluence through their new brickmaking enterprises.

In a community assembly of April 12, 1960, the following resolution was passed:

> That the purchases already made of these communal lands be cancelled and that the lands be distributed by lot to the comuneros in order to provide economic benefits to the junta comunal [which would receive the purchase price instead of the church receiving it].

It proved impossible to cancel the purchase contracts, so the opponents of the 1954 agreement concentrated upon obtaining the distribution of lands still rented to community members. In 1965, the church agreed to turn over the rental lands to the community on condition that the proceeds of their sale be used for the building of the new church.

This new agreement led to a conflict between the established renters

139

and those who sought to supplant them. In a community meeting in September 1966, the president of the junta comunal reported that as he had tried to carry out the new distribution of lands, he had been insulted by several of the men and women currently using those lands and one had threatened to kill him. The president stated

> that Messrs. R. C. and H. S. had betrayed the community. Yesterday they went to the parish priest to sign contracts for the purchase of the comunal lands and that last Sunday they planted crops upon them. . . . He urged that the community dispossess these traitors to the people. . . .

This led to the community decision to cancel all previous purchase and rental arrangements and seek to recover the "communal lands" from the church through legal action.

While this legal struggle was going on, the church apparently decided that the small income from its rentals was not worth the trouble of maintaining ownership. In 1968, the community was able to take over all remaining church land. The final solution was a compromise. The brickmakers fought off all claims to the land they had bought from the church, but the community achieved a redistribution of the lands that were still being rented from the church.

A second conflict that occurred during this same period involved the change in location of the municipal offices and village square. In an earlier period, the center of town was between the barrios of Aywán and Chaupi, and the other three barrios (Bolognesi, Awako, and Yaulí) were thought to be on the periphery. The decline of Aywán and Chaupi began in the years following 1930 as a result of population growth in the other three barrios. This growth was due to three factors:

1. The land holdings of Awako and Yaulí were smaller, which allowed for a larger population per unit of land.
2. The barrios of Bolognesi, Awako, and Yaulí were located close to the highway, which provided them with easy access to Huancayo.
3. The brickmaking industry grew in Awako and Yaulí.

While the traditional farmers and hat makers fought to maintain the original location of the village square and the municipal office, the brickmakers succeeded in organizing support to outvote them in 1960 and thus shift the center of Cajas to a location most convenient to the barrios of Awako and Yaulí.

In 1958, the community voted that for the purpose of determining the best location for a potable-water reservoir, each barrio should dig a test well. Months later, in 1959, when only Yaulí had made good on its commitment, the community voted to base the reservoir project on the Yaulí well.

The brickmakers sought to consolidate their leadership through lobbying with APRA representatives in Congress, and at last, in 1963, the Ministry of Health agreed to provide financial support and technical assistance. The expert sent by the Ministry to evaluate the project reported that the Yaulí reservoir would not be high enough to provide sufficient pressure to get water to all sectors of the community. He recommended that the project be constructed some distance from the barrio of Yaulí.

The community voted to accept the recommendations, to form a project committee with a representative from each barrio, and to sign a contract with the Ministry of Health and with a UN agency that was also supporting the project. Shortly thereafter, the representative from Yaulí resigned, and the comuneros from that barrio declined to contribute their labor, announcing that they would go ahead instead with their own reservoir. The community records report (December 16, 1964) a resolution to declare *persona no grata* the leaders of Yaulí for their opposition to the collective decision of the community.

Working through their APRA representative in Congress, the leaders of Yaulí secured a grant of 80,000 soles for their reservoir project. Later, through the intervention of administrative authorities in the APRA-led university at Huancayo, Yaulí received a grant from AID for 47,000 soles together with technical assistance.

Since the brickmakers were allied with APRA, the traditional leaders of the community lined up with Popular Action and in 1963 retained control of the municipality by a vote of 266 (69.5 percent) to 117 (30.5 percent). The brickmakers' divisive stand on the reservoir had been costly. Popular Action candidates also won out in the annual election for the junta comunal of the community.

The new political leadership of municipality and community went to work vigorously to finish the Cajas reservoir, to organize a bus coopera-

141

tive, to repave the new central plaza, and to construct a new municipal building.

During the three-year period between municipal elections, the leaders of the APRA faction continued their political efforts. In late 1965, they arranged a visit to Cajas of national APRA representatives. Such efforts resulted in the following government grants in 1965 and 1966:

1. 13,000 soles for unspecified public works.
2. 50,000 soles for construction of a bridge providing access to the sport stadium
3. 200,000 soles for paving the Plaza de Armas or the park
4. 90,000 soles for finishing construction of the boys' school
5. 235,000 soles for establishing the coeducational industrial institute, to provide secondary education in industrial arts

In contrast, the local government officials were not able to arrange visits of Popular Action politicians or financial support from the Belaúnde government.

In the 1966 municipal elections, the APRA faction nominated a Cajas lawyer who had gained considerable professional prominence. The candidate was actually a resident of Lima, but this may have worked in his favor, for the local APRA leaders had demonstrated that access to the top national APRA leaders was essential to the flow of resources into the community. The 1966 election gave the APRA-brickmaking faction 266 (63.4 percent) against 142 (34 percent) for the Popular Action–Democratic Christian candidates. (An independent list got 2.6 percent.)

The new municipal government was inaugurated with a good deal of popular enthusiasm and the participation of important APRA politicians and the rector of the University at Huancayo. In his inaugural speech, the mayor announced an ambitious program of public works and proposed local taxes on commerce and industry to promote the industrial development of Cajas.

Performance fell far short of initial promises. Opposition leaders claimed that the new taxes were light on the brickmakers and weighed unfairly upon other segments of business and industry. After 1966, funds from the national government for local community projects dried up, so the APRA channel to Lima no longer produced results. At the same time, the mayor was so occupied in Lima that he could only spend

142

a few days a month in Cajas. Other members of the council were unable to fill the leadership gap.

Although APRA had won control of the municipality, the Indian community remained under the control of the Popular Action faction. Relations between the two groups were such that municipality and community were not able to agree on any common projects. Meetings of these bodies declined in frequency and in member attendance.

In 1968, the military government named a municipal council without regard to the two factions and mainly from individuals who had not been politically active. A government-required reorganization of the junta comunal, with an election supervised by a government representative, brought to office a similar group of non-party members.

Under the auspices of the new national government, Cajas again got money and other assistance to carry forward projects that had been stalled: the reopening of the industrial institute and completion of the boys school. The junta comunal formed a cooperative sheep-grazing operation. Also, a regional electrical cooperative enrolled 80 percent of the Cajas families, with the result that Cajas gained electricity by the end of 1969.

MITO

The story of Mito already has been told in substance. Mito remains today a town living in its past. Agriculture continues to be the main activity, and there has been some development of commerce and artisanship but nothing to rival the new types of agricultural and other economic activities we had found in our other two communities.

Applying what we had learned in Pucará and Cajas, we sought to identify an "emergent group" that was challenging the traditional leadership for control, particularly in the era of popular elections from 1963 to 1968. This effort broke down when we found members of the same families taking different political positions.

National political struggles were reflected in Mito, with Popular Action winning the municipal election of 1963 and APRA winning in 1966. However, these divisions seemed to represent personal rivalries rather than the occupationally based groupings we found in Pucará and Cajas.

143

In spite of divisions in Pucará and Cajas and the apparent lack of community movement in Mito, we find respondents in all three villages seeing signs of progress, with only a slight decline shown from 1964 to 1969 (except for sharper drops for the women of Cajas and Pucará). (see Table 13-3).

Realistically, Miteños are least inclined to see their community as progressing.

The record also shows signs of material progress in all three villages, as indicated in Table 13-4.

In figures to be presented later, we find declines in both perceived conflict and perceived cooperation in all three communities from 1964 to 1969. In both years, Mito is the lowest in both cooperation and conflict, as if the Miteños were telling us that they had nothing to get together on and nothing to fight about either. The declines in conflict and cooperation for Pucará and Cajas may reflect increasing stagnation over the five-year period.

Experience of the 1960s seems to have led to a decline in the perceived value of working with other people, especially in Pucará and Cajas. We would not expect any change in Mito, and, indeed, there we find a slight increase in collective orientation among males but a more marked decrease among females, as Table 13-5 indicates.

In terms of the theme of this chapter, the most interesting changes are

TABLE 13-3
Perceptions of Village Progress

What would you say about the progress of this village? Would you say it is (progressing rapidly, progressing slowly, not progressing, going backward)?

	PUCARA, %		MITO, %		CAJAS, %	
	M	F	M	F	M	F
Progressing rapidly or slowly						
1964	96	96	69	65	90	87
1969	92	74	64	60	85	53

TABLE 13-4
Percentages of Families Possessing Modern Artifacts, 1964 and 1969

	PUCARA, %		MITO, %		CAJAS, %	
	1964	1969	1964	1969	1964	1969
Radio	43	72	45	59	36	56
Sewing machine	30	46	28	39	36	48
Kerosene stove	33	64	20	44	23	48
Clock	37	39	39	48	27	30
Bicycle	19	28	25	46	19	34
Car or truck	1	4	3	4	7	13
Phonograph	—	10	—	9	—	9
Typewriter	—	16	—	17	—	7
Electric light	—	69	—	36	—	0

Note: The 1964 survey did not include questions on phonograph, typewriter, and electric light. Cajas did not yet have electrical service available by 1969.

TABLE 13-5
Collective vs Individualistic Orientation

In general, do you prefer to work with others or alone?

	PUCARA, %		MITO, %		CAJAS, %	
	M	F	M	F	M	F
With others						
1964	45.3	19.4	21.3	20.0	26.4	16.0
1969	28.0	14.4	24.0	7.7	17.5	8.0

the sharp declines in confidence in the municipal council and in the junta comunal in all three communities (see Tables 13-6 and 13-7).

Although we conclude that any explanation of the shortcomings of the local governments must give special attention to their relations with the national government, apparently the villagers were more inclined to blame their local institutions. To be sure, Mito did show a marked negative shift in its evaluation of the national government—perhaps a product of increasing recognition that the government was not going to do much for Mito. However, evaluations of the national government in Pucará and Cajas became only slightly more negative and the shift was very small in comparison to loss of faith in their own institutions.

TABLE 13-6
Atitudes toward Municipal Council

In general, would you say that the activities of the municipal council:

| | 1964, % | | | | | | 1969, % | | | | | |
| | PUCARA | | MITO | | CAJAS | | PUCARA | | MITO | | CAJAS | |
	M	F	M	F	M	F	M	F	M	F	M	F
Improve conditions	46	29	39	55	23	14	13	9	0	5	5	3
Improve conditions at times	48	66	45	33	66	65	47	56	36	51	34	51
Do not improve conditions	6	5	16	13	11	10	40	35	64	60	42	46

TABLE 13-7
Attitudes toward Junta Comunal

In general, would you say that the activities of the junta comunal:

| | 1964, % | | | | | | 1969, % | | | | | |
| | PUCARA | | MITO | | CAJAS | | PUCARA | | MITO | | CAJAS | |
	M	F	M	F	M	F	M	F	M	F	M	F
Improve conditions	63	31	37	56	27	23	18	8	2	6	3	10
Improve conditions at times	36	65	52	31	48	66	56	67	54	58	69	66
Do not improve conditions	1	4	10	13	25	10	26	24	33	36	28	24

Note: The 1964 survey had two unfavorable alternatives: "Make no difference" and "Would be better off without them." These two have been combined into "Do not improve conditions" for comparison with 1969 figures.

THE CHANCAY VALLEY IV

The Evolution of the 14
Chancay Valley

The Chancay valley links highland communities to the coast. It is formed by the Chancay River, which has its source at an altitude of about 15,000 feet and which flows westward into the Pacific. On the coast, the river is less than 50 miles north of Lima, and the Pan-American Highway carries heavy traffic from Lima to the Chancay valley and on to the north.

The valley is made up of three distinct ecological areas. In the high area of the valley, between 6,000 and 11,000 feet, we find 27 scattered indigenous communities with a total population in the 1960s of about 16,000. Between about 4,000 and 1,600 feet, the river valley falls into a canyon, and only a few small farmers have been able to make a living out of the sharply sloping land. Below 1,500 feet, the valley fans out to form the coastal delta, where most of the inhabitants lived during our period of study. Here we find haciendas, four villages, and two small cities: Chancay on the coast and Huaral on the road from Chancay up the river to the highlands.

Chancay resembles other coastal valleys in that its agriculture is completely dependent upon irrigation. In size and economic importance, it is dwarfed by the valleys that have given rise to the cities of Trujillo, Chiclayo, and Piura to the north and Ica to the south. Apart from its relatively small area, the Chancay valley's growth has been limited by its closeness to Lima. Since businessmen and farmers can get to Lima within an hour by bus or colectivo from Huaral, that small city has not been able to develop the range of economic activities that have grown up in coastal cities farther away from the capital.

In Part IV, we will examine three highland communities and two coastal villages. For purposes of comparison, we will also make occasional references to our study of the coastal village of Virú, farther to the north.

DEVELOPMENT OF THE DELTA

We begin tracing the history of the Chancay valley with the delta, because that has been the dynamic center of economic and political development and has had major influences on the highland communities.

The rural area of the delta is dominated by 21 haciendas. In the 1960s, only two of them were owned by the same families that held them before Peruvian independence. Thirteen came under the control of the families that owned them in the 1960s during the period between 1901 and 1926. Japanese owners were briefly prominent in the valley from 1925 to 1941.

Cotton became the predominant crop in the delta during the United States Civil War. Fruits, particularly seedless oranges and melons, have been grown in large volume since 1930.

When the international market for cotton was down, hacendados moved toward indirect cultivation, shifting risks to sharecroppers. In boom times for cotton, the owners used various illegal and legal devices to push the sharecroppers out and take over the cultivation of the land. Thus, the boom of the World War I era led to a marked shift toward direct cultivation. This shift also accounted for part of the impetus for the development of the irrigation project of La Esperanza. The owners of one of the most modern and efficient haciendas of the valley felt that it

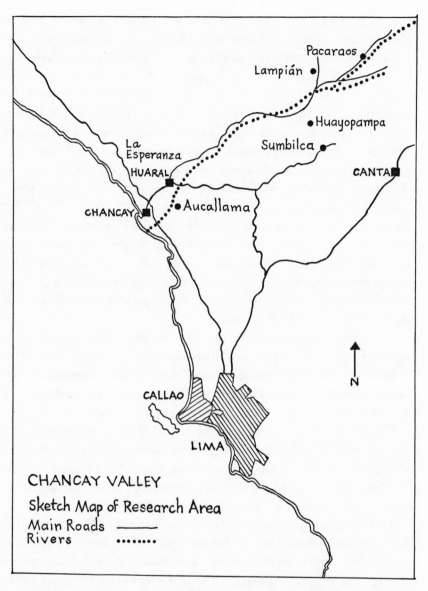

CHANCAY VALLEY
Sketch Map of Research Area
Main Roads ———
Rivers ••••••••

would be easier to evict the sharecroppers from Huando if, at the same time, they could offer them small properties of their own within the new irrigation project; and they were able to persuade the Leguía government to develop the project, upon which we focus attention in the next chapter.

World War II established the conditions for another sharp reduction of sharecropping in many of the haciendas. It also provided a political as well as economic opportunity, as Japanese sharecroppers and owners alike were rounded up and sent to the United States for internment.

During the first part of the nineteenth century, the highlands were still underpopulated, so that population pressure did not provide a stream of migrant workers. The hacendados sought to meet their labor needs by importing slaves from Africa until 1853, when President Castilla decreed the abolition of slavery. From then on, hacendados imported "coolies" from China and Japan. In both periods, it was only the more prosperous hacendados who could invest in such importation. This led to increasing concentration of land ownership in few hands, as owners unable to import labor were forced to sell out to wealthier owners. The slave trade has left traces in the valley, particularly in the village of Aucallama, where we find many dark-skinned people. Particularly along the coast, the Asiatic immigrants have moved up and out into many occupations. The Japanese influence on farming methods was particularly felt until they were expelled in 1941, and we still find major signs of Asiatic influence in La Esperanza.

Around the beginning of the twentieth century, demand for labor in the delta and increasing population pressure in the highlands opened up a steady stream of migration to the coast. Some migrants stayed for years or permanently, whereas others came down for about four months a year for the cotton harvest.

Chancay on the coast had been the capital of the *corregimento* under Spanish rule, but it faded in importance in the twentieth century as Huaral became the junction for passenger and freight traffic to the highlands and north and south along the coast. We found Huaral a lively commercial and political center of about 15,000 population.

Until after the beginning of the twentieth century, the power of the hacendados was unchallenged. Around 1919, arising out of the agitation in the cities for the eight-hour day, anarchosyndicalist activity spread through the valley, and we see the first short-lived efforts at union organization. The rise of APRA in the 1930s spurred the spread of unionization into the major haciendas of the valley. Huaral also became a provincial center for political and union activity, with Communists increasingly competing with APRA after the 1930s.

Union organization and political mobilization brought forth legislation first protecting sharecroppers from expulsion by hacendados and later, in

1964, providing for the sharecroppers to become owners of lands they worked.

Although the 2 cities and 21 haciendas dominated the delta, squeezed in among the haciendas were 4 peasant villages, two of which will be examined in the following chapter. The precarious position of the villages is illustrated particularly in the case of Aucallama, the two parts of which are separated by haciendas.

HIGHLANDS HISTORY

The history of the 27 indigenous or peasant communities falls into two distinct stages.

In the early years after the Spanish conquest, Canta, in the highlands part of the Chillon valley, was not only the political capital of the Chancay highland area but also the center of economic domination. Canta was first settled for its silver-mining potential, and the conquerors pressed Indians from the Chancay valley into service in the mines. As silver mining in and around Canta declined and practically disappeared, the mine owners no longer needed Indian labor, so they released their hold upon the native population along the Chancay River. Since there were no large landowners in this area at that time or since, the 27 indigenous communities were left alone to follow their own lines of development.

These communities were not entirely cut off from the outside world. In fact, there was a missionary school established in the high area of the valley around 1850, and in the last quarter of the nineteenth century, we find growing agitation for education in the community records. We also find in those records going back a hundred years references to the need to get the community in touch with the coastal cities and thus in tune with modern times.

Relations between highland and delta grew rapidly after 1900 with the flow of temporary and permanent migration. The opening up of vehicular roads connecting the highland communities with Huaral, in the late 1940s, made possible a growing stream of daily traffic up and down the mountain. Canta remained the capital of the province, but few people from the upper part of the Chancay valley ever visited Canta.

153

During the colonial period, these Indian communities clung to their native culture and agricultural practices. As in the days of the Incas, land within a community was held in common, being redistributed from year to year according to the needs of the various families and especially to provide land for newly formed families. The catastropic drop in population following the conquest made it possible to provide each family with enough land for subsistence.

In 1824, the Liberator, Simón Bolivar, proclaimed a law to grant Indians equal rights to private property just like any other citizen. That law had drastic and unintended consequences. In other parts of the highlands, it opened the way for exploitation and encroachment on Indian lands by large landowners with powerful political connections. That did not happen in the high area of the Chancay valley, where no large landowners were present.

The law did have the effect of slowly increasing social and economic differentiation within the Indian communities. Up to that time, these communities had been structured very largely in terms of an age-grading system in which political and religious offices were intertwined in terms of progression from the least to the most important office. When families were more or less equal in wealth, it was assumed that every male would take his turn moving up the political-religious hierarchy. As land came to be owned by private families and the more resourceful grew in affluence, many men became unable to meet the expenses of the higher religious offices, and these offices fell within the small circle of more affluent comuneros.

Around the turn of the century, unoccupied cultivable land practically disappeared in these communities. Young peasants could no longer assume that, upon marriage, they would have land allotted to them. As control remained in the hands of the older and more affluent citizens, this led to increasing friction between generations. We will examine a striking case of such intergenerational conflict in Lampían.

There was more than one way of adjusting to changing conditions. In Chapter 16 we will examine Pacaraos, a fragmented and individualistic community, and Huayopampa, which had progressed spectacularly on the basis of collective effort but was beginning to show signs of a deepening crisis.

154

Villages among the Haciendas 15

Aucallama and La Esperanza represent varying adaptations to a common situation: small-farmer settlements surrounded by haciendas. Before showing the differences between them, let us consider what they have in common. The common elements will stand out more clearly as we compare these villages with the village of Virú, farther to the north.

Virú is practically without a highlands hinterland. Peasants to the east of Virú do indeed come down to the coast in large numbers, but they migrate farther to the north, to the city of Trujillo and the sugar cane plantations, or farther to the south, to Chimbote, a steel mill and fishing center. Like the haciendas, Aucallama and La Esperanza have absorbed a stream of migrants from the peasant communities in the high area of the Chancay valley. These differences among the villages are reflected in the 1969 survey item on place of birth: 70 percent of the respondents in Virú had been born where they were interviewed, compared with 17 percent in La Esperanza and 24 percent in Aucallama. We find the same story in responses to questions on language: no Viruñero could speak Quechua and none said he had a parent who spoke it; one-third or more of our Chancay villagers had at least one Quechua-speaking parent. (La Esperanza had retained more of this linguistic heritage than had Aucallama, 38 percent of the males and 11 percent of the females in La Esperanza saying that they spoke Quechua, compared with 4 percent and 2 percent, respectively, in Aucallama.)

Villages in the Chancay and Virú valleys differed also in their relations to cities. Virú is about three-quarters of an hour by bus from the nearest city (Trujillo), which means that the village itself is the commercial center for its valley. Thus, although agriculture is the predominant economic activity in all three villages, 33 percent of our male respondents in Virú, compared with negligible percentages in the Chancay villages, were engaged in commerce. In Chancay, there was an important occupational difference within the farming population: 50 percent of the La Esperanza male respondents were farm laborers whereas 39 percent were farm owners; in Aucallama, the proportions were reversed, with independent farmers outnumbering farm laborers 49 percent to 29 percent.

Some of the large landowners of the Virú valley lived in Virú—or at least maintained legal residences there. The Chancay valley hacendados lived either on their haciendas or in Lima. Thus, the division of interests between large and small farmers was built into the social structure of Virú, whereas this separation and potential conflict was acted out between the village and the surrounding haciendas in the Chancay valley, particularly in the case of Aucallama.

Turning now to the comparison between Aucallama and La Esperanza, we find small differences in level of education but major differences in land ownership, wealth, and income. In 1969, about two-thirds of our respondents in Aucallama, compared with about three-quarters in La Esperanza, claimed to be able to read and write. Over 20 percent of the La Esperanza respondents, compared with 11 percent in Aucallama, had gone beyond elementary school. Such figures put these villages well above average for rural Peru but on roughly the same level as the Mantaro valley communities.

In 1962, La Esperanza showed the distribution of land ownership shown in Table 15-1.

TABLE 15-1
Distribution of Land Ownership in La Esperanza

SIZE OF INDIVIDUAL PROPERTIES, HA	PROPRIETORS		TOTAL AREA OWNED BY GROUP	
	NO.	%	HA	%
Up to 5	55	23.9	129.7	4.9
5–10	73	31.7	510.1	19.1
10–100	100	43.5	1,747.7	65.3
100–500	2	0.9	289.0	11.8
Totals	230	100.0	2,676.5	101.1*

*Total of rounded percentages.
Source: Portugal (1966).

Although we do not have a comparable table for land ownership in Aucallama, such detailed information would be of little use for our present purposes because there is so small a range in land size, with the largest property being only 21 hectares. On the basis of our 1969 population estimate of about 900, with an average of slightly over 6 persons per household, and with total holdings for Aucallama of 430 hectares, the size of the average family property was about 3 hectares. These figures indicate that the average Aucallama family was in roughly the same situation as those in the lowest quartile for La Esperanza. In addition, Aucallaminos had access to 120 hectares of hacienda land, or a little less than 1 hectare per family, as sharecroppers.

We estimated that in 1964, the average Aucallama farmer, raising principally cotton, did not net more than $200 per year on his own property. Most of the farmers therefore sought to supplement this income by working as laborers or sharecroppers on the haciendas. We have no comparable income estimates for La Esperanza; however, the average figures there were clearly far higher.

On this economic base, few Aucallaminos could afford modern technology, and their cotton yields per hectare were far below those of the haciendas. La Esperanzans spent much more on modern technology, and some of them appeared to have as high yields in fruit per hectare as did the leading fruit hacienda, Huando.

157

These economic differences are also reflected in our 1969 household survey of artifacts. There was only a small difference in favor of La Esperanza in the percentage of households having radios (81 percent compared with 71 percent for Aucallama), there were major differences in percentage of families owning cars, trucks, or tractors (25 percent versus 5 percent) and in those owning bicycles (35 percent versus 3 percent).

In both villages, control of water was the central issue of economic life, but the control problem took different shape in the two cases. Aucallama was engaged in a never-ending struggle with the haciendas for water rights, whereas in La Esperanza the issue divided the large from the small landholders.

AUCALLAMA

In the years just after the conquest, the Indians who had lived in what is now Aucallama either died out or migrated. When the cotton haciendas developed in the eighteenth and nineteenth centuries, the owners imported slaves, and Aucallama is the only one of our 12 communities with a significant proportion of Negro blood. In our 1969 survey, the largest proportion of males (30 percent) identified themselves as Negroes, *zambos*, or *morenos* (the latter two being local terms for people with some Negro blood). For females, the proportion was much smaller (19 percent) but still substantial.

Aucallama became a district capital in 1825 but in 1890 was put under the direct control of Huaral. The later history of the village is marked by its struggles to defend and expand its land area. In 1917, haciendas brought suit to claim an area known as Monte San Luis. A court decision in 1920 confirmed Aucallama ownership. The hacienda sharecroppers who had banded together to fight the case now divided Monte San Luis among themselves, each family getting about 1.5 hectares.

In 1931, Aucallama won official recognition as an Indian community as a means of protecting its lands. In 1933, Aucallama won still another court case and thus further expanded its lands at the expense of the haciendas. After decades of political efforts, in 1940 Aucallama regained its status as a district capital.

In 1940, laborers on haciendas banded together to claim 360 hectares of uncultivated lands in the desert. To have a large enough group to support their claim, the laborers sought to recruit additional members through radio and newspaper advertising in Huaral. This campaign did bring in additional members, but the leaders found that they could not finance a court battle against the haciendas, so they simply moved in and occupied what is now called San Graciano. From 1879 to 1940, the population of Aucallama rose from 366 to only 457. By 1961, the population had reached 861, an increase of 92 percent over 1940, due largely to the opening up of San Graciano.

Along with the marked population increase came an increase in the hetereogeneity of the inhabitants. Aucallama also suffered the effects of geographical dispersion. Aucallaminos lived in five distinct neighborhoods, with an hacienda actually separating the two main parts of the village.

Cultural differences coincided with location in Aucallama. The major differences were described in this way by Oscar Alers (1969):

> There was a contrast between the coastal style of life practiced in El Pueblo and Andean culture that is more characteristic of San Graciano. While El Pueblo primarily mirrors the coastal criollo culture, it also contains elements of Negro culture, with its distinctive songs, dances, and magical-religious rites. The San Graciano culture is influenced by the culture of the highlands, with some of its people retaining habits according to highlands custom. They chew coca, wear indigenous clothes, play huaynos [sierra folk music], and have transplanted their religious beliefs and practices from the Andes. Conflict exists between these groups, and a few Aucallaminos have in fact blamed this for the retarded development of the community. They perceive the situation as one in which "lack of solidarity" and the "separation of the people of San Graciano from those of San Luis" are at fault for the slow pace of progress.

In the years following the opening up of San Graciano in the 1940s, Aucallama seemed a dynamic and advancing community, but the water shortage in the 1950s blocked progress and led to frustration. The development of La Esperanza greatly increased the drain upon the Chancay River, and in 1956 the government water administration decreed that no new irrigation ditches could be built. This meant that any water that Aucallama gained would be at the expense of surrounding haciendas and vice versa. In this period, the village set up its own irrigation junta, but when the government declined to give the Aucallama junta official recognition, the organization passed from the scene.

In the early 1960s, there was one major effort to integrate the community around the water issue, and the rise and fall of this effort tells us much about the problems of Aucallama.

The effort began in 1962 with the election of a San Graciano man as president of the junta comunal. The new president and his supporters set in motion a reorganization of the Indian community to conform with national legislation, a step that was essential if the community was to press its legal claims. They then assembled documents to demonstrate that the original Indian community known as Aucallama had included the entire left bank of the Chancay River—which meant that parts of six haciendas should belong to Aucallama.

The organizers called several meetings that stirred up broad community interest, and for a time there seemed a real possibility that Aucallama might mount a formidable challenge to the haciendas. The organizational efforts fell apart in the face of two problems.

San Graciano was the most populous section of Aucallama, but it was also the section where land ownership was the most precarious, since its existence depended upon an "invasion" and squatter settlement that had never been legally recognized. Furthermore, many of the residents of San Graciano were also sharecroppers or laborers on haciendas involved in the conflict. They feared reprisals by the hacendados, and they also anticipated that if Aucallama instituted a suit against the six haciendas, the hacendados would counterattack by seeking to invalidate the claims of San Graciano residents to the land they had been occupying. In the face of growing anxieties and resistance to his efforts, the president of the junta comunal resigned, and the movement collapsed.

LA ESPERANZA

The first section of the irrigation project of La Esperanza was opened for settlement in 1929 under the following terms:

1. The price per hectare was 1,000 soles, which then was about 320 United States dollars.

2. A colonist could purchase up to 10 hectares if single, 15 if married.
3. Payment was to be made in 24 annual installments of 80 soles per hectare to cover principal and 6 percent interest.
4. Payments were to begin after the third year of ownership.
5. The director of immigration was empowered to sign purchase contracts with foreigners.

The first settlers were sharecroppers and owners of small plots in other parts of the valley and foreigners, especially Japanese. Thirty-one percent of the present colonists settled in La Esperanza between 1940 and 1948. The population was 782 in 1940 and had risen to 1,261 in 1961, largely due to the opening of new areas of irrigation.

The egalitarian initial land distribution had been eroded in subsequent years as some of the plots were divided through inheritance, and unsuccessful farmers sold out to the more successful, so that at the time of our studies the range in ownership per family was from under 5 to 153 hectares. Socioeconomic stratification in La Esperanza followed the lines of land ownership and the use of technology. Our studies found five socioeconomic levels in the community. The characteristics of these segments were as follows:

1. 2.1 percent of the families owned land from 40 to 153 hectares. None of them had been among the original settlers, and two-thirds of the owners were foreigners or sons of foreigners.   All operated highly mechanized farms and hired full-time laborers. Only a third lived regularly in La Esperanza although all of them had comfortable homes there. They played no part in community activities except on the *junta de regantes* (irrigation board), where they played influential roles.
2. 3.5 percent of the owners had properties running from 15 to 39.9 hectares. None of them had been among the original settlers, and half were foreigners or sons of foreigners. All of them used tractors, and half of them owned their own machines. They employed two or three full-time laborers. Like group 1, their participation in community affairs was largely limited to the junta de regantes.
3. 12.6 percent of the families owned properties from 5 to 14.9

hectares. Like those below them, they were all Peruvians and not of recent foreign extraction. They rented tractors and hired part-time laborers. They were the most active participants in the occasional community events characteristic of La Esperanza.

4. 34 percent of the families had holdings under 5 hectares. In contrast to the more affluent fruit growers, they cultivated vegetables and cotton. They worked without either permanent or temporary labor.

5. 48.2 percent of the families, mainly recent migrants from the highlands, did not own any land in La Esperanza. They made a precarious living primarily as permanent or temporary laborers in La Esperanza or on the haciendas.

La Esperanza was part of the district of Huaral and had no local government. The only institution that played an integrating role in La Esperanza was the annual fiesta of the patron saint. The most important organization for La Esperanza was the junta de regantes. The smaller landowners (predominantly in group 4 in the structure described above) complained that the big landowners used their political control to secure more than their fair share of water. At one time the small landowners had tried to form a rival junta to represent their interests, but failing to receive government recognition, they were not able to wrest control of the water system from the official body.

La Esperanza was a highly stratified community with a population heterogeneous in social and cultural background as well as in economic interests. Although this hetereogeneity made community cooperation difficult, it did not lead to a high level of internal conflict. There was friction between the smaller and larger property owners, but almost 50 percent of the families owned no property at all and thus were unaffected by these issues. Nor were the laborers organized to present a common front against the property owners. Efforts to unionize the 90 farm workers on the largest property had failed.

HOW THE VILLAGERS VIEWED
THEIR COMMUNITIES

We found the population of La Esperanza far more favorable than the population of Aucallama in its views of past progress and future possibilities. In neither case did the villagers see progress as depending upon collective efforts. When asked in 1969 "Do you prefer to work with others or alone?" the vote was predominantly for "alone" in both cases: males 84 percent and females 96 percent in Aucallama; males 72 percent and females 82 percent in La Esperanza.

For the two villages, in 1969 we found sharp differences in expressed satisfaction with one's own village, as Table 15-2 indicates.

In both 1964 and 1969, the average score for most villages we studied fell between "Like others" and "Better than others." Its evaluation had improved slightly over the five-year period, but Aucallama remained by far the most negatively regarded of the 12 villages in our surveys for both years.

The surveys confirm our picture of Aucallama as a fragmented and frustrated village. We found a low level of cooperation in La Esperanza, but progress there did not depend heavily upon collective efforts, and so we find La Esperanzans well satisfied with their situation and prospects.

TABLE 15-2
This Village Compared with Others

How do you feel your village compares with other villages?

	AUCALLAMA, %		LA ESPERANZA, %	
	M	F	M	F
(3) Better than others	13	36	65	64
(2) Like others	31	21	21	24
(1) Worse than others	56	43	14	12
Mean score	1.6	1.9	2.5	2.5

Note: No answer and other responses omitted.

Pacaraos and Huayopampa: 16
Stagnation and Dynamism

Above the Chancay valley, Pacaraos and Huayopampa have evolved in markedly different directions. In Pacaraos, the traditional community organization and culture gradually disintegrated, leaving the village poor, fragmented, and stagnating. In Huayopampa, the villagers built new integrating organizations upon the traditional groups and moved together into an era of widely shared prosperity.

Although the two villages had been very similar in culture, they differed markedly in economic opportunities. Huayopampa's extraordinary economic progress was based upon a shift from traditional agriculture to commercial fruit farming. That alternative was closed to Pacaraos because fruit could not be grown commercially in the climate prevailing at an altitude of 10,000 feet. Huayopampa, at an altitude of about 6,000 feet, had superior opportunities, but Huayopampa exploited those opportunities in an extraordinarily effective manner.

Up the mid-1960s, the history of Huayopampa was a success story.

164

But in the late 1960s and beyond, we find the village undergoing a severe crisis. The Huayopampa case will therefore enable us to examine both the potentialities and the limitations of its development strategy.

ECONOMIC AND DEMOCRAPHIC COMPARISONS

Figure 16-1 provides a visual representation of income distribution for the two villages. How these income estimates were made is described elsewhere (Matos Mar et al., 1969); here we simply point to the relationships revealed by the figures.

We see in the illustration that the bottom income grouping in Huayopampa is above all except the top income grouping in Pacaraos. To put the figures in an urban perspective, the average family in the lowest grouping in Huayopampa had the income of a reasonably good white-collar job in Lima in 1967.

The shapes of the income distributions also differ markedly. We find that the range in earnings from top to bottom levels was about 18 to 1 in Pacaraos compared with about 4 to 1 in Huayopampa. Furthermore, the largest grouping (close to 35 percent) was in Pacaraos at the bottom, whereas the largest grouping (35 percent) in Huayopampa was in the middle. The distributions suggest that Huayopampa had a large and affluent middle class, whereas Pacaraos had a very small affluent group far separated from the poor and the very poor.

We found marked differences also in the occupational pattern of the two villages. Although some families were also engaged in other activities, all the landowning families of Huayopampa had agriculture as the chief source of income. Our field studies indicated that the 14 families in the top stratum in Pacaraos gained less than 7 percent of their income from agriculture; the number of families whose income came primarily from agriculture rose steadily with each step down the economic strata, reaching 83 percent of Pacaraos families at the bottom. The top stratum earned 69 percent of its income from commerce and 24 percent from cattle.

As we might expect from the occupational pattern of Pacaraos, there was little relation between family income and the amount of irrigated land owned. Top stratum families averaged 0.89 hectares, whereas the next three levels held from 0.94 to 0.99 hectares. Families at the bottom

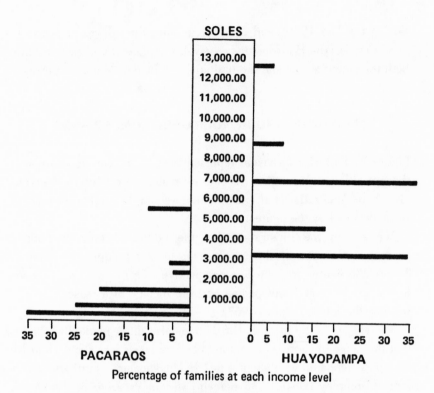

SOLES

PACARAOS   HUAYOPAMPA

Percentage of families at each income level

FIGURE 16-1
Income Distribution in Huayopama and Pacaraos

Note: For Huayopampa, although the principal income is from fruit, additional income from other sources is estimated from field reports. At the time of these estimates (1967), the sol was valued at 26.80 to the United States dollar.

held over half as much irrigated land (0.52 hectares) as did those at the top yet had incomes little over 6 percent of top families.

Between the top and bottom strata in Huayopampa there was somewhat greater spread in the size of average plots of irrigated land owned. Both villages were far more equal in land holdings per family than were La Esperanza and even Aucallama.

In our 1964 survey (29 males and 22 females in Huayopampa; 37 males and 40 females in Pacaraos), we found marked differences between the villages and the sexes in migration and travel experience. Forty-eight percent of the males of Huayopampa, compared with 19 percent of the males of Pacaraos, had never lived outside of their village. At the other extreme, only 14 percent of Huayopampa males, compared with 44 percent of Pacaraos males, had lived outside the village for more than three years. For females, the differences were reversed and smaller: 50 percent of the Huayopampa women and 65 percent of the Pacaraos women had never lived away from home.

In frequency of travel to the coast generally and to Lima, Huayopampa was much more closely linked to urban life. Forty-one percent of the men and 46 percent of the women compared with 19 percent and 10 percent, respectively, of Pacaraos men and women, reported going to a coastal town or city at least "several times a month!" For those reporting a trip to Lima within the past month, among the males there was just a small difference (38 percent to 30 percent) in favor of Huayopampa, but the Huayopampa females not only were far ahead of the Pacaraos women (60 percent to 15 percent) but also traveled to the capital substantially more often than their own men.

These figures are explained in part by the differences in interests and conditions of life in the two villages. Pacareño men had to leave home for extended periods so as to return with money to survive back home—but the women generally remained behind them. Huayopampinos could make a much better living at home, so they had much less need to migrate—except to go on with their educations, since Huayopampa did not have its own high school. Huayopampinos had much more to buy and sell, which led them naturally to the urban centers. Also, at the time of our study, half the families in Huayopampa owned homes in Lima, which accounted for a good deal of traveling back and forth for family reasons. The Huayopampino women were especially active in both commercial and family affairs.

Huayopampa had the highest educational level of the 12 villages in our study. Eighty-six percent of the males had had at least a complete elementary school education. Pacaraos males were also relatively well educated for our rural villages, with 73 percent having had at least a complete elementary education. At the high end of the educational scale for males, the two villages were farther apart: 17 percent of the Huayopampinos, compared with 3 percent of the Pacareños, had had some education beyond high school. In both villages, the females were less educated than the males, as is nearly always the case in rural Peru, but the Huayopampa women had far outdistanced the Pacaraos women in education, as indicated by a 44 percent to 22 percent difference in those having at least completed elementary school.

167

PACARAOS

Pacaraos remains, as in the past, the district capital and the dominant village in its area. We find two important dates in the twentieth-century history of Pacaraos.

By 1902, population had increased to the point where the village government was running out of agricultural land to distribute to new families. The end of land distribution to new families meant that increasing numbers of young villagers had to migrate to the coast or to the mines.

The growing land scarcity also tended to sharpen border disputes among neighboring villages. A dispute with Ravira in 1925 escalated into a gunfight in which two Pacareños were killed. Some years later, when the leaders of Pacaraos were considering improving and extending their irrigation system, they concluded that a joint project with Ravira would be most efficient, but the Ravirans rejected the idea.

Over the years, Pacaraos retained the traditional pattern of an integrated politico-religious hierarchy in which only those who have served at each step in the religious *cargo* system are eligible for top community-government positions. Only the more affluent Pacareños could meet the expenses of sponsoring the more important religious fiestas, so top government leadership was restricted to this small group, and among those individuals, succession to top political positions followed simply from completion of religious responsibilities.

From 1930 onward, we find increasing signs of strain within Pacaraos. Through 1931, all heads of households in Pacaraos were comuneros and their average age was 30.3 years. In 1966, the average age of comuneros was 50.1 years, whereas the average age of the residents (nonmembers of the Indian community) was only 38.5. Comparison of the 1931 and 1966 figures indicates that some of the sons of comuneros were failing to take over the community obligations of their fathers. Furthermore, at age sixty a communero becomes a *notable*, which means that he is free of community obligations while he continues to enjoy the benefits of membership. Thus, by 1976, half of the 1966 comuneros would be retiring from active service to the community, and we found few young men stepping in to replace them.

The benefits of community membership (preferential access to irrigation water and to pastureland and nonirrigated land) are most important to full-time farmers, and the obligations (faenas to clean and repair irrigation ditches, for example) are of greatest benefit to farmers. (Furthermore, our research team, balancing land use benefits against the value of labor in faenas at current prices, calculated that over a 40-year period, obligations for even a full-time farmer would slightly outweigh the value of benefits received. When we added the costs of obligatory service in religious cargoes over this period, the costs of membership outran the benefits by about 50 percent.) The residents constituted 11 out of 26—almost half—of Pacareños engaged in commerce and services, and the richest man in the community (a trucker) was a resident.

When 28 residents were asked "Would you like to become a comunero?" only 5 said yes and 1 could not decide. Still more serious for community prospects were the responses of 78 comuneros to the question, "Would you like your son to become a comunero?" Only 6 gave an affirmative response, and 1 was undecided. When asked to explain, they all responded along the same lines: "You lose time, and it is a lot of work." "You are a slave, you are not free to work as you wish or to leave the village; those who are not comuneros have less worries and benefit more." "Because the duties are heavy and without reward."

As community membership became more burdensome, the junta communal experienced increasing difficulties even in restricting the potential benefits to comuneros. For example, residents were supposed to pay twice as much as comuneros per head of cattle for use of communal pastureland, but many residents evaded this surcharge by placing their cattle through comunero relatives. Presumably, the residents had to reciprocate by doing some service for their comunero relatives, but the channeling of the exchange among individual families deprived the community of benefits to which it was legally entitled.

The strength of the community government depends in part upon the penalties it is able to impose for noncompliance with community rules and customs. In the period 1964–1966, an average of 59 percent of Pacaraos families participated in the faenas called for work on maintaining the irrigation system or other community projects. The family that failed to provide a worker for an official community faena was fined an amount equivalent to the prevailing wage for a day's work. In Pacaraos, the collection rate for fines ranged from 13 percent to 32 percent of fines

169

owned—with the bottom socioeconomic stratum paying 32 percent of the fines it owed and the top stratum among those paying 13 percent.

When fines failed to secure compliance, the junta had no success with other means. When the junta cut off electricity from one recalcitrant comunero, he appealed to national authorities. Since the electric power system had been built by the national government and did not belong to Pacaraos, these authorities simply ruled that the electric service must be reinstituted.

HUAYOPAMPA

The differences that set Huayopampa apart from Pacaraos and other communities in the upper part of the Chancay valley are not of recent origin. A Catholic missionary elementary school was established in Huayopampa around 1850. Although it was short-lived, this early exposure to education left a lasting mark on that community. In 1874, people of a number of communities in the upper part of the valley drew up a petition requesting the national government to establish a school. All but 20 percent of the petitioners from other communities signed with their thumbprints, but two-thirds of the Huayopampinos signed their own names.

When petitions to the government brought no action, in 1886 Huayopampa took matters into its own hands, building its own school and hiring a teacher. It was 1922 before any other community in the area got its own school.

In 1902, as did Pacaraos, Huayopampa faced the decision regarding its final distribution of land to new families. Instead of simply turning over the remaining plots, Huayopampa retained ownership for the community and rented the land for three-year periods. Thus, 30 families eventually received farmland on a rental basis. These rents have been a major factor in the superior resources of Huayopampa's communal government.

In 1904, Huayopampa built a new shcool and attracted two remarkable teachers, the Ceferino Villars. As their two sons succeeded them as teachers in Huayopampa, the community remained under the influence of the Villars family until 1925. They are still remembered today, the

170

main street bearing the name of Ceferino Villar and one of the school buildings being named after his wife.

Around 1920, the archbishop of Lima was contemplating establishing a school somewhere in the upper part of the valley. During a period of education in Lima, one of the sons of Ceferino Villar had met the archbishop and, hearing of his plan, urged him to visit Huayopampa. After spending the night in the Villars home, the archbishop met with the villagers, who offered to build a new school if the church would supply the teachers. On this basis, the Seminario Menor was established to provide several years of education beyond that previously available. Along with all the other structures of Huayopampa, the new school was burned to the ground in 1927 as a means of killing the rats that were spreading bubonic plague. Again the church's direct educational contribution was short-lived, but its impact was lasting. Most of the leaders in the development of Huayopampa in the 1940s and 1950s had been students in the Seminario Menor.

Schoolteachers shaped the development of Huayopampa both in educating the young and in providing leadership in civic affairs. In the 1960s, all 10 teachers in Huayopampa were natives, and the pattern of native sons and daughters returning from higher education to teach in Huayopampa had prevailed for many years. At the time of our studies, only two of the teachers in Pacaraos were natives of that community, and only one of these was a comunero. None of the teachers played an active role in community affairs in Pacaraos.

Huayopampa teachers modeled the organization of school activities upon the communal traditions of the Indian community—while injecting new activities and responsibilities into that framework. The boys and the girls each elected juntas to govern their activities. Each faena work group was under the leadership of a teacher and an elected brigadier. There was a weekly faena for cleaning the school, making repairs, scrubbing the floors, etc. Every pupil was responsible for the cleanliness of the doors, windows, and walls of his home and for the neatness of the space around it. There were severe penalties against writing on walls or throwing trash out of the house. The juntas made regular inspection rounds, and a child could be sent home to remedy the defects found. If adults refused to clean up trash they had dumped, the school juntas did the job for them—and the junta comunal levied fines.

The teachers sought to integrate their instruction with the life of the area. For example, the children studied local plant diseases and their prevention and regional archaeology—from a book by Pedro Villar Cordova, son of the pioneering schoolteachers.

The 1944 village archives contain this statement by the teachers, in response to parental complaints against the school's emphasis on manual labor:

1. It is true that the children come to study, but also to study the characteristics and uses and the ways of treating plants and other things that are good or harmful for men;
2. The children learn to value the work of their parents and of the comuneros, working for their good and for the good of others;
3. Work teaches the child more and better than books and the words of the teacher, because work teaches scientific knowledge and technical discoveries;
4. Through working, the children learn that only work creates wealth and transforms villages;
5. Children who study and work do not look down on practical activities and care much more for their school, their village, and their family;
6. The children through working, cultivate their best sentiments: fraternity, union, and mutual aid;
7. Work does not exhaust the children because the tasks are graded according to their strength.

The schoolteachers also played major roles in the agricultural development of Huayopampa. On plots ceded by the community in 1940, 1943, and 1945, they established experimental gardens and a reforestation project to teach the children—and, indirectly, their parents— modern methods of agriculture and control of soil erosion. Schoolteachers were not alone in leading Huayopampa into commercial fruit growing, but they played prominent roles in providing information and linking the village with professors of the National Agrarian University, with extension agents, and with officials of the Agricultural Development Bank. Before 1960, rapidly growing demand for credit and a good repayment record led to the establishment of a branch office of the bank in Huayopampa.

172

The spirit of hard work and achievement was still very much alive among teachers in the late 1960s. One of them closed a discussion with us with these words: "Querer es poder" (equivalent to "Where there's a will, there's a way.") But the emphasis remained upon *collective* achievement.

Huayopampinos did not express their devotion to religion through going to church. In our 1964 surveys, only 3 percent of the males and 38 percent of the females reported going to church once a month or more often—compared with 8 percent of the males and 48 percent of the females in Pacaraos. Nevertheless, although religion seemed little more than ritual in Pacaraos, it continued to play an important integrating role in Huayopampa.

This integrating role was dramatized in the ceremonies of Holy Week. From Thursday until Sunday, the community was symbolically transformed into a sacred society. No work was permitted. Stoves in the homes could not be lit. Men and women limited their contacts in public. Smoking and drinking were forbidden. The villagers had to maintain in public the serious demeanor appropriate to mourning. Special authorities chosen to enforce the rules patrolled the community.

During the whole period, the church was open, and the authorities were active there also. With long poles, they prodded those who were behaving in an irreverent manner. As was the case for other activities, the political officials of the village were fined double for any infraction. The villagers submitted willingly to controls and fines as dramatic representations of the dominance of the sacred world over the secular at the climax of the religious year.

At the regular monthly assembly, comuneros were elected to the major positions in the religious fiesta system, indicating that villagers viewed these positions as obligations owed to the community. A comunero might try to avoid such service, but only the weightiest excuses were accepted and the asemblea itself was the final authority.

As the following account of a confrontation indicates, the fiesta served more to integrate the community than to represent religious beliefs. A schoolteacher had been nominated for *depositario* two or three times. Each time, he had avoided the obligation with excuses that the villagers reluctantly accepted. Meanwhile, a number of the villagers had been claiming that the teacher had arbitrarily eliminated the teaching of religion from his classes. When he was again nominated, they refused to accept any excuses and demanded the real reason. Finally he said, "I am an atheist, so I cannot lead a fiesta in honor of a God I don't belief in."

His critics told him this was no excuse; he owed it to the community to become a depositario. When the teacher remained adamant, the community proceeded to take the following steps:

1. A fine was levied.
2. His electricity was cut off. (Huayopampa had built and owned its power system, so no appeal from this decision was possible.)
3. Irrigation water was cut off from his land.
4. The parents refused to permit their children to go to school until this teacher was removed.
5. The teacher was formally expelled from the community.

He went to Lima and, a year later, petitioned the community for the return of his lands. The comuneros agreed on condition that he become a depositario. Thus, an athiest came to play the leading role in a Catholic folk festival.

Although some of the villagers were concerned about the teaching of religion, this issue was not enough to mobilize the whole community against the teacher. Only when he refused to discharge the obligations of a comunero did the community act against him. And note the severity and the effectiveness of the sanctions.

The community solidarity fostered in the educational program built up a far stronger junta comunal in Huayopampa than was the case in Pacaraos. Faena attendance was higher in Huayopampa (70 percent versus 59 percent), but the main difference was in enforcement. In Huayopampa, 100 percent of the fines levied were collected. The accounts on fines due were closed yearly at the time of the community cattle roundup. If delinquents did not then pay up, officials sold one or more of their animals to collect the fines. These levies, together with the annual rental of farmlands and the fees per head of cattle for grazing on community lands, gave Huayopampa an income substantially above that of Pacaraos.

The effectiveness of communal government in Huayopampa rested upon a common set of economic interests. Fruit growing provided the primary source of income for every comunero family. The families in the five socioeconomic strata differed mainly in the way they worked the land and in the size of land holdings.

Five families at the top, with an average of 1.64 hectares of irrigated land, hired labor and owned their own machines. Nine families at the second level, with an average of 1.15 hectares, hired labor and rented machines. Fifty-seven families in the third stratum, with an average of 1 hectare, made little use of hired labor or machines and depended upon traditional forms of reciprocal labor among relatives and close friends. In the fourth stratum, 28 families, with an average of 0.76 hectare, supplemented their income from fruit with part-time labor for more affluent communeros. At the bottom, with an average of 0.54 hectare, 52 families concentrated on their own properties and did not enter into reciprocal exchanges or seek part-time employment.

Below these five strata were two small groups of families: landless farm laborers and sheep and cattle herders who worked in the pastures far above Huayopampa. Being migrants into the community, being generally illiterate, and not being comuneros, they played no active role in local affairs.

The top social stratum earned a higher income from fruit growing than did the lower social strata entirely because of differences in land holdings. The difference in fruit-growing income *per hectare* between the top and bottom strata we estimated at an insignificant 28 soles per month. And since the families in the bottom stratum did not hire labor or use machines, their net income per hectare from fruit growing was markedly higher than the top families' net income per hectare from fruit growing. The greater affluence at the top levels depended not only upon more land but also upon professional and commercial incomes. Since families in the third stratum, depending upon reciprocal labor, not only saved on labor costs compared with those above them but also had more sheep and cattle than any other stratum, their net family income was close to that of stratum 2.

In contrast with men in the top strata in Pacaraos, men in the top strata in Huayopama were highly active and influential in community affairs. Men of the third stratum were the most faithful in discharging their community obligations.

Upon this base of widely shared prosperity, common economic interests, and strong communal government, Huayopampa had developed its own series of cooperative enterprises: a communal store, a trucking firm, a bus line, a system of potable water, and an electric power plant. Ownership of these enterprises gave the junta comunal powerful rewards and penalties to use in getting support for its decisions.

Huayopampa had much more active competition for local political offices than did Pacaraos, although both communities had retained the requirement of passing through the religious fiesta obligations in order to be eligible for top political offices. With increasing affluence, there was active competition for the top religious position of depositario, and there were always enough men who had gone through this step so that succession to political office was not automatic. Competition did not take the form of campaigning for office. In fact, it was customary for the nominee to claim that he was not qualified or available, but the assembly could assure competition by requiring nominees to run.

The internal strength of the community was paralleled by its success in intervillage conflicts. Huayopampinos reported that they had not lost a court case with a neighboring village since 1900. But this success had its costs. Shortly before 1940, Huayopampa and neighboring Sumbilca became interested in constructing roads that would connect them with the coast. There were two alternatives: from Huayopampa to Huaral in the Chancay valley or from Huayopampa through Sumbilca over the mountains south to the Chillon valley; the second road would provide more direct access to Lima. Leaders of Huayopampa proposed that the two villages work together on the Lima route. Leaders of Sumbilca agreed— if Huayopampa would relinquish its claims in a long-contested boundary litigation between the two communities. Huayopampa refused and plunged into building the road toward Huaral. Its completion in 1948 made it possible for the first time to sell fruit to coastal markets.

When Huayopampa purchased a bus and established regular service to Huaral, village leaders recognized that the enterprise would be more successful if they could attract customers from other villages. To do this, the authorities established fines for Huayopampinos who insulted non-Huayopampinos on the bus and an even heavier set of fines for those who expressed their feelings physically. The residents of other communities now travel unmolested on the buses; however, the strenuous measures taken are evidence of the magnitude of the problem. The persistence of these frictions was dramatized for us during a visit to Huayopampa when we encountered a man standing outside a bar, swaying drunkenly and proclaiming; "I am from Sumbilca. Huayopampa is always taking advantage of Sumbilca."

Huayopampa spent much less of its local government money on sending delegations to Lima than did Pacaraos. Huayopampinos had recognized that the help they got from the national government was not without substantial costs. One of the community leaders put it this way, in describing an earlier community project:

> Over a period of fifteen years we sent delegation after delegation to Lima to get the government to provide us with the material and the technical knowledge we needed to carry out the project. This was a very frustrating experience because we were always getting promises and no action. Besides, when we came back and nothing happened, there were always people in the community saying that we had just spent their money to have a good time in Lima. Finally, after fifteen years the government did provide the material and the engineering help we needed so we could complete the project. But then we sat down and figured out how much it cost us in expenses for those trips to Lima over the years, and we realized that we would have got the job done much faster and cheaper if we just had bought the materials and hired the engineers ourselves.

In the early 1960s, Huayopampa changed its strategy and was hiring its own engineers, buying its own materials, and so on.

WILL SUCCESS SPOIL HUAYOPAMPA?

In the early 1960s, Huayopampa was at the peak of its success both in economic performance and in organizational effectiveness, yet even then danger signals were clearly visible on the road ahead. The paradox of Huayopampa is that to a considerable extent, its later difficulties were the product of its early successes.

When young people emigrated from Pacaraos, they entered the labor markets of the coast and the mines at the bottom. Even though they earned more than ever before, they remained around the bottom of the labor force, so that life in Pacaraos continued to attract them; many returned to settle down permanently in the old home town.

Most young people from Huayopampa followed the route of higher education on the coast and entered the urban labor market close to the top. By 1966, Huayopampa had produced 95 males and 52 females who either were established professionals or were studying for professional careers. As further evidence of the profound influence of schoolteachers in Huayopampa, we found that 50 (52.6 percent) of these professional men and 43 (82.7 percent) of these professional women had become or were becoming schoolteachers.

When we met with a group of Huayopampino university students in Lima, we found them very proud of the progress of their home town and committed to frequent visits to family and friends there; but not a single one was considering settling down in Huayopampa.

In the short space of five years, our surveys revealed the kinds of shifts in attitudes and beliefs that reflected a developing community crisis. To put the changes in context, we compared Huayopampa with Pacaraos for both 1964 and 1969.

The most striking shifts for Huayopampa are found in perceptions of conflict and cooperation. Huayopampinos perceived an extraordinarily high level of cooperation in 1964; by 1969, this level had dropped sharply, although it still remained above the level perceived in Pacaraos. In 1964, Huayopampinos perceived far less community conflict than did Pacareños; by 1969, this difference was practically eliminated by the marked increase in conflict perceived in Huayopampa. These comparisions are shown in Table 16-1.

A marked decline in collective orientation was reflected in responses to the question, "Would you rather work with others or alone?" From 1964 to 1969, Huayopampino males opting for "with others" dropped from 59 to 41 percent, and females choosing this response dropped from 54 to 23 percent. In Pacaraos, the changes were in the same direction but much smaller: males dropped from 27 to 22 percent and females from 28 to 13 percent.

On the five items used for our measure, we found Huayopampa in 1964 higher in interpersonal trust than any of our 11 other villages. By 1969, the trust level in Huayopampa had dropped on all five items and had dropped especially sharply for the statement shown in Table 16-2.

We found in Huayopampa a marked drop in the perceived power of the communal government to solve community problems, as shown in Table 16-3.

What happened between 1964 and 1969 to account for these changes in attitudes and perceptions? We did not carry on intensive studies of Huayopampa after 1967, but field trips have provided enough informa-

TABLE 16-1
Perceptions of Cooperation and Conflict, Huayopampa vs Pacaraos, 1964–1969

When it comes to cooperating on some project for the community, how well do the people cooperate? Is there:

	HUAYOPAMPA				PACARAOS			
	MALES, %		FEMALES, %		MALES, %		FEMALES, %	
	1964	1969	1964	1969	1964	1969	1964	1969
Much cooperation	97	38	86	30	68	33	55	18
Fair cooperation	3	54	14	53	30	58	38	53
Poor cooperation	0	8	0	17	3	8	8	29

Is there much conflict or division between the people of this village?

Much conflict	0	29	9	11	24	19	18	27
Some conflict	41	50	27	68	46	47	30	62
No conflict	59	21	59	21	30	33	45	11
NA	—	—	5	—	—	—	7	—

TABLE 16-2
Interpersonal Trust, Huayopampa vs Pacaraos, 1964–1969

Would you say most people like to help others or like to watch out for themselves? They are more inclined to:

	HUAYOPAMPA				PACARAOS			
	MALES, %		FEMALES, %		MALES, %		FEMALES, %	
	1964	1969	1964	1969	1964	1969	1964	1969
Help others	45	7	59	3	19	22	13	13
Look out for themselves	55	93	41	97	81	69	85	82
NA	—	—	—	—	—	8	3	5
N	29	27	22	30	37	36	40	39

TABLE 16-3
Perceived Power of Communal Government, Huayopampa vs Pacaraos, 1964–1969

To solve the problems of this village, how much power do you think the junta comunal has? Would you say it has:

	HUAYOPAMPA				PACARAOS			
	MALES, %		FEMALES, %		MALES, %		FEMALES, %	
	1964	1969	1964	1969	1964	1969	1964	1969
All the power necessary	90	68	91	59	27	53	20	31
The power to make certain improvements but not others	7	20	0	31	51	19	30	39
Very little power to make any improvements	0	12	0	10	19	28	18	31
NA	3	—	9	—	3	—	32	—
N	29	27	22	30	37	36	40	39

tion to suggest the following factors in the decline of community solidarity:

1. *Changes in Intercommunity Relations.* Huayopampa had been exceptionally successful in conflicts with other villages. By the end of the 1960s, these conflicts had subsided, and Huayopampinos were no longer concerned over external threats. Intervillage conflict may have been one force promoting internal solidarity.

2. *Demographic Changes.* From 1964 to 1969, the average age of heads of household appears to have increased. This increase cannot be demonstrated directly from the questionnaires because of changes in our age categories: In 1964, we surveyed a sample of adults from 21 to 60 *and over;* in 1969, the sample ranged from 18 to 60. However, indirect evidence is provided by an item on number of children living in the home. In 1964, 52 percent of the households contained three or more children; in 1969, this figure had dropped to 37 percent. In 1964, 25 percent of the households were without children living in them; in 1969, this figure had risen to 39 percent.

To fill the gap, the farm owners steadily increased the number of hired laborers. With declining physical energy and endurance, the Huayopampa farmers themselves had to shoulder an increasing workload and were also compelled to provide closer supervision for the laborers than for members of their own families. These burdens made the farmers increasingly reluctant to take on the responsibilities for managing communal enterprises.

3. *Managing and Monitoring Communal Enterprises*. Each collective economic activity had been managed by a three-man elective board serving for a three-month period. Each head of household was required to serve (without compensation) when his turn came.

Here the problem was not simply the number of three-man boards that had to be manned; some of these assignments were far more time-consuming, difficult, and frustrating than others. The crucial distinction was between locally self-contained enterprises and those that operated largely outside of Huayopampa.

Many Huayopampinos had participated in the construction of the potable water and electric lighting systems and thus had gained familiarity with the technical side of their operations. The communal store was an operation of no great complexity, since it was limited to the staple products frequently purchased, and the hired storekeeper could readily maintain the financial records as well as wait on customers. Furthermore, monitoring of these three activities was almost automatic. When anything went wrong, it would quickly become obvious to large numbers of comuneros.

The bus line and the trucking enterprise presented problems of quite a different order. No Huayopampino had experience in auto mechanics, and there were no local repair and maintenance facilities. The Huayopampino bus passengers provided some informal monitoring of that activity. The communal government tried to check on the trucking enterprise by requiring that the paid driver be accompanied by an adult volunteer, in order to make sure that the driver did not use the truck for his own purposes, that he did not enter into kickback agreements with repair shops, etc. But this responsibility added heavily to the load of community obligations to be borne by the comuneros.

During our 1967 fieldwork period, the monthly meetings of the asemblea comunal were largely given over to discussion and arguments

181

concerning the management—and alleged mismanagement—of these two enterprises. Responsibility came to be increasingly costly both in time required and in community complaints received.

In order to ease the burden, the community voted to reduce the term of service for the trucking committee from three months to one month. If a three-month term was already too short to allow committee members to learn much, the monthly rotational scheme guaranteed inefficient management.

The communal trucking enterprise also suffered from increasing competition from middlemen from Huarochirí, who brought their trucks to Huayopampa and offered to buy the produce on the spot. The outsiders not only were enterprising businessmen; they also plugged themselves into the social network of Huayopampa by hiring a band for the fiesta, by delivering messages, and by doing other collective and individual favors.

Huayopaminos may have recognized that they would make more money if they sent their goods to market through an efficiently operating communal enterprise, but they could not always count on a Huayopampino truck when they needed it, and they bore all the losses when that truck broke down. Besides, in increasingly affluent Huayopampa, time and energy were scarcer than money.

In the mid-1960s, Huayopampa owned and operated two trucks. At this writing, the communal enterprise is struggling along with one aging vehicle. Unless Huayopampa establishes and supports a paid and competent management for its vehicular enterprises, the communal trucking company will soon come to an end.

As Huayopampa was entering the decade of the 1970s, the collective political economy of earlier years was breaking down. Huayopampinos were finding their collective obligations increasingly burdensome and were more inclined to seek individualistic solutions to their problems.

Generational Conflict in Lampián 17

We will now examine a case in which migration was the dominant factor in the restructuring of a community. This is the story of an integenerational conflict that precipitated the expulsion of the young men and of their return to remake Lampián with the ideas they had learned in school and in their migratory experience.

THE SHAPING OF CONFLICT

Along with Huayopampa and Pacaraos, Lampián is one of the 27 communities in the Chancay valley highlands. Located 7,800 feet above sea level, Lampián had a population of 485 in 1967.

Up to the late 1940s, the people of Lampián had practiced subsistence agriculture on inadequately irrigated lands and on land dependent upon rainfall. During this period, the peasants grew the crops of their ancestors with traditional methods and tools.

Lampián was recognized as an Indian community in 1926. In effect, the local government was a gerontocracy, with the higher positions being reached only through increasing age. This traditional system began to break down under the stress of population pressure. Population rose 25 percent between 1926 and 1936, and by 1938 one-quarter of the comuneros (30 of 120) were without land.

During the 1930s, the young men of Lampián came to feel that they were bearing the burdens of community membership without enjoying the benefits. They took part in faenas in place of their fathers and attended the monthly communal assembly—where they had neither voice nor vote. Without land, they had to postpone marriage, and what little they had to look forward to in the community was in the uncertain future.

Their position led to increasing frustration, but it was a schoolteacher who channeled this discontent. Pedro de Verón Marquina, a teacher from the provincial capital of Canta, became director of the primary school in 1927 and remained in that position for 10 years. He pursued two principles: manual and intellectual work should be combined, and the knowledge acquired in the classroom should be applied to the conditions of life of the community.

De Verón Marquina turned the patio of the school into a garden plot so he could teach the children to cultivate crops according to modern methods. He concentrated upon agriculture and animal husbandry. To extend his program, he sought in vain to get the community to cede the school a strip of irrigated land. He had to settle for planting potatoes in an unirrigated area.

One of his former pupils told us:

The teacher who has left the best memories with the community has been Pedro de Véron. . . . He taught us very well. Listen, after 25 years, we remember him well. . . . The teacher made his classes like telling a story, and then, so we could understand well, he drew pictures for us. That teacher worked day and night. We cultivated a garden, and our parents came gladly to help us in faenas there. It was because he taught us so well. . . . And he loved the community (Celestino, 1972:28).

The impact of the teacher went beyond classwork. In his earlier experience on the coast, he had met Haya de la Torre, and he became a dedicated exponent of the political ideology of APRA. Beginning in 1934, he organized his former students into four APRA party cells, each one with six or seven members. Outside of school he conducted a four-month training course for cell members. He then encouraged them to go out to the neighboring communities to spread the APRA message.

The young men had already let their discontent be known in various ways, but the crisis came to a head in 1938 with the parcelization of a 10-hectare plot. The young men without land were not the only claimants, for some of the older men felt that completion of all of their obligations to the community entitled them to share in the distribution of new parcels, as had been customary in the past.

The commission to distribute the land was not chosen by the assembly but by the *sindico apoderado* (principal trustee) himself. Members of the commission allocated to themselves and to some of the older comuneros the best parts, leaving the young men with the roughest terrain, in nonirrigable sections, and even smaller than the preannounced minimum dimensions. The authorities explained their decision by pointing out that the majority of the young claimants were not yet active participants in the community.

The public announcement provoked bitter arguments even while the land was being marked out for its new owners. The young men refused to accept the decision and at first were supported by some of their fathers. In a public meeting, the young men vigorously denounced the community officials and the older comuneros, accusing them of "betraying the necessities of the youth."

This open challenge to the authority of the old men provoked an even stronger reaction. The elders attacked the young men for their lack of allegiance to traditional values and voted to expel all 30 from the community immediately. Thus began the exile of the younger generation of Lampián.

SEVEN YEARS OF EXILE

Fifteen of the exiles went directly to Lima. Ten found work in the valley delta, particularly on the haciendas of Huando and Palpa. Five settled in the vicinity of San Miguel, a narrow point in the valley between the highland and the delta. There they worked as farm laborers and in jobs with middlemen engaged in the buying and selling of highland produce and in supplying the highland communities.

Although he had left the community a year earlier, Pedro de Verón had kept in touch with Lampián, and now he stepped in to help his former pupils and political protegés. He arranged with the Ministry of Education to get four of them scholarships to continue their studies in the better secondary schools of Lima. He encouraged others to continue in school and called upon their parents to provide whatever help they could.

The young men who went to school were short of money and often did not have enough to eat. As one of them described this period, "We ate quinua [a grain] and zapallo [squash] daily. I got very thin, but I did not give up; I wanted to study. My teacher, de Verón, would come to see me every time he came down from Canta."

The students from Lampián had no trouble with their schoolwork. As one of them explained, "De Verón, he taught us very well, he was a good teacher. In nearly all of the courses, we were better prepared than our Lima classmates."

Success in school opened up new social horizons. As one said,

> My classmates were rich people, gringos but good people, and I worked with them and solved their mathematical problems. . . . To have more contacts and to go out more with the rich gringos, we forced ourselves to be the best in the class. In that way we had opportunities to help the lazy students, so as to be invited out to their houses for weekends or to get good pay for tutoring.

Five of the young men worked in the shoe business in Lima—as artisans, factory workers, or salesmen—and several ended up making and selling their own shoes. Three got jobs as waiters, both working and living in the restaurant building, getting their meals free, and saving money from tips and wages.

Two entered the army. Four others had a variety of jobs, mainly in construction and domestic service.

All of the migrants visited Lampián from time to time. At first, they were cooly received outside of their immediate families, but with the passage of time, tensions diminished. The migrants were also visited

186

occasionally by people from home, and the young men took pride in showing how well they were doing and what they had learned. One young man, working on a delta hacienda, put it this way:

In spite of all they had done to us, we used to help them. We would invite them to eat and drink, and they could see that we were doing better than they were and that we had money from our work and they had nothing compared to us. We would tell them everything about our work and the places we were seeing. They were impressed; some wanted to come down and work but they could never quite bring themselves to do it. They weren't like us. *Caramba*, when you are young you do many things and you learn much! We knew more than they did.

PROBLEMS BACK HOME

Back home, the comuneros of Lampián were learning that with the expulsion of the young men, they had solved one problem but created other problems they could not solve. The most immediate one was the filling of the bottom positions in the politico-administrative hierarchy. The strength and energy of youth was required to patrol the community lands day and night to protect the cattle and crops. The youngest men remaining in the community had already taken their turn at these positions and could not be forced back into them. The community voted to put the jobs on a paid basis. The new system was in continuous difficulties because the community could not afford large enough payments to make the positions attractive, and the men designated served reluctantly and sporadically.

Lampián was also beset with a variety of human and environmental problems. On two occasions, diseases caused heavy losses of cattle. The local government was involved with a series of problems with the surrounding communities and the national government. Although Lampián was legally recognized as an Indian community in 1926, this recognition was to be followed by the preparation of a community map establishing the boundaries of Lampián and the distribution of ownership within the community. In 1936, Lampián had secured an engineer from the Ministry of Labor and Indian Communities to draw its map. Then followed the necessary steps to get the map legally accepted by the government.

187

When the proposed map was shown at a meeting with representatives of surrounding communities, they immediately protested, claiming that Lampián had upsurped lands not belonging to it.

It took seven years of political efforts for Lampián to get its map recognized by the ministry, but then two neighboring communities challenged that decision in the courts. For many months more, Lampián had to spend its scarce funds to cover legal costs.

During the long land struggle, Lampián faced two new problems. A 1942 law required the reorganization of local government of the Indian communities. A ministry representative came to explain the new system, but several Lampián delegations had to go to Lima to make sure they were following official procedures.

In 1943, the national government established a new system requiring payment for the irrigation water taken from the river. In the past, Indian communities had not been charged. Lampián repeatedly sent representatives to Lima to protest, thus incurring further costs—and still the government declined to remove the water changes.

These problems exhausted the community treasury and required assessments on individual families. In a subsistence agricultural community, these charges weighed heavily. They also provoked conflicts as to how the charges would be levied: whether the larger farmers should pay more than the smaller ones and if so, how much.

The growing complexity of Lampián's problems led to a sense of frustration among the villagers. Increasingly, they came to feel that they were not able to cope with their problems without help.

Lampián faced two pressing needs:

1. Increased agricultural income to meet the rising costs of local government.
2. Community leaders with greater negotiating skills and more experience with the urban world.

There was only one way to meet both needs: invite back the rebel young men. In February 1945, an asemblea comunal voted to rescind the expulsion order and establish a committee to call for their help. By the end of the following year, all 30 were back in Lampián.

THE RETURN OF THE YOUNG

Until this time, age had determined the passage of individuals up the political hierarchy. Now it was agreed the individual best able to perform the functions required of the position should be elected.

This did not mean that the older comuneros simply turned the government over to the youth. In 1949, the old guard even won an apparent victory in a community decision to abolish the official structure imposed by the national government and go back to the traditional system in which power was concentrated in the hands of a sindico apoderado.

That was the last stand of the old guard. The young men responded by withdrawing their participation from the customary community activities, such as faenas. The official structure was shortly reestablished, and the young men assumed unchallenged control.

The young men brought back with them not only their savings and knowledge of the urban world but also a political ideology and a set of organizational ideas. Their experiences with unions and political organizations in the delta and in Lima had strengthened their links to APRA. The years of 1945 to 1948, when APRA participated in the government of President Bustamante, were also the high point of APRA power and prestige. The young community leaders of Lampián worked actively, under the APRA banner, with their counterparts in other nearby communities on such projects as shifting the provincial capital from Canta to Huaral.

THE RESURGENCE OF LAMPIAN

In a few years after returning to Lampián , the young men had consolidated their key positions through solving community problems. To meet the costs of land disputes, 15 of the returnees lent money to the community—taking in return the use of certain community lands. (Later they continued to rent these plots.) In 1947, the disputes were finally settled, with Lampián retaining control of all the land it had claimed.

It had been the custom for Lampián to grow potatoes along the borders of its land, so as to protect its claims. This custom had been abandoned because of a serious potato blight. In 1948, the community moved to reestablish the potato planting. Land parcels along the borders were divided equally, but the poorer families were given additional parcels.

The new community leadership took steps to fortify the local economy. A cycle of dry years and an epidemic of hoof and mouth disease in 1943 had sharply reduced the Lampián herds and pasturage use. In fact, some of the pasture had passed out of Lampián's control. In 1946, the new community leaders recovered these lands.

It had long been customary to levy assessments to pay for community projects, but the levies had become small and infrequent as Lampián grew poorer and fewer projects were undertaken. Now at least the younger generation had increasing resources and new project ideas, so the assessments began to grow.

The surge of the village economy is shown in income figures from 1935 to 1967. For both 1935 and 1936, village government income was about 1,500 soles. In 1946, when the migrants were still in the process of returning, the income was about 5,500 soles. By 1951, income had almost tripled to (16,113 soles). The 1955 figure (44,210 soles) was, again, almost triple of that for 1951. Income continued to rise—going over 94,000 soles in 1964 and over 138,000 soles in 1967.

In 1946, the community voted to launch the construction of a vehicular road that would link it with Huaral and other coastal cities. Community leaders got tools, explosives, and technical assistance from the national government and committed the labor of all the males sixteen and over in faenas lasting a week every month. Completion of the road in 1954 enabled Lampián to follow Huayopampa into commercial fruit growing.

Before 1960, with some national government assistance and faena labor, Lampián had built its own systems of potable water and electric power. The community also built a new school and municipal building, covered the streets around the Plaza de Armas with asphalt, built cement pathways within the plaza, and planted shrubbery.

The returned migrants were not concerned only with economic development. They participated actively in the religious *cofradias* (brotherhoods) and took increasingly prominent positions in the annual religious fiesta. As the returned migrants assumed ceremonial leadership, the fiestas became more elaborate, bringing prestige to their sponsors and to Lampián.

These various projects were based, in large measure, upon increased agricultural income, produced primarily by the returnees. Between 1945 and 1950, they experimented with vegetables grown in the delta: tomatoes, sweet potatoes, yucas, string beans, lima beans, and cabbage. None of these crops did well in Lampián, but at the same time they were planting apple and peach trees. By 1950, it was evident that the fruit trees were going to pay off handsomely, and the innovators extended their plantings rapidly until orchards covered about half of the land under their control.

With fruit growing came the application of modern agricultural methods. For example, the returnees began the use of insecticides with small hand pumps and began shifting to power sprayers in 1955. By 1967, 28 families owned power machines and an additional 11 rented them from their neighbors.

Guano, the traditional fertilizer, is a state monopoly, and in recent years it was in short supply, which led to a system of rationing. The former migrants, with their superior contacts and negotiating skills, were generally able to meet their needs and sell their surplus to their less favored neighbors. At the time of the study, guano was sold at 40 soles per sack at the port of Chancay and could be resold in Lampaián for from 60 to 70 soles.

Chemical fertilizers had been used only by the fruit growers, but with good results on fruit, they extended the use of fertilizers to other crops.

Ten of the former migrants have become wholesalers, buying fruit and produce in Lampián and selling to retailers in coastal markets. Others of this group sell their own crops directly in the markets of Lima and Huaral and along the northern coast. Four Lampián families own their own trucks. Nonowners rent from them or from another community.

In animal husbandry, the returnees introduced better strains of animals and used vaccines and pills to protect the herd against disease. They read the bulletins issued by SIPA and the agricultural–animal husbandry page of Lima newspapers. Some of them sought out SIPA agents for special instructions on cattle, and they arranged for agents to visit Lampián for lectures and demonstrations. The three most successful cattlemen began to provide technical services to their fellow comuneros, and SIPA agents were called in only for serious problems.

191

With modernization of methods and increased income has come a decline in traditional forms of work reciprocity and a growing belief in commercial strategies. One man expressed his views in this way:

> The new municipal building was constructed with lightning speed, in one year. I believe it cost 200,000 soles, but the work was done through contracts with a Work Society [*Sociedad de Trabajo* within Lampián] and through hiring skilled masons. That is how the job got done quickly. If the community had taken on the job, we would still be working on it. With more people, you make less progress (Celestino, 1972:83).

The most successful farmers completely dropped out of the traditional labor exchange patterns. They had no time to work for someone else, and they hired the labor they needed.

No one could afford to drop out of the faenas because access to irrigation water was dependent upon meeting these obligations. However, the system allowed for alternatives to one's own labor. The community established a schedule for annual payments, ranging from 200 to 800 soles depending on amount of land, for those who did not participate in the faenas. It was sometimes more profitable to hire a substitute.

The returnees were also the heaviest users of agricultural credit. Eleven of them have been borrowing at a rate over 100,000 soles per year. Only two of the traditional farmers have had agricultural credit and only in small amounts to cover emergencies.

The economic and political success of the returned migrants has led to the development of a social structure with two distinct segments. At the top are 40 families, the original 30 migrants plus friends and relatives who have entered the new world with them. In 1967, these families, making up about 36 percent of the population, controlled 80 percent of the land, with average holdings of 4 hectares per family. The remaining 64 percent of the families held an average of about 0.9 hectare. The land use was also strikingly different. Whereas the 40 families devoted 45 percent of their cultivated land to fruit, the traditional segment devoted less than 6 percent of their cultivated land to these crops.

A similar split was observed in animal husbandry. The 40 families owned 73 percent of the cattle, averaging 23.7 head per family, while the traditional segment averaged slightly under 5 head per family.

Average wealth had increased greatly in Lampián, but marked socioeconomic distinctions had accompanied this change. After the first years of enthusiasm over community progress under the returning migrants, Lampián appeared to be experiencing a marked decline in community solidarity, with the older generation increasingly feeling left out and discriminated against. One comunero *pasivo* (passive, over 60 years old) gave this view:

> There are coming to be more and more people who do not respect the traditional customs of the community. Often neither the old agreements nor the new decisions of the community are respected. There is a lack of consideration for the ideas of the old people. Because of that, we passive comuneros no longer go to the community meetings. Neither do the authorities have the power to lead the community as before. They are just interested in their own private benefits (Celestino, 1975:95).

LAMPIAN COMPARED WITH HUAYOPAMPA

The comparison between Huayopampa and Lampián is of special interest. Both communities made striking economic advances by shifting into commercial fruit growing. In both communities, schoolteachers played a vital role. But Huayopampa moved ahead economically with a broad sharing of benefits, whereas in Lampián the benefits of change were largely monopolized by that segment of the community that engineered the change.

Closer examination of the ideologies of the teachers in Huayopampa and Lampián might point to significant differences, but that hardly seems likely. The ideology of APRA in the 1930s appears to have been as collectively oriented as the ideologies of the pioneering schoolteachers in Huayopampa, and as APRA sentiment grew, it became customary for the men of Lampián to address each other as *compañero* "comrade" in approved APRA style.

The differences appear to be due to two factors: the earlier introduction into Huayopampa of a new educational philosophy and the concentrated migratory experience of the young men of Lampián between completing school in the community and coming back to take it over.

In our 1964 surveys, we used two items to measure respect for age and tradition: the choice between a younger and better educated person for mayor as against an older person who knows the village better and the statement that "These days the advice of old people has no value." In

193

general, we found that communities making economic progress were more inclined than stagnating communities to vote for the young man and agree that the advice of the old is without value. Huayopampa was an exception, voting significantly more for the old man and showing more respect for age than Pacaraos.

This apparently paradoxical survey finding makes sense in the context of Huayopampa's history. There the modernization of the community began many decades ago, stimulated particularly by the pioneering schoolteachers. We have noted that most of the leaders of the community's development in the 1940s to 1960s had been students in the Seminario Menor in the mid-1920s. At the time of our field studies, many old men of Huayopampa retained the prestige they had won through their innovations in agriculture and community organization.

Huayopampa's progress was based upon collective foundations and constantly reinforced through its educational system. The land distribution of the 1960s was somewhat more egalitarian for Huayopampa than for Lampián, creating a ratio in amount of irrigated land of 3 to 1 between top and bottom strata for Huayopampa compared with 4 to 1 for Lampián. We do not have systematic income data for Lampián, but the ratio of incomes of top and bottom strata must have been far greater in Lampián than in Huayopampa, for we have noted that all landowners in Huayopampa were heavily engaged in fruit growing and that those below the top 40 families in Lampián devoted only 6 percent of their land to fruit. Furthermore, the data for Lampián suggest a wide gulf in economic resources and way of life between the top 40 and the rest of the population, compared with much smaller gradations from stratum to stratum in Huayopampa.

We do not have survey data for Lampián to measure attitudes toward old people and old customs, but our anthropological data demonstrate that there was a deep-seated cleavage between old and young in that community from the 1930s into the 1950s. However, as the returning young men grew older, the age cleavage gradually gave way to a social class cleavage, with 40 families enjoying the increasing affluence of modern agriculture while the majority of the community remained traditional and poor.

From 1927 to 1937, Pedro de Verón had an enormous impact upon his pupils, but he had only a tangential impact upon the older generation. When the young men had the traumatic experience of being expelled from their home town, they could hardly view the old customs as worth preserving—or adapting to new conditions (as happened in Huayopampa). Furthermore, before returning, they had spent seven years in situations in which survival and progress depended primarily upon their own efforts. They had been sufficiently successful in the coastal world of individualism and private profit to reinforce individualistic orientations. Returning to the community, they acted out a belief that community welfare would be best served if subordinated to the demands of individual economic advantage.

THEORY, V
METHODOLOGY,
AND PRACTICE

Power and Peasant Progress 18

The purpose of Part V is to place the empirical materials into a theoretical framework. We told the story first so that we could illustrate our framework with materials already familiar to readers.

A further objective of this chapter is to examine the relationship between two quite different conceptions of the nature of power and of changes in the distribution of power. The main line of sociological thinking on power tends to place that concept in an interpersonal context, focusing upon the dominance of one individual over others. Latin American sociologists tend to focus upon power at the macrolevel, examining the way the major structural elements of a society shape behavior.

Each of these approaches is insufficient by itself. As the student of interpersonal relations recognizes that the behavior of individuals is influenced by forces beyond the immediate situation he studies, he seeks ways of relating the micro to the macro. Those committed to the macro approach run the risk of reifying power and failing to account for the ways in which power is exercised in observable human behavior. Beginning with a macrolevel analysis, in this chapter we propose to link together the two approaches to the study of power.

Up to this point, we have followed a regional and historical organization, in order to place the cases in the context of time and space. We will now highlight those sequences of events whose strategic importance provides the theoretical basis for the structural-historical framework that enables us to generalize beyond the cases studied. To develop our analysis of peasant movements, we distinguish among (1) long-run structural determinants, (2) precipitating factors, and (3) the process of development of peasant movements.

LONG-RUN INFLUENCES
FAVORING PEASANT MOBILIZATION

As a basis for explaining change, let us assume a preexisting stable state in the relations between hacendados and colonos. This does *not* mean that the peasants were satisfied but simply that they accepted the conditions imposed upon them. The peasant decision to challenge the status quo grew out of the following factors:

1. *Changes in the Regional and National Class Structure.* Occupational differentiation on the countryside undermined the monopoly power of hacendados as increasing numbers of merchants, traders, schoolteachers, and government professionals and white-collar workers entered the arena to compete for resources and power. In the nation as a whole, the growth of industrial and commercial activities brought to the fore new elites whose power and influence did not depend on rural land ownership. These people were concentrated particularly on the coast. Since they tended to regard the sierra as a backward region and a drag upon the Peruvian economy, they could not be counted on to rally to the support of the highlands hacendados when that help was needed.

2. *Weakening Position of the Mestizo Elite.* As the hacendados became increasingly involved in urban life, the customary income from the land was no longer adequate to maintain their urban standard of living. During the same period, many of the younger

200

members of the old mestizo elite in the small towns left the rural areas to settle in large cities. Thus, the hacendados were steadily losing potential allies in their coming struggle with the peasants.

3. *Expansion of Economic and Political Involvement of the Peasantry.* This expansion took two interrelated forms: (a) new economic activities that increased peasant resources (coffee for La Convención, mining wages for the Yanamarca valley) and (b) new contacts and new organizational experiences (involvement in union activities and contacts with union leaders, politicians, lawyers, and merchants). Paige (1975) stresses the importance of peasant involvement in export-crop cultivation as the key to the success of peasant movements. This was important for the Convención valley movement, but the case is much less clear for the Yanamarca valley. Wool was indeed an export product and was grown on some of the haciendas there, but we have no data to indicate a marked growth of peasant involvement in raising sheep and selling wool in the period leading up to the Yanamarca peasant movements. We are not in a position to check the Paige hypothesis systematically, but the record appears to show that peasant work in the mines and experience with unions provided the critically important resources: money, information, ideas, and personal contacts beyond the villages.

Perhaps we are simply broadening the Paige formulation. Entry into export agriculture is one important way—but not the only way—for peasants to acquire the resources necessary to shift the distribution of power in their favor.

Changing social experiences were accompanied by changes in peasant psychological orientations. As peasants experienced alternative ways of life and heard of others like themselves improving their conditions, they came increasingly to question the legitimacy of the old order. Passive acceptance evolved into passive resistance.

PRECIPITATING FACTORS

We see three precipitating factors so closely linked that it is difficult to discuss them separately. They are (1) a decline in returns for both labor and land on the hacienda, (2) a worsening of market conditions, and (3) threats to recently achieved peasant gains.

As the population continued to grow in the rural sierra, sons divided the land of their fathers so that their work obligations remained the same and yet each family could make less out of its own lands. Even when peasant work obligations remained the same, hacendado income from the land did not keep pace with the rising cost of urban living. To get more out of the land, the hacendado could put more into it, investing in modern technology; indeed, we have noted such cases. However, such a strategy could be successful only if the hacendado was prepared to increase greatly his own time and energy devoted to his farming operation. Few hacendados were prepared to give up the gracious living of the city. This left them only one alternative: to drive the peasants harder in hopes of squeezing more out of the land. For the peasants, this involved a marked negative shift in the exchange rate.

In the Convención valley, the peasants did not suffer from the fragmentation of their lands through inheritance; in fact, they occupied far larger tracts than the average colono in the highlands. Furthermore, the exchange rate had turned much more favorably toward the peasants than they or the hacendados had anticipated when they discovered that their lands were well adapted to the cultivation of coffee. The threat to recently achieved gains occurred when the hacendados began trying to get land back from the peasants. The peasants' situation also worsened through forces beyond the control of the hacendados. The drastic decline in coffee prices from 1954 to 1961 required them to work harder for smaller economic returns. Although other agricultural commodities did not suffer the sharp drop of coffee prices, the peasants generally found their buying capacity being reduced at a time when the spread of education, mass communication, and off-farm experience had raised their level of expectations.

THE PEASANT MOBILIZATION PROCESS

Peasant mobilization appeared to go through the following five stages:

1. *The Formation of Upward Linkages*. Young men with migratory experience assumed leadership roles. They became acquainted

with union leaders, lawyers, and politicians who could deal with important power figures.

In the Yanamarca valley, these upward linkages were forged first around education. Since the hacendados were clearly in violation of the law in not establishing schools, the peasants found some receptivity among officials at the Ministry of Education. The establishment of a local school provided a rallying point for further organizational efforts. Hacendados tried to discourage the colonos, but education was not a direct attack upon hacendado interests, and the hacendados could not expect prominent city people to support efforts to keep the peasants in a state of ignorance.

In some cases, linkage with the banking system proved important. If the hacendado was unable to meet his loan payments, and if the bankers thought that the peasants were going to win in the long run, it was only good banking to accept the peasant offer to pay off the debt—thus strengthening peasant claims to the land.

2. *The Internal Organizational Effort.* The hacendado retained his control by dividing the peasants through favoring some with benefits not accorded the others. These favored individuals stood between the administrator and the rank and file, transmitting and enforcing the hacendado's orders. The importance of these intermediary figures to the control structure was out of proportion to their numbers. When the hacendado lost the loyalty of these intermediaries, he could no longer block the peasant movement.

In the Convención valley, on Hacienda Chawaytirí, and in the Yanamarca valley, these intermediaries cast their lot with fellow peasants. We lack information on how this shift came about, but we will venture an interpretation.

When there was a shared understanding of the rights and obligations of the colonos, the intermediary role was viable. Under shifting conditions, the intermediary found himself in a bind. The hacendado sought to increase work obligations and put pressure on the intermediaries to police the system. They found themselves caught between the hostility of their fellow peasants and the pressures from hacendado and administrator. In educational background, social contacts, and economic resources, the intermediaries resembled rank and file colonos far more than they did the administrator or the hacendado. Compliance with the hacendado's orders would not gain them higher social class position. If the peasants won, the intermediary who remained on the hacendado's side would have no future in that community. As expectations of peasant victory increased, the intermediaries broke away from the hacendado.

The organizing process involved the development of indigenous leaders, the establishment of new organizational roles for stimulating and channeling participation, the abandonment of customary submissive behavior, the creation of new norms for group-oriented behavior, and the holding of organizational and political meetings and mass demonstrations designed to build peasant solidarity. Particularly in the Cuzco region, the leaders emphasized the Indian heritage not only through conducting union affairs in the indigenous language but also through shouting Quechua slogans of defiance to mestizos in the public squares of the cities.

3. *The Strike*. Under the conditions prevailing in the Peruvian sierra, a strike by the colonos was a peculiarly effective weapon. When the hacienda serfs go on strike, they simply withdraw their labor from the hacendado's land and continue to cultivate crops on their own plots. They give up only the token daily payment of 3 or 4¢ (United States currency) and a single day's work elsewhere brings in 10 to 20 times as much.

The hacendado could and did bring in "scab" labor to do the work of the strikers, but this was costly. He had to pay far more than he was paying his own colonos. If the peasant movement was widespread and many hacendados were competing for labor, the result was a general rise in wages.

4. *The Hacendado's Counterattack*. Such a strike could be settled in only two ways: by important concessions to peasants or by the intervention of government to drive the peasants off the land or put their leaders in jail.

The modern commercial plantations on the coast were in quite a different economic and political situation. There labor was paid for in wages and fringe benefits comparable to those received by urban workers. Having no farm plots of their own on the plantation, the laborers were entirely dependent upon their cash income. The owners could afford to make wage concessions with the hope of balancing increased labor costs with improvements in technology and higher prices in the export market. As the plantation owners also had important commercial and industrial interests in coastal cities, they had stronger political influence than did the highlands hacendados. As Paige (1975) points out, under these conditions, union and management bargain over the distribution of the surplus. The traditional sierra hacienda produced very little surplus. Even small financial concessions could turn profit into loss.

Since he could not win an economic struggle, the hacendado had to fall back on physical force. The peasants possessed far more physical force than he, so the hacendado could hold his position only with the force of arms provided by government.

The hacendados claimed that the peasants were being misled by Communists and called for police and military intervention. In some cases, peasant leaders were jailed, but this was not enough to stop the movement. The peasants maintained their solidarity, developed new leaders, or waited for their leaders to get out of jail to begin a new push. Only government repression on a large scale, as in early 1964, could halt such peasant movements. This kind of massive intervention appeared only when peasant movements became so extensive as to threaten the power structure throughout a large region of the country.

Meanwhile, the military was evolving its own orientation to rural development, and its leaders were increasingly unsympathetic to the traditional sierra landlord. Military intervention in the Convención valley did *not* reestablish the domination of the large landlords but rather supported peasant control of the land.

Some of the landlords we studied were defeated only after struggling to the end. Others, observing what was going on around them, concluded that the day of the large hacienda was passing and that they should try to sell their lands. In this period the peasants were the only people interested in buying.

5. *The Legal Struggle*. Consolidation of peasant victory required legal services and court proceedings. Doctors were scarce in rural areas, but the supply of lawyers was large and increasing. They appeared to fall into three categories. There were the lawyers for the elite, necessarily few in number because the people they

served were few. Beyond this favored group, many lawyers made a living through handling cases involving boundary disputes between one peasant community and another or land disputes within a given community.

There was also a type of rural lawyer who specialized in representing peasants against large landowners. Although some of these lawyers undoubtedly believed in the peasants' cause, they also lacked alternative ways of making a living. They had little to lose in turning against the hacendado and if the peasants won, stood to gain not only economically but also in peasant support if they went into politics.

DIAGRAMING STRUCTURAL CHANGE

If it makes sense to talk in terms of structure, then we should be able to diagram the structure of the hacienda and to draw the structural changes arising out of peasant mobilization. The titles of the functionaries vary, and generally there were more levels from top to bottom than indicated in Figure 18-1, but the basic characteristics were the same wherever the traditional hacienda system prevailed. We see a straight-line hierarchical organization with the individuals at each level simply directing the work and enforcing compliance. At the bottom, we find what Julio Cotler has called the "triangle without a base" (Cotler, 1967–1968), designed to indicate each individual having linkage only with the line of authority and the peasants being unorganized among themselves. As mobilization advances (Figure 18-2), the peasants close the base of the triangle, forming their own organization, and they establish upward linkages to local union officials who relate them to a peasant federation or to other union officials. The intermediaries now respond to the local union leadership and not just to the hacendado. The peasant leaders are further linked upward with local lawyers and politicians and through them to the Ministry of Labor, the Ministry of Education, the Agricultural Development Bank, and so on. Figure 18-2 also shows the weakening of the hacendado's linkages downward, upward, and horizontally.

It should be emphasized that the diagrams are not designed simply to reflect channels of communication. The vertical positions show differences in power. The lines and open spaces between points signify or-

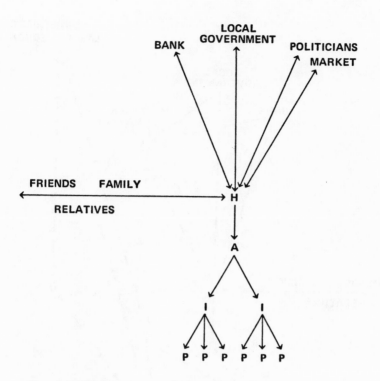

H = hacendado
A = administrator
I = intermediary (supervisor)
P = peasant

FIGURE 18-1
Hacienda Before Peasant Mobilization

ganization or the lack of organization. The direction of the arrowheads indicates the direction of initiation of new activities.

In a rural society dominated by haciendas, the structure of power over the traditional Indian village is more diffuse, yet the domination over the Indians is hardly less extreme. Figure 18-3 represents the preintervention situation for Kuyo Chico. Mestizo domination was exercised through the cabecilla (Tomás Díaz), who was responsible for rounding up the Indians for faena service and other labor Again we see at the bottom the triangle without a base.

Beyond their official ties through the cabecilla, we see individual mestizos exploiting individual Indians. The multiplicity of these upward

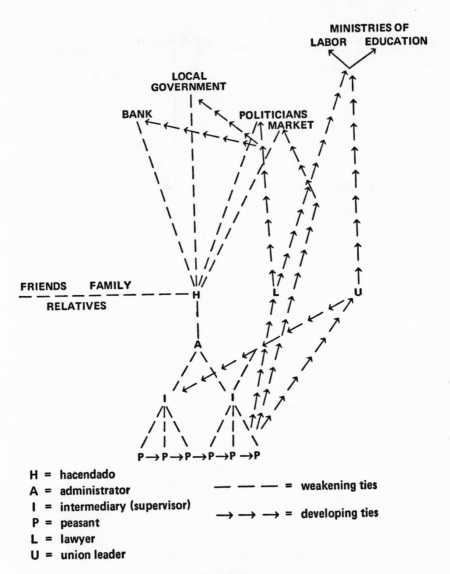

MINISTRIES OF
LABOR   EDUCATION

LOCAL
GOVERNMENT

BANK

POLITICIANS
MARKET

FRIENDS   FAMILY
RELATIVES

H

L

U

A

I

I

P→P→P→P→P →P

H = hacendado
A = administrator
I = intermediary (supervisor)   — — — — = weakening ties
P = peasant
L = lawyer   →→ → = developing ties
U = union leader

FIGURE 18-2
Peasant Mobilization on the Hacienda

ties does not provide the Indians with alternatives because there was a general understanding among mestizos regarding the exchange rate that should prevail in their transactions with Indians. To be sure, some mestizos treated "their" Indians better than others, but such differentiation simply tended to inhibit organization among the Indians.

In Figure 18-4, under PNIPA, we see the applied anthropology pro-

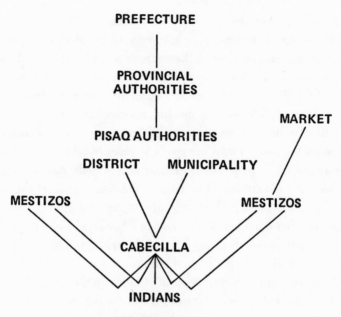

FIGURE 18-3
Kuyo Chico Dominated

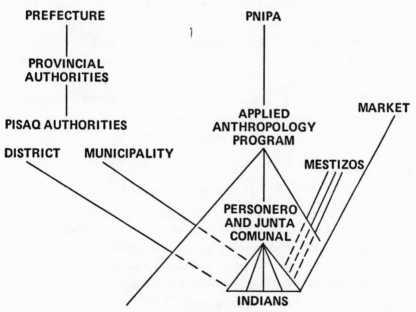

FIGURE 18-4
Kuyo Chico Within the Applied Anthropology Program

gram taking over responsibility for community development. With the establishment of a community government, headed by the personero and junta comunal, the base of the triangle was closed. The diagonal lines extending down from the program indicate that the project sharply reduced the influence of the Pisaq authorities over the Indians.

In Figure 18-3, we see the Indians blocked off from the market as mestizos come in to requisition their produce and alcanzadores waylay them on the road to take the goods at below-market prices. Figure 18-4 shows the opening up of direct Indian access to the market.

We have not attempted to diagram the intervention of the new schoolteachers, but our information suggests that the effects were similar to those of other outside interventions in Chawaytirí and Kuyo Chico: helping the Indians to close the base of the triangle, blocking the mestizos who were seeking to maintain the traditional relationships.

This suggests a structural parallel between the union in the hacienda and the applied anthropology project in the community. When they had the project, the Kuyo-Chicons had the functional equivalent of a union and thus viewed the union movement more negatively than did respondents in any of the other villages in that area. When the project was abruptly terminated, the 1969 survey shows the moderation of antiunion attitudes in Kuyo Chico.

We do not mean to suggest that only an applied anthropology project or a union can break the domination of the mestizo elite over Indian communities. In the case of Sicuani, that domination was eroded away over the years with the growth of occupational differentiation; the opening of the export market to peasant producers; and the spread of peasant commercial, social, and political organization.

FROM MACRO TO MICRO

As we come down from the macro- to the microlevel, we are, in effect, studying the exercise of power in interpersonal relations. As we explore these relations, it is important to see them in the larger context because the distribution of resources and the use of rewards and penalties are, to a large extent, dependent upon macrolevel structures.

To conceptualize power at the microlevel, we need to answer three questions: (1) What is power? (2) How does one recognize the exercise of power? (3) On what bases is power gained, maintained, and lost?

To define power, Blau begins with Max Weber's definition (Blau, 1964:115): "the probability that one actor within a social relationship will be in a position to carry out his own will despite resistance." Blau gives his own definition in these words, stating that power

> is the ability of persons or groups to impose their will on others despite resistance through deterrence either in the form of withholding regularly supplied rewards or in the form of punishment, inasmuch as the former as well as the latter constitute, in effect, a negative sanction (1964:117).

We find such definitions difficult to apply to practical cases because they involve determination of three elements: what Person wants to do, how successful Person is in doing it, and what degree of opposition is manifested by others. Furthermore, the definition leads us into statements that seem to violate common sense. For example, let us compare person A with person B, assuming that each of them imposes his will on an equal number of other people, but the others submit to A gladly and comply with B's directions with great reluctance. Would we then say that person B has more power than person A? The combination of acts of leadership with the mental state of the followers involves us in unnecessary confusion.

We propose to separate the state of mind of the followers from the action process itself so as to be able to examine the relationship between the actions involved in exercising power and the attitudes and emotions of followers. For this purpose, we will simply say that *Person has power over Others when he initiates activities for them*. Although we do not want to draw a sharp line between power and no power in terms of the frequency and the duration of the activities initiated, clearly we are not concerned with casual or sporadic events. The greater the frequency and duration of the activities initiated by Person over Others, the greater we assume the power of Person over Others to be.

How do we determine that Person has power over Others? We observe Person and Others in action. We interview them and those who have observed them in order to determine how events have come about. We also might find certain documents that make it clear that Others acted in response to initiatives from Person.

To say that Person commonly initiates activities for others tells us nothing about the bases of his power over them. We assume that the bases of power are Person's control of the resources required to reward Others for acts desired by Person and to penalize Others for failing to act in the manner desired by Person or for taking actions contrary to the wishes of Person. The study of the gaining, maintaining, and losing of power thus involves examination of the resources at the disposal of Person and Others and of the way these resources are brought to bear in the action situation.

We focus our attention on the production, transfer, and distribution of goods. This seems an economic focus, but our concerns are broader than those of the traditional economist, for we consider a *good* anything that is of value to human beings. Material goods are of obvious importance, but nonmaterial values such as respect or status, affection, sociability, and so on also fit within our definition of goods. We are not so much concerned with the question, What goods do people value? as we are with the question, How do they go about trying to get what they want out of life?

The answer to that question involves *objectives,* the *means of achieving those objectives,* and the *distribution of costs and benefits* involved in reaching the objectives.

Objectives (goals or purposes) are the aims toward which a set of activities are directed. Although we are particularly concerned with collective phenomena, we will clarify what we mean through examining the key questions faced by individuals participating in the scene we examine. For the activities Person carries out, does he himself set the objectives, or does someone else set them for him? Or does he share in the determination of the objectives?

By *means* of achieving the objectives we refer to a set of activities or projects. Do the means require the coordinated activities of a group? Or can Person reach the objectives on his own—or at least outside of the group or groups upon which we are focusing our attention? In the case of objectives that can be reached only through collective activities, does Person determine the means to be used, are they determined for him by somebody else, or does he share in the determination of means?

The *distribution of costs and benefits* involves the question of who puts in what to the activities and who gets what out of the product of these activities. Is the distribution of costs and benefits decided by the individual, is it decided for him by somebody else, or does he share in decisions regarding distribution?

The power of A over B, C, and D is perceived by him and them to be greatest when A can unilaterally determine objectives, means, and distribution. This is the situation in the monolithic power structure of the traditional hacienda. The power of subordinates increases as they gain influence in these decisions.

The bases of power that enable the hacendado to initiate activities for peasants are control over rewards and penalties. For the control of goods to be a basis of power for the hacendado, these goods must be desired and/or needed by peasants. If they do not desire or need goods controlled by the hacendado, then he cannot influence their behavior through offering or withholding these resources.

The resources may be either material or nonmaterial. Material resources can be money, land, or other physical goods. Prestige is one nonmaterial resource. Another nonmaterial resource, information, may at times be even more important to subordinates than material goods, for access to accurate information may enable them to increase their material resources, and lack of access or false or misleading information may cause subordinates substantial losses. Thus, the control of information is of vital importance in the distribution of power.

Similarly, access to important people may be required by subordinates if they are to increase or preserve their material goods. If A is able to provide or withhold such access, his personal connections are a source of his power. Spiritual resources may be viewed in the same manner. If subordinates believe in God or other supernatural forces, then A, directly or through allies, may gain power by offering or withholding the blessings of the religious institution.

Although withholding of resources customarily offered can be regarded as a penalty, it is not the only negative sanction that may be available. Person may be able to impose further penalties by his direct action or through the actions of those allied with him. For example, the traditional hacendado himself could whip the peasant, get the political authorities to put him in jail, or—in the extreme but not unknown case—get him killed.

There are a number of ways in which the hacendado's power over peasants may be reduced. Even before he is challenged by his subordinates, the hacendado may lose control over some of the resources he has been using to reward subordinates. The parties do not exist in a social vacuum. Some of the resources the hacendado has been relying upon may be available only through relations he has cultivated with other figures of equal or superior power in the society. This dependence on others is likely to be particularly important for the application of penalties. Even when the hacendado has the strength to administer corporal punishment, he cannot do so successfully unless he is assured at least of the neutrality of people more powerful than himself. Similarly, his use of weapons to punish or threaten depends upon his assurance that in case he injures or kills a challenger, law enforcement officials will not punish him. To the extent that the hacendado's relations with superior power figures are weakened, he loses some degree of control over the resources needed to secure compliance or to punish noncompliance.

Peasants may find the resources the hacendado has customarily offered them to be of decreasing value. Peasants can reduce his power over them through reducing their desire for resources controlled by the hacendado. We introduce this theoretical possibility for the sake of completeness because, although it may be important in other situations, we find it of no use in our analysis of the struggles of Peruvian peasants. When the key resource controlled by the hacendado is land, and peasants have only enough land to keep themselves alive on a near-starvation diet, the option of stopping eating altogether does not seem worth consideration. Of course, individuals can escape the power of the hacendado through migrating to the city, but this does not change the distribution of power between the hacendado and those remaining on his land.

Peasants can reduce the hacendado's power over them through finding alternative channels for gaining the resources they need. The power of hacendado over peasants is most extreme when he has a monopoly over the resources they desire and need. As peasants open channels for securing any of these resources independent of the hacendado (see Figure 18-2), to that extent they weaken the hacendado's power over them.

Peasants can reduce the hacendado's power over them through forming a coalition to resist his orders. If one of them refuses to follow orders, the hacendado can readily withhold resources and impose penalties. If one peasant resists, the hacendado can seek support of other power figures to protect himself and punish the individual who challenges his authority. But if peasants collectively refuse to carry out the hacendado's orders, then the power situation becomes drastically altered. Although

214

the hacendado can dispense with any of these subordinates without serious loss, he cannot get rid of them all and have anyone left to carry out his orders. Furthermore, if he tries to penalize his subordinates collectively, he finds that this confrontation attracts far more public attention than sanctions imposed upon an individual, and therefore the hacendado needs more secure ties with power figures above him if he is to put down a collective challenge.

If peasants are able to form a union, now, for the first time, they are in a position to impose penalties upon the hacendado. They can appeal for support to other power figures who are not closely allied with the hacendado. On a more elementary level, as isolated individuals, peasants may have lived in physical fear of the hacendado, but he now finds himself surrounded by hostile subordinates, and he may fear for his life.

It is at this point that the organic link between micro- and macrolevels becomes most apparent. When the colonos form a union and go on strike, they impose heavy penalties on the hacendado and at the same time increase their immediate rewards as they shift work formerly performed for the hacendado to their own plots and to paid employment elsewhere. When this happens, the hacendado is completely disarmed—at the microlevel. He can hope to mount a counterattack only if he is able to secure from those higher than himself in the national structure the legal sanctions and physical force necessary to put down the peasant challenge.

PEASANT MOVEMENTS AND REVOLUTIONARY THEORY

A peasant movement bears some resemblance to a revolution. It is an organization of lower-class people directed toward the overthrow of the power elite of a local area. This resemblance naturally suggests the question, Why should it not be possible to build upon peasant militance a military force that would eventually be able to seize the power of the state?

Peru's revolutionists of 1965 and 1966 were inspired by the example of Fidel Castro, who seized power in Havana only after many months of guerrilla warfare in the Sierra Maestra. Héctor Béjar (1969) describes the Peruvian revolutionists' hopes of being able to build the Castro model upon peasant movements such as those led by Hugo Blanco. It seems likely that Luis Uceda de la Puente decided to launch his guerrilla operations in and around the Convención valley to take advantage of the well-known militancy of its peasants. Two other guerrilla groups opened fronts in the departments of Junín and Ayacucho, both of which had been marked by colono struggles against their masters and peasant community "invasions" of hacienda lands.

Revolutionary theory was then based upon two key assumptions that turned out to be false. The first was that the militant peasants would support the guerrillas in the struggle for a national revolution. Peasant militancy had been focused upon winning ownership of the land on which the peasants worked. In the Convención and Yanamarca valleys, they had won what they had been fighting for; in the Mantaro valley, the peasants had owned the land for generations and had no large landowners against whom to mobilize. In this situation, it was not clear what they had to gain through joining the guerrillas, and it was all too clear what they had to lose: their land and their lives.

The second assumption was that the situations in Cuba and Peru were similar before the outbreak of Cuban hostilities, so the Castro model might work in Peru. Let us compare the situation in the two countries, relying here upon a recent very detailed study, *The Cuban Insurrection* (Bonachea and San Martín, 1974).

1. *National Political Situation.* When Fidel Castro landed his small force in Cuba on December 2, 1956, it was more than four and a half years since Batista had established a military dictatorship. Batista had been ruling for the benefit of a small clique. He had little popular support, and passive and active opposition was widespread. Furthermore, since Batista showed no inclination to give up office voluntarily, it was evident that major changes could come about only through violent attack upon the government.

Peru had had democratically elected governments since 1956 (except for the interim military junta of 1962–1963). Belaúnde's election and the first few months of his regime stirred widespread hopes for basic reforms and social and economic progress. The frustration of Belaúnde's reform program and the repression of peasant movements in 1964 dampened these hopes, but it was by no means obvious that an insurrection provided the only hope for progress. Political freedom was maintained, and the leaders of the competing parties could continue to prepare for the national elections of 1969.

2. *Effectiveness of Government Military Forces*. Batista's forces were highly unprofessional and politicized.

Throughout his years in power, Batista had played one officer off against another, dividing and conquering, thus creating an attitude among the officers which was not conducive to any kind of serious military undertaking. The troops were aware of these conflicts, and they were highly demoralizing. Discipline among the enlisted men was at a low ebb even before the first encounter with the guerrillas (Bonachea and San Martín, 1974:231).

Whereas Batista appointed commanding officers whose only qualifications appeared to be loyalty to his regime, the Peruvian military establishment held nearly full control over its own appointments and promotions. According to Einaudi (1969), for years promotions in Peru had been based primarily on merit—as determined by performance in educational programs. The Peruvian military was a far more formidable counterrevolutionary organization than were the forces under Batista's command.

To this should be added the advances that had taken place in the technology, strategy, and tactics of counterinsurgency since Castro had begun his campaign. When Castro's men barely escaped with their lives and fled into the Sierra Maestra, few considered his small group a serious threat to the government. By the time Castro had won, military planners were giving serious thought to counterinsurgency programs, and the Vietnam war provided the United States military with a testing ground for antiguerrilla warfare. United States material and technical assistance were freely available to Peru's counterinsurgency forces, and some of Peru's officers had participated in United States counterinsurgency training programs.

3. *Terrain*. The Andes are a much more difficult setting for guerrillas than is the Sierra Maestra. In Cuba, a guerrilla force could disappear into the thick underbrush of the forest, evading its pursuers, setting ambushes, and then moving on again. There is little ground cover in the high Andes. Guerrillas could seek refuge by going east into the jungle, but the jungle is sparsely populated and offers little in food and other necessities to support the guerrillas.

Castro's forces had to put up with hardships, but they did not have to master the extremes of altitude and cold. As Béjar describes one phase of the action on the Ayacucho front,

We discover that the population of this village is sparse and seasonal. Most people live farther up and only come into the ravines and to the banks of the Apurímac River for a few months. We want to contact the entire population, but going up to the high areas poses the tactical problems of how to travel and where to hide. It is not just a matter of terrain but also of equipment. It's no laughing matter to spend a night under the stars at 15,000 feet. We would need overcoats, scarves, and thick clothing, but we don't have them, and even if we did they would be too heavy to carry on the 10,000-foot climb to the peak. Nevertheless, we take the risk, climbing painfully up one night with a pitiless rain soaking us to the bone (1969:97).

The physical problems of resupply from the cities to the guerrilla fronts were more difficult in Peru than in Cuba. Not only were the distances far greater, but also the access routes were fewer. In Cuba, the military found it impossible to cut off the many relatively short routes into the Sierra Maestra from a number of coastal cities. In Peru, to reach the Central Sierra or Ayacucho fronts from coastal cities, supporters of the guerrillas would have had to travel up the Central Highway, going over a pass at 15,800 feet, readily subject to air and ground surveillance nearly all of the way. The military also could (and did) establish checkpoints to stop and search all vehicles that approached the fighting areas. It would have been possible for some guerrilla supporters to escape this surveillance by going on foot and moving only at night, but they could hardly carry more supplies than were needed for themselves.

Cuzco was the logical point for resupply to the Convención valley, but at the time, there was no road from Cuzco into that valley, and the train could easily be checked by government troops. Furthermore, the entry to the valley from Cuzco and the outlet to the northeast were through narrow ravines. The army could plug up both outlets, maintain a close watch on those who tried to slip through on foot or muleback, and take its time to comb the valley for the guerrillas. Although Luis Uceda de la Puente could seek refuge above on the Mesa Pelada, that frigid plain offered very little sustenance for human beings, so he was forced to go into the valley to get the supplies he needed.

4. *Knowledge of Peasant Life*. The guerrillas in both countries started from the same base of ignorance common among urban intellectuals. This is more understandable in the case of Castro, for he did not plan to fight in the countryside and found himself there only when his original plan failed. The Peruvian guerrilla leaders had been planning for many months to launch their insurrection on the countryside, so one might have expected such intelligent and dedicated men to have concentrated on field trips to get acquainted with the social and physical conditions of life in the rural highlands and on reading and discussion of the nature and problems of Peruvian rural life. On the contrary, the guerrillas-to-be read little beyond ideological tracts and made no efforts to learn anything in the field. No one who reads the account of the military intervention in the Convención valley in 1962 and 1963 can fail to be impressed by the intimate knowledge of the local scene upon which the leaders based their civic action and military campaign. Of course, the army had an enormous advantage in the resources it could devote to the study of rural conditions, but this does not seem to have been a critical difference. Before the attempted insurrections, we find no recognition of the importance of knowledge of peasant society and culture on the part of the guerrillas.

The severest criticisms of the guerrillas are those written by one of their few survivors. As he describes the debates of the "new left," Béjar draws this conclusion:

It [the new left] fervently denounced the Communist Party's tendency to allow itself to be guided by political formulations that were alien to our country's reality, but it made no systematic effort to study that reality and, in general, it can be said that it knew nothing about it (1969:51–52).

Castro's guerrillas learned about peasant life through experience and developed great skill in dealing with the peasants. The Peruvian guerrillas had too little time to learn from experience.

5. *The Language Problem*. In Cuba, peasants and guerrillas alike spoke Spanish. On the Ayacucho and Convención valley fronts, few of the peasants were fluent in Spanish, and even those who were felt more comfortable with their native Quechua. As Béjar puts it,

The language is another barrier. Very few of us speak Quechua (I know only a few words, and those I pronounce very badly). One comrade knows the Quechua spoken in the Cuzco region, which is pronounced differently. Only one of us knows the local pronunciation (1969:96).

6. *Numbers and Organization.* The leftists advocating revolution were perhaps no more unified in Cuba at the time of Castro's landing than they were in Peru in 1965. At first, Castro was denounced by Communists as a foolish adventurer, and it was only after he had demonstrated that his forces could hold out indefinitely in the Sierra Maestra that leaders of various revolutionary factions rallied to him.

However, when the guerrilla campaigns began in the two countries, there were far more Cubans prepared to risk their lives in the struggle than was the case among Peruvians. Many Cubans, especially those among city groups supporting Castro, were killed, and yet there were men and women ready to replace them and carry on.

7. *Urban-Rural Linkages.* Since public attention has focused upon the drama of Fidel Castro challenging the Cuban army in the Sierra Maestra with his 20-man force, the critical role of the urban underground and of urban-rural linkages may easily be overlooked. The urban underground movement in Cuba was large and active long before Castro's landing in December of 1956. As soon as Castro demonstrated that he had a chance to survive in the mountains, urban leaders focused their activities upon the support of the rural guerrillas. This has been well recognized in Cuba, where the martyred Frank País, the most effective urban leader, came to be one of the heroes of the revolution.

The Peruvian guerrilla leaders seriously underestimated the importance of urban organization and support. As Béjar puts it,

Both for the MIR and the ELN, the guerrilla war had to move from the countryside to the cities. . . .

The goal was to establish a leadership in the countryside. It was feared that if an urban organization began to move too soon it would act on its own, thus creating problems of authority. . . .

It was practically impossible at the same time to set up an organization that would operate in both rural and urban regions. Therefore, almost all of the cadres were in the countryside when the uprising began (1969:112–113).

8. *The Logic of the "Foco" Strategy*. The guerrillas were following the strategy described by Régis Debray (1967) on the basis of his analysis of the success of Fidel Castro. The guerrillas were to begin by establishing a *foco* on the countryside. As they moved around this point, ambushing and harassing government troops, the oppressed peasants would be inspired by the example and would gradually move to their support. The government troops would seek to strike back with heavy-handed and cruel reprisals against both those who were guilty and those who were innocent of aiding the rebels, and these methods would further alienate the peasants. Eventually the rebels would establish a territory they could defend from fixed positions, and as more peasants joined the guerrillas or helped them with supplies, that territory would expand—and so on and on.

Within a few weeks of reaching the Sierra Maestra, Castro's 20-man force began successful attacks upon the small and isolated outposts of Batista's army in the Sierra Maestra. In the dense tropical forest, the rebels could move rapidly without being detected from land or air, pick their times to attack, and then slip away with captured munitions and supplies. Thanks to the nature of the terrain and the reluctance of the regular troops to fight, especially in the forest, the peasants quickly learned that the regular army was only passing through their area while the rebels were there to stay and would execute military justice upon anyone who collaborated with the government.

The situation was far different in Peru. For example, Béjar reports peasant reaction to the guerrilla capture of Hacienda Chapi and their execution of the hated landowners:

> There are discontented people everywhere and they receive us enthusiastically. When we begin our operations against the landowners . . . their enthusiasm grows. . . . All our actions have their support. . . . After we take Chapi, many of them dance with pure joy (1969:99).

But within a few days came the army patrols, and the guerrillas were forced to move on.

> When the invasion finally comes, all of our supporters are tortured and shot. The terrible vengeance extends to their nearest relatives, their crops, even

their homes, which are remorselessly burned. . . . It is planned barbarism to terrorize the population and inflict exemplary punishment for their friendship toward us (Béjar, 1969:101).

In the open terrain of the Peruvian sierra, it was the army that could occupy and hold any area it chose. What counted here was not the attitudes of peasants but the terribly unequal abilities of the contending forces to reward peasants who aided them and to kill peasants suspected of aiding their enemies.

Although peasants provided sporadic help to the Peruvian guerrillas, there is no record of even a single peasant joining to fight with them. The same lack of success among the peasants doomed the 12-month guerrilla campaign led by Che Guevara in Bolivia in 1966 and 1967. That internationally celebrated enterprise suffered from many of the same problems that doomed the Peruvian guerrillas—with one additional complication: Guevara's forces were made up of Cubans and Peruvians as well as Bolivians, and the diary of the commander (Guevara, 1968) shows that Guevara frequently had to wrestle with international frictions that had no right to exist according to his ideology.

We are not, of course, denying the possibility of devising a successful revolutionary strategy based in part upon peasant militancy. It has been done in China and elsewhere. How it has been done or how it may be done in the future are themes far beyond the scope of our research in Peru. Now we are concerned simply with demonstrating the lack of fit between Peruvian realities and the theoretical conceptions of the Peruvian guerrillas.

The guerrillas failed to understand the macrostructural conditions that made Peru different from pre-Castro Cuba, and they also had minimum knowledge of the social, economic, and physical conditions where they intervened. They acted in terms of what their ideology told them the world *ought* to be. These brave and idealistic men gave their lives for a cause that was doomed to failure.

Conflict, Cooperation, and **19** Power in Peasant Communities

Much of our discussion of peasant communities has centered upon conflict and cooperation—again without defining what we mean by these terms. In this chapter, we have three objectives:

1. To relate our studies to the anthropological literature on peasant communities
2. To examine the pattern of peasant *perceptions* of conflict and cooperation so as to produce a theoretical reformulation of processes of peasant community life
3. To define *conflict* and *cooperation* so as to focus on their objective linkages with *power*

223

DEBATE ON THE NATURE OF
THE PEASANT COMMUNITY

Before presenting our own definitions of these concepts, let us examine the *perceptions* of conflict and cooperation found in the anthropological literature in relation to peasant perceptions measured in our surveys.

The debate on the nature of the peasant community was joined when Oscar Lewis published his study of Tepoztlán (1951), a community that had been studied earlier by Robert Redfield (1930). Redfield described a well-integrated village. Lewis wrote as if he had examined a different village. His findings

> emphasized the underlying individualism of Tepoztecan institutions and character, the lack of cooperation, the tensions between villages within the municipio, the schisms within the village, and pervading quality of fear, envy, and distrust in interpersonal relations (Lewis, 1951:428).

Julian Pitt-Rivers (1960–1961) came to the support of Redfield, and George Foster (1960–1961) joined ranks with Lewis. In "Peasant Society and the Image of the Limited Good" (1966), Foster presented a cognitive orientation that served to explain the prevalence of conflict, mistrust, and envy. He found peasants looking upon the world as made up of good things (from land to health) available in limited quantities and not subject to increase, at least in the short run, through human efforts. The gains made by a peasant in any good important to the community are made at the expense of his fellow peasants.

Another debate has raged over the value of conflict and cooperation. Lewis Coser (1956) has persuasively argued that writers in the mainstream of sociology and anthropology have tended to treat cooperation as "good" and conflict as "bad." He is concerned with pointing out the positive or functional aspects of conflict.

In general, we agree with Coser's position. A low level of conflict may characterize a situation of stagnation and frustration, whereas a higher level may lead the actors toward economic progress and increasing social satisfactions. But under other sets of conditions, cooperation may involve people reaching their goals together, and conflict can destroy the social unit or lead to a persisting impasse wherein each faction has the power to prevent the other faction from reaching its goals.

When we can make such opposing statements with equal confidence, we need to clarify the meanings and interrelations of the two concepts and then identify and examine different patterns of conflict and cooperation that are actually found in various settings.

We have found the Foster conception a better fit for our Peruvian peasant community data than the vision provided us by Redfield. In a series of items designed to measure interpersonal trust, we found Peruvian peasants below the level of samples of Peruvian high school seniors, white-collar utility workers, and department store employees in Peru and much further below samples of United States college students, high school students, department store employees, and army recruits. For example, when asked to choose between two statements, "Most people can be trusted." and "You can't trust people." the peasants selected the trusting alternative in only 21 percent of the cases in 1946 and 17 percent of the cases in 1969. We also found peasants very preoccupied over the envy they attributed to people around them (Núñez del Prado, 1973).

In spite of this general fit between the Foster formulation and our data, we saw limitations in "the image of the limited good." Such an ideal type can be useful in pointing out underlying similarities, but it does not help us to cope with variation. We found a number of Peruvian peasant communities that fitted the Foster model reasonably well, but we also found three or four that did not seem to fit at all. When we reexamined our data on conflict and cooperation, we discovered a second deficiency in the Foster formulation: the one-continuum model.

The debaters differed sharply on the amount of cooperation or conflict within the peasant community, but implicitly they agreed on putting these two concepts at opposite ends of the same continuum. In other words, a community that is high in conflict should be low in cooperation and vice versa. If the single-continuum model had been reasonably correct, we would find a high negative correlation: respondents perceiving a high level of cooperation would report a low level of conflict and vice versa. The actual figures for 1964 and 1969, respectively, were −.08 and .06.

To measure conflict and cooperation, we used the following two items in 1969: "Is there much conflict or division among the people of (this

225

village)?" ("Much conflict," "some conflict," "no conflict.") "When it comes to cooperating on some project for the community, how well do the people cooperate? Would you say there is (much cooperation, fair cooperation, poor cooperation, no cooperation)?" In 1964, we used the identical item on cooperation, but the conflict item was expressed in terms of the cherished notion of intellectuals regarding the struggle between progressives and conservatives: "Is there much conflict in this village between the people who want to change things and the people who want to keep to the old ways?" In our studies, we encountered a number of conflicts that did not fit the conservative-progressive split. Therefore, we used the question in more general form in 1969. Since the two items produced similar distributions of responses in 1964 and 1969 and since the conflict-cooperation correlations for the two years were nearly identical, we felt justified in assuming that the peasants interpreted our 1964 questions simply in terms of their perceptions of the degree of conflict in the community.

If we set two continua, conflict and cooperation, perpendicular to each other (see Figure 19-1), we divide our conceptual space into four boxes,

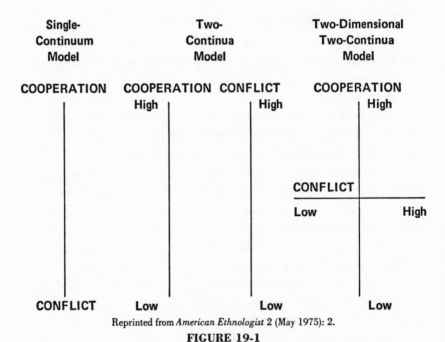

Reprinted from *American Ethnologist* 2 (May 1975): 2.

FIGURE 19-1

Theoretical Models for Conflict and Cooperation

representing high-cooperation–low-conflict, low-cooperation–high-conflict, and high-high and low-low combinations. Figure 19-2 shows this arrangement of the data in detail. To produce these four boxes, we have drawn the dividing line between high and low at the mean values for the total of the 12 communities. So as to avoid giving extra weight to the scores in the more populous communities where our sample sizes were larger, we have simply summed the mean scores for each community and divided by 12.

So as to show the mean values for both years, we have drawn the 1969

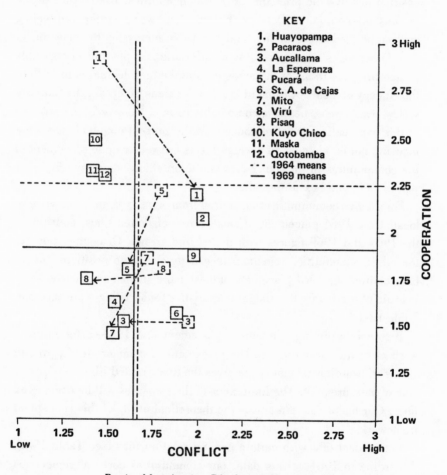

KEY

1. Huayopampa
2. Pacaraos
3. Aucallama
4. La Esperanza
5. Pucará
6. St. A. de Cajas
7. Mito
8. Virú
9. Pisaq
10. Kuyo Chico
11. Maska
12. Qotobamba
- - - 1964 means
— 1969 means

Reprinted from *American Ethnologist* 2 (May 1975): 2.

FIGURE 19-2

Perceived Cooperation and Conflict, 1964 and 1969

values in solid lines and the 1964 values in dotted lines. The reader will note a slight drop in the level of perceived conflict. Since the change in conflict is so small as to be within the range of measurement error, no further comment would be useful. The drop in perceived cooperation may reflect a broad national trend. One of the first acts of President Fernando Belaúnde Terry (1963–1968) was to provide for popular elections at the municipality level. The months following the Belaúnde inauguration seemed to be a period of general optimism in rural Peru, with increasing numbers of people feeling that they were now in a better position to solve the problems of their communities. By the time of the military intervention in October of 1968, there was a widespread feeling of disappointed expectations, and the 1969 survey figures may reflect this. Other items show increasing manifestations of pessimism regarding village progress in all of the areas we studied and decreases in faith in the efficacy of local government in all of the areas except for the Chancay valley, where we do not have comparable figures. However, the adequacy of this explanation is not of concern in the present chapter, for we are focusing not on changes in average levels but rather upon placement of the communities in the four boxes and upon changes over the five-year period from one box to the other.

For the five communities that shifted from one box to another, we have located the 1964 placement in small boxes of dotted lines, connecting the 1964 and 1969 figures with dotted-line arrows. Of course, none of the other communities remained in exactly the same position, but we have omitted the 1964 placement of these more stable communities so as to avoid cluttering up the diagram. (Statistics for all villages are shown in Table 19-1.)

Before interpreting community placement and 1964–1969 shifts, a word of caution is required. The placement of communities at precise points in two-dimensional space gives the unwarranted illusion of precision of measurement. The limitations of the measures will be considered later. Our major concern now is the theoretical utility of this conceptual framework.

Let us deal first with certain general relationships (see Table 19-2). According to 1961 census data, our communities cover a tremendous range in population size from a low of 139 (Qotobamba in Cuzco) to 2,647 (Virú on the northern coast). As might be predicted, perceived conflict tends to increase and perceived cooperation to decrease with

TABLE 19-1

Cooperation and Conflict in Relation to Village Size and Differentiation*

VILLAGE	1964 CONFLICT	1964 COOPERATION	1969 CONFLICT	1969 COOPERATION	POPULATION	RANK ON POPULATION	RANK ON DEFEREN- TIATION
Huayopampa	1.44	2.92	1.98	2.20	541	9	3
Pacaraos	1.83	2.57	2.01	2.07	803	6	5
Aucallama	1.94	1.54	1.58	1.51	582	8	8
La Esperanza	1.63	1.77	1.54	1.61	1,205	5	9
Pucará	1.79	2.22	1.61	1.80	2,010	3	2
San Agustín de Cajas	1.97	2.04	1.88	1.56	2,306	2	6
Mito	1.71	1.89	1.53	1.47	627	7	7
Virú	1.80	1.81	1.38	1.75	2,647	1	1
Pisaq	1.87	2.08	1.97	1.90	1,230	4	4
Kuyo Chico	1.27	2.69	1.42	2.48	305	10	10
Maska	1.61	2.55	1.42	2.32	168	11	11
Qotobamba	1.22	2.92	1.47	2.30	139	12	11

*The population data are from the 1961 census. The higher the number, the higher the perceived conflict or cooperation. Data on differentiation being unavailable for Maska, it is assumed to be tied for last place.

To simplify the presentation, we lump male and female responses for each community. We found the male and female responses highly similar on these two items, and treating the sexes separately does not change the quantitative pattern presented here.

TABLE 19-2
Conflict and Cooperation Related to Village Population

	KENDALL RANK ORDER CORRELATION	SIGNIFICANCE LEVEL
Conflict		
1964	.545	.006
1969	.181	N.S.
Cooperation		
1964	−.363	.049
1969	−.424	.026
Same Relations but Excluding Three Smallest Villages		
Conflict		
1964	.277	N.S.
1969	−.220	N.S.
Cooperation		
1964	−.110	N.S.
1969	−.110	N.S.
Conflict and Cooperation Related to Structural Differentiation		
Conflict		
1964	.35	.055
1969	.38	.041
Cooperation		
1964	−.04	N.S.
1969	−.20	N.S.
Same Relations but Excluding Three Smallest Villages		
Conflict		
1964	−.05	N.S.
1969	.14	N.S.
Cooperation		
1964	.44	.06
1969	.33	N.S.

increasing population. This relationship is high in 1964 and has dropped to a nonsignificant level (but one going in the same direction) in 1969. The negative correlation between size and perceived cooperation is strong in 1964 and somewhat stronger in 1969.

Further analysis indicates that the relationship depends primarily upon the three smallest communities (Kuyo Chico, Qotobamba, and Maska), which are all perceived as high in cooperation and low in conflict. When these three are removed, the correlations drop below .05

significance levels. The negative correlation between cooperation and size persists, but at the very low level. A positive correlation between perceived conflict and size is still found for 1964, but the relationship is negative for 1969.

Next, we examine how perceived conflict and cooperation are related to complexity or differentiation, according to a scale devised by Frank Young (1964). Differentiation is based upon the number of publicly identified specialized roles (doctor, teacher, truck driver, etc.) and the number of specialized facilities (post office, pharmacy, health clinic, etc.) to be found in the community. As is to be expected, differentiation tends to increase with increasing size of community (Kendall rank correlation of .62), but there are several marked discrepancies. For example, Huayopampa is ranked third in differentiation whereas it is only ninth in population size.

Again as expected, we find a positive correlation between level of perceived conflict and level of differentiation. However, we find no relationship between perceived cooperation and differentiation for 1964 and only a slight and nonsignificant negative relationship for 1969.

Again when we leave out our three smallest communities, the correlation of perceived conflict and level of differentiation disappears or drops to a nonsignificant level. The differentiation-conflict relationship shows a significant positive correlation for 1964 and a somewhat lower but still positive correlation for 1969.

The highest correlation cited in these sets of figures accounts for less than 30 percent of the variance, and even those other correlations that are statistically significant at or close to the .05 level account for little over 10 percent of the variance. We can therefore say that although these figures point to possible trends that may be worth investigating further, they also suggest that we will not get very far in our study of conflict and cooperation until we examine the dynamics of behavior in particular communities, which we now propose to do.

RELATIVELY UNCHANGING COMMUNITIES

We begin our case examination by considering first those communities that remain in the same box in our fourfold classification in both 1964 and 1969.

In the high-cooperation–low-conflict box, we find the three small Indian communities in Cuzco (Kuyo Chico, Qotobamba, and Maska). These communities also occupy the last three positions on the social differentiation scale, meaning that they are highly homogeneous in population (predominantly small independent farmers and others who divide their time between farming in their own community and working additional land as serfs on neighboring haciendas).

In the high-conflict–low-cooperation box, we find two villages. Pisaq (fourth in size and differentiation) was the center of mestizo domination of this area, but even by 1964, the power of the dominant mestizos in Pisaq had been considerably eroded, and this erosion continued in later years, with increasing conflict as the once dominant families left the community or struggled to maintain their power against the rising strength of lower-status groups.

In San Agustín de Cajas, conflicts were difficult to resolve because each important issue facing the community in the 1960s divided the inhabitants along the same lines of occupational and geographic cleavage.

The high-high combination for both years is represented by Pacaraos, a traditional community that had maintained its communal activities but was experiencing increasing difficulties in mobilizing the community for collective action. In the low-low category for both years we find La Esperanza, which may be considered more a geographical area than a genuine community.

SHIFTING COMMUNITIES

Of the five communities that changed boxes, four shifted from high-conflict–low-cooperation to the low-low box. It was as if these villages had given up fighting because they had given up trying to accomplish anything collectively. Such was the case in Aucallama with the collapse of the movement to regain lands from the haciendas.

In 1964, we found Mito only slightly higher than the average in perception of conflict, so that its placement in the low-low box in 1969 did not represent a major shift. We found Mito a village living in the past, unable to find projects upon which people could cooperate, and not involved in any issues that provoked conflict.

We found Pucará a dynamic community that was losing its ability to pull together on community projects after a period of impressive successes. Pucará was beset by threefold divisions in economic activities (traditional farmers, truck gardeners, and teachers plus university students) and in political organization (Popular Action, APRA, and Marxists). When the control of the municipality and of the Indian community fell to opposing factions, Pucará became politically paralyzed.

The most striking feature of Virú during the period of our studies was the extreme inequality in the distribution of land among farm families. In 1965, 456 farmers were registered in the records of the irrigation system. Of a total of 16, 409.44 hectares farmed, six farmers (1.3 percent) owned 14,579.50 hectares (89 percent), with holdings averaging 2,483.25 hectares. Six other farmers (1.3 percent) owned 900.39 hectares (5.4 percent), with holdings averaging 75.03 hectares. Forty-one small farmers averaged 9.2 hectares each, and 397 *minifundistas* held only 1.4 hectares per family. The minifundistas, making up 87 percent of the farm families, owned only 3.3 percent of the farmland.

Virú was a community dominated economically and politically by the large and medium-size farmers. For people with these sizable farm operations, there were no advantages in cooperation at the community level, and cooperation among the small farmers and minifundistas might have resulted in claims that would threaten the land boundaries and water supply of the big operators.

All observers (see Greaves, 1969) have agreed on the social characteristics of Virú as expressed by Victor Antonio Rodriguez Suy Suy (field report):

> Individualism is clearly defined among Viruñeros. Everyone wants to act independently. There is no cooperative grouping. SIPA [the agricultural extension agency] is studying the possibility of introducing some sort of agricultural or animal husbandry cooperative but finds neither the support nor the interest necessary. . . . Sr. C. P. Pulido, graduate of the University of Trujillo and a native of Virú, has tried a number of times to organize the fruit producers into a cooperative so that they can eliminate intermediaries in selling their products . . . but he has not found any support either.

José Elias Minaya (field report), writing several years later, made a similar comment:

> The comunero of Virú has practically converted himself into the inhabitant of Virú. . . . His movement toward individualism has been decisive.

The low level of cooperation in Virú both for 1964 and 1969 is well documented in both surveys and anthropological reports, but our field data do not explain the shift of Virú from high to low conflict (as measured by the surveys) over this five-year period.

In 1964, Huayopampa had manifested a level of perceived cooperation far above any other village in our sample, and it was among the lowest in perceived conflict. The level of cooperation dropped sharply, though still remaining above the 1969 mean for the 12 villages, and Huayopampa shifted from a low- to a high-conflict box. The magnitude of these shifts drew our attention to the disintegration of community solidarity, which we have examined in Chapter 16.

RATIONALE FOR THE FOUR BOXES

The figures should demonstrate the inadequacy of the single-continuum model, but we need to look beyond figures for a rationale for the two-continua, or four-box, model.

Paradoxical as it may seem, the levels of perceived conflict and cooperation both depend upon the existence of projects intended to bring about some improvement in the community. A new project of broad concern to the community will require the commitment of labor and/or money in order to carry it out. It then becomes a potential rallying point for the building of community solidarity, as people work together to bring about a generally shared improvement. Conversely, a new project may be the focal point of conflict. It may benefit some people more than others and/or involve an inequitable sharing of the contributions required to put the project into effect.

A low-low community such as Mito in 1969 makes sense as we recognize that people have abandoned hope of bringing about any improvements on a community-wide basis. They have no focal point for cooperation but also no focal point for conflict.

We have described the conditions prevailing in communities in each of the four boxes. Let us go beyond the cases to make a more abstract statement (in Table 19-3) regarding the social processes that we should expect to find in each box.

TABLE 19-3
Conflict-Cooperation Typology

CONFLICT	COOPERATION	SOCIAL PROCESSES
Low	High	Integrated village moving ahead with broad sharing of costs and benefits
High	High	Factional strife but projects moving ahead with unequal sharing of benefits
High	Low	Divisions too sharp to permit much progress but factional leaders still struggling
Low	Low	Village going nowhere. Potential leaders have given up struggle

CONFLICT OR COOPERATION AND SOCIAL ORGANIZATION

So far, we have focused attention on the whole community. Conflicts do not take the same form from one community to another, and we therefore need to go below the level of the community to examine the lines along which conflicts tend to take place.

The modernization literature is of no help to us. The tendency there is to see conflict in terms of the struggles between the moderns and the traditionalists. Our studies suggest that this is an oversimplified and distorted view of the peasant world. Furthermore, although we can sort out survey responses along modern-traditional lines, we have difficulty in linking these attitudes and perceptions to aspects of social organization that can be observed.

We have even less success if we attempt to examine conflicts in terms of political ideologies. In the first place, concern with political ideologies is rare or completely absent in many of our peasant communities. When such concern does arise, it tends to be reflected in organizational phenomena, for example, a younger generation of students and teachers in Pucará forming their political organization around a leftist ideology. We can thus study the role of ideology in organizational terms.

Since perceptions are subjective, we cannot say exactly what "conflict" or "cooperation" mean to anthropologists or to survey respondents.

If we are to leave the subjective realm to apply the concepts of conflict and cooperation to social organization, we need to define these terms and relate them to our discussion of power.

For cooperation, common definitions are inadequate because they contain two quite different elements: a coordinated set of activities carried out by two or more individuals *and* favorable sentiments of the participants toward these activities and generally also toward other individuals participating in the activities. (Favorable attitudes toward the activities and toward the persons generally go together, but this is not necessarily the case. The men of the famous double-play combination of many years ago, Tinker to Evers to Chance, did not speak to each other off the field but nevertheless took pride in the activities they jointly carried out so well.)

For analytical purposes, it is important to separate the coordination of activities aimed toward a given objective from the attitudes of the participants toward these activities. Otherwise, we run into the confusion illustrated by the following example. When we observe a group of peasants working together toward some objective set by themselves, we call this cooperation. When we observe them working together under the orders of the hacienda administrator and toward objectives set by him, this does not look like cooperation, and we are more inclined to call it "compliance." But where do we draw the line between cooperation and compliance? At the extremes, the distinction is easy, but we often find, in situations of marked power differentials, that subordinates come to accept the status quo to some extent and may even report that they really want to do what they are doing. It is only when a structural change is in process that subordinates come to question the previous structure of relationships and manifest hostile sentiments toward those seeking to give them orders.

For this reason, we prefer to separate the coordination of activities aimed toward a given objective from the sentiments of participants toward these activities and the persons involved in initiating them. A shift to negative feelings toward the persons previously holding power occurs when the vertical organization of coordinated activities declines in frequency and the horizontal coordination of activities among those previously in the subordinate position increases in frequency. It is at this point that the concepts of cooperation, conflict, and power are linked.

The attitudes of the participants toward the coordinated activities will be shaped in part by the *objectives* toward which the activities are directed, by the *means* (activities) used to reach those objectives, and by the *distribution of costs and benefits* involved in trying to reach the objectives. There is another factor involved in shaping attitudes: the extent to which the actors influence decisions regarding objectives, means, and costs and benefits. In situations that may be described as stable paternalism, we may find the power figure unilaterally determining objectives, means, and distribution of costs and benefits while the subordinates remain reasonably contented with their lot. We are not concerned here with the conditions under which a paternalistic relationship remains stable. We assume that, in general, participants will have more favorable attitudes toward the activities in which they are engaging and toward those directing these activities when they participate to some extent in decisions regarding objectives, means, and distribution of costs and benefits.

When people do not participate in determining objectives, means, and distribution of costs and benefits, and when they are in serious disagreement regarding any or all of those matters, we have a situation commonly described as at least latent conflict. The conflict becomes overt when the coordination of activities breaks down and the parties are unable to agree as to how to get the activities going again.

On the traditional hacienda, the hacendado unilaterally determines objectives, means, and distribution of costs and benefits. When the hacendado is removed, vertical coordination of activities gives way to what we have described (in oversimplified terms) as horizontal coordination. Although the word "horizontal" focuses attention on the contrast with the previous condition of monolithic power in the hands of the hacendado, in fact the liberated peasants are not all equal in power or status. But compared with the social and power gulf that previously separated them from the hacendado, the differences among them are far less in these respects. Nevertheless, when coordinated activities arise among them, they do not spring up spontaneously. Local leadership, with its accompanying differences of power and status, emerges. Coordination of activities may take place on a community-wide basis (as in Kuyo Chico) or on the basis of conflicting factions (as in Cajas). In the latter type of situation, villagers will report a high degree of *conflict* within the whole community, although they may find much *cooperation* within each faction.

237

Conflict on the traditional hacienda involves issues on all three levels: objectives (ownership), means (coordination of activities by hacendado or by peasants themselves), and distribution of costs and benefits (exchange of peasant labor for land-use rights and money). In the community, a serious disagreement on objectives naturally involves also disagreement on means and distribution of costs and benefits, as occurred in the project to relocate the Cajas central square. The villagers may agree on objectives but fall out on means and cost-benefits, as occurred in the issues involving managing the Huayopampa communal trucking enterprise. Or they may agree on objectives and means yet fall out on costs-benefits, as occurred in the Cajas reservoir case or in the school-location issue in Pucará.

Conflicts within villages do not occur in random form. We have found them structured in terms of the following types of cleavages.

1. *Age Grading or Generational Divisions*. Some old-young frictions are inevitable, but we find enormous differences among our villages. In some cases (the Cuzco Indian communities), there seems to be little evidence of this type of conflict. At the other extreme is Lampián, where the conflict resulted in the expulsion of 30 young men from the community. Pucará shows less extreme conflict, but we saw the young students and schoolteachers challenging their elders by forming their own political organizations.

2. *Differences in Wealth*. Here we view social class or status in terms of the material bases of wealth (especially land and access to water). We note that the top stratum in Pacaraos had an estimated income 18 times that of the bottom stratum; whereas in Huayopampa, the same comparison yielded a difference of less than 4 to 1. The Indian communities of Cuzco are examples of very poor villages where the range of differences in wealth were very small. By the late 1960s, Lampián had become a village divided by wealth rather than by age grades.

3. *Differences in Economic Activities*. Such differences do not necessarily correspond to differences in wealth. In Cajas, the most prosperous members of the community were among the brickmakers, but the more affluent farmers had incomes higher than those of many brickmakers. Nor is this just a question of occupational

homogeneity versus heterogeneity. A community with a wide variety of economic activities might have difficulty getting people together on cooperative enterprises, but this dispersal of interests might result in a low level of conflict. Cajas ranked relatively low on the Young Social Differentiation Scale, and yet its two groups of farmers and brickmakers polarized the community.

4. *Sociocultural Differences.* Here we see communities whose members identify each other in groupings defined in social and cultural terms. In Pisaq, these differences were seen by the people in terms of mestizos, mozos (cholos), and Indians. In Aucallama, two of the sections of the community had distinctively different social and cultural features, one representing the coastal criollo culture, with a strong Negro mixture, the other keeping alive some of the traditional customs of the highlands.

5. *Neighborhood (Barrio) Divisions.* In Aucallama and Cajas, neighborhood divisions were particularly marked and were recognized as important by the inhabitants.

6. *Religion and Religious Organization.* The church may serve to integrate the community, as in Huayopampa, or it may be a source of divisions. Since the percentage of at least nominal Catholics in rural Peru is probably at least 95 percent, this religious cleavage will show up only in a rare community where some Protestant sect has made substantial inroads. Unfortunately, we have no such community within our sample. But even where Protestants are a small minority, when the issue involves rebuilding the Catholic church, as in Pucará, the non-Catholics decline to cooperate.

   As owner of property, the church has an important impact, but the direction of that impact depends upon the characteristics of those who rent church land. The struggle to regain church lands was a unifying force for Pucará, since the renters were members of the rival community of Zapallanga. The same issue accentuated divisions in Cajas, where the renters were mainly brickmakers.

7. *Political Party Membership.* If only one party has substantial strength in a community, party membership may have a unifying influence, as was the case with APRA in the 1930s and 1940s in the Chancay and Mantaro valleys. The effects will be divisive if two parties are represented in substantial strength, as was the case in the Mantaro valley in the 1960s.

239

The foregoing list certainly does not exhaust the theoretical possibilities. We are simply suggesting a framework for analyzing the cleavages that we found.

INTERRELATIONS OF SOCIAL CLEAVAGES

This framework suggests an examination of overlapping versus cross-cutting cleavages. The cross-cutting situation would be found where the most well-to-do do not live clustered together, come from different sociocultural backgrounds, are of different ages, and so on. This situation is likely to reduce the level of perceived conflict, although it may not necessarily increase the level of perceived cooperation. The village can be divided in so many ways that people are immobilized.

The overlapping-cleavage situation may be illustrated with the case of Cajas. In 1964, it ranked highest in perceived conflict and fourth from the bottom in perceived cooperation. In 1969, it was fourth highest in perceived conflict and ninth in perceived cooperation.

We have no evidence regarding age grading or generational conflict for Cajas. Differences in wealth did not appear to be important. Divisions in economic activities between farmers and brickmakers were of great importance. These were reinforced by the neighborhood division and by the divisions in membership between the two major parties. The church-land issue also fell into the framework of brickmakers versus farmers. Eleven percent of the 1964 respondents in Cajas identified themselves as Protestants, and an additional 3 percent either called themselves atheists or declined to answer the question. It may be important to note that this 11 to 14 percentage of non-Catholics was by far the largest percentage of non-Catholics found in any of the communities we studied. Pucará, in second place, reported 5 percent non-Catholics.

Does our analysis mean that these cleavages *determine* the degrees of conflict and of cooperation within a community? Not entirely, but they do provide the potential organizational base for channeling of conflicts. To understand the intensity of conflict, we need to examine the social change process with particular reference to the framing of issues and the roles played by leaders. We will pursue this theme further in Chapter 20, where we seek to draw some practical implications from our research.

The present chapter is focused primarily on problems of theory and methodology.

CONFLICTS: FUNCTIONAL OR DYSFUNCTIONAL?

Coser makes the following distinction between functional and dysfunctional conflicts:

> Internal social conflicts which concern goals, values or interests that do not contradict the basic assumptions upon which the relationship is founded tend to be positively functional for the social structure. Such conflicts tend to make possible the readjustment of norms and power relations within groups in accordance with the felt needs of its individual members or subgroups.
>
> Internal conflicts in which the contending parties no longer share the basic values upon which the legitimacy of the social system rests threaten to disrupt the structure (1956:151–152).

Although this distinction sounds plausible, we suspect that it has little predictive power. If we find a group pulling together once again after a conflict, we can say that the conflict did not "contradict the basic assumptions on which the relationship is founded," or if the group falls apart, we can say that the conflict was "dysfunctional."

Before we can make any reasonable judgments as to whether conflict is functional or dysfunctional for a given community, we need to go beyond global consideration of conflict in order to determine the nature of conflicts and the lines of social cleavages upon which they are structured.

Planned Change and 20
Political Processes

We have been studying changes in which the villagers have been the principal actors. This focus does not imply that development planners should leave the villagers alone. Government neutrality in rural development is impossible. Government policies and actions inevitably have impacts upon rural people. For the planner, the problem is to understand these impacts so that plans fit the ends the planner hopes to reach.

Analysis of government policies for rural development is beyond the scope of this book (see Whyte, 1975b). Here we shall confine our attention to the local level to set forth, for the change agent, the lessons that may be drawn from our research.

ABANDONING THE MYTHS
OF RURAL DEVELOPMENT

The first step involves abandoning some popular myths.

1. *The Myth of the Passive Peasant*. The peasant is seen as a tradition-bound man, set in his ways, who resists changes even when they would benefit him. Curiously enough, this myth is accepted by people with radically different political views and objectives: by community developers, who seek only to improve conditions of life for the peasants, and by would-be revolutionists, who seek to involve the peasants in their struggle. Both groups believe that the peasant is standing still and that it is up to somebody else to move him. They differ only as to who is to do the moving and what direction the movement should take.

Instead of assuming a static peasantry, the change agent should make the contrary assumption: that the peasant world is in movement. Only as he discovers the direction of movement will the change agent be able to offer the kinds of assistance that the peasants need and will accept.

2. *The Outside-the-System Myth*. It is often said that in Peru, millions of Indians live largely outside of the market economy and also outside of the dominant national culture. It is true that Indians lack purchasing power and do not sell their products in large volume in the marketplace, but they are very much in the economy as a source of cheap labor for those with greater economic resources and political power. And they are in the political system even when they are not allowed to vote. In the past, representation in Congress has been determined by size of total population rather than by the number of eligible voters, thus giving the rural mestizos political power out of all proportion to their numbers (Cotler, 1967).

The myth is important for its action implications. The Indians are not to blame for their depressed condition. Mestizos explain that the Indians were once a noble race. By their cruel subjugation and exploitation by the Spaniards, the Indians lost their spirit and became a passive, fatalistic, coca-chewing people who would rather get drunk in a fiesta than make serious efforts to better their lot. But placing the blame on the Spaniards provides no solution. Whatever the presumed causes, the outside-the-system myth leads to a diagnosis in terms of the deficiencies of the peasants themselves. The solution is to give these outsiders the education, ambition, and social values that will integrate them with the national society.

A contrary diagnosis indicates that the problem for the Indians and poor peasants in Peru has not been their exclusion from the system but rather their incorporation within it in a manner highly disadvantageous to themselves. This view calls for structural change so as to reduce the disadvantages attached to the bottom positions in rural Peruvian society.

3. *The One-Way Flow of Initiative Myth.* Since the technical innovations affecting rural life have their origins mainly in urban institutions, it is common to think in terms of a one-way flow in which city people always have the initiative. This is a natural corollary of the passive-peasant myth.

In the records of Pacaraos and Huayopampa, we have encountered statements dating back more than a hundred years pointing to the desirability of the community adopting some of the modern ways of the city. The peasants were not passively waiting for change to be brought to them. They were actively reaching out for it.

Change does not come to a rural community because all or most of its citizens become ready to move ahead at the same time. For any change that is generated at least in part from within the community, we should expect to find internal change agents, people who belong to the community but at the same time are committed to changing that community. In rural Peru, these people were most likely to be returned migrants or schoolteachers.

Returned migrants have taken the lead both in agricultural innovation and in political mobilization and community development. Schoolteachers have been leaders of agricultural innovation in some communities and more generally they have provided ideas and ideology for political mobilization.

The change agent from outside cannot assume that he will find

244

strategic allies among these people. In some communities, the returned migrants have played only a peripheral role in village affairs. In the past, most rural schoolteachers have been alienated from the communities they served. However, we did not begin with any expectation regarding the strategic roles of returned migrants or schoolteachers. Therefore the prominent roles they have played suggest phenomena of broad and general significance.

THE BREADTH AND DEPTH OF CHANGE

Our studies should have a sobering effect upon those who think that a change agent, equipped with the right technical knowledge and with social skills and sensitivity, should be able to help a peasant community to move ahead within a short space of time.

We have studied communities that have made impressive progress, and yet we must emphasize the time that was required to bring about the changes. Huayopampa shifted successfully into commercial fruit growing within a few years after the completion of the road to the valley, but the roots of Huayopampa's progress were laid in the nineteenth century and the early years of the twentieth century. Changes came to Lampián more rapidly and dramatically, yet even here we have to think in terms of decades.

The forward thrusts of Pucará and San Agustín de Cajas were rooted in political struggles to establish themselves as independent communities. The backward slide of Mito must be traced to the breaking down of its control over the surrounding communities.

Time and intensity of exposure to new experiences must also be considered at the individual level. The peasants of Huayopampa and Lampián did not move into fruit growing nor did those of Pucará move into truck gardening in response to information from an extension agent or to the offer of loans from the Agricultural Development Bank. The men who led the way had previously spent months to years as farm laborers on the coast. They learned by doing, under supervision, what it took to grow the new crops under coastal conditions. They also learned from talking to people more experienced and knowledgeable than themselves. And when they returned to their home towns, it took some years more for them to adapt their knowledge to highland conditions.

This does not mean that extension agents and bank loans were unimportant. It does mean that the peasants had to reach a certain level of knowledge and resources before they could make effective use of technical assistance and bank financing.

When these returned migrants were ready to launch their new activities, they could make far better use of the extension agent than was possible for peasants without such prior experience. They knew what they wanted to accomplish, and they could tell the agent what they needed to know. If he could supply the information, they put it into practice. He did not have to persuade them of the value of modern technology.

In an industrialized country, we take it for granted that the seeds, fertilizers, insecticides, and other supplies will be available to the farmer when he needs them. Not so in rural Peru. There peasants have often been frustrated by their inability to get the inputs when they were needed. Having previously learned their way around the market economy and having established ties with people in the urban world, the returned migrants were better able than other peasants to get supplies when they need them.

In developing countries, credit tends to go predominantly to the larger farm operations, and this has certainly been true in Peru. The Agricultural Development Bank did not serve to lift the poorest farmers up from the bottom of society. Only as the peasants began to move upward with their own resources and knowledge did the bank facilitate further progress.

COMMUNITY DEVELOPMENT

Past literature on community development has presented us with a social psychology of interpersonal relations in a structural and political vacuum. The change agent is advised to discover the felt needs of members of the community. As he learns to communicate with the inhabitants, he *involves* them in discussions of what should be done. He gets them *participating* in decision making and then working together to implement these decisions.

The community is seen as structurally undifferentiated. To be sure, the exponents of community development recognize differences in social prestige and in leadership abilities, and they advise the change agent to take these differences into account. But structural differentiation in terms of patterns of land ownership and use, occupation, and political power are seldom taken into account.

Discussions of politics are notably lacking in the community-development literature. The community-development process is conceived as apolitical, bringing the good things of life to all members of the community. The idea that basic change in the rural community may come about only through some sort of political mobilization is not found in this literature.

Suppose a change agent wanted to intervene in the traditional sierra hacienda to help the peasants to help themselves. He would first have to seek permission of the hacendado in order to spend time on the property: "Mr. Hacendado, would it be all right with you if I came in and tried to help the Indians to organize themselves so that they can better meet their needs?"

The change agent can get nowhere without confronting the power of the hacendado. In a rare case, the change agent may be able to solve the power problem through buying or renting the property, thus himself becoming, in effect, the patrón and, from that position, working toward a more participative society. That was the strategy carried out by anthropologist Allan R. Holmberg, representing Cornell University, whose officials found to their surprise that the university had suddenly become the renter of some thousands of acres and 1,700 Indians at Hacienda Vicos (Dobyns et al., 1971). Provocative as the Vicos case is, it hardly provides an intervention model that can be widely used. There just are not enough available people or institutions with money to invest in taking over haciendas for the purpose of transforming them into progressive, democratic communities, nor are there enough change agents with the skills and sensitivities of a Holmberg to use the power position of the hacendado to bring about a democratic transformation.

In the more usual situation, if the change agent is to intervene on the hacienda so as to help the peasants, he must do so from outside. And he must help organize the peasants against the hacendado and link them with other outsiders in this struggle. In other words, he must become a leader or supporter of a peasant movement.

The peasant community does not provide the same barriers to physical access as does the hacienda. The outsider does not have to have permission from anybody to spend time in the community, and it is a rare outsider who can make himself so obnoxious as to be physically thrown out. But being there and being effective are two different things—even though the second depends on the first.

MODERNIZATION OR STRUCTURAL CHANGE?

Until recently, "modernization" was the dominant theme of social change research in developing countries. The approach arose out of the contrast between the rural agricultural sector, with its archaic technology for subsistence farming, and the large city, with its factories and modern means of transportation and communication. It was also observed (Inkeles and Smith, 1974) that men in the modern sector of society tended to have a different world view than men in the traditional sector.

This suggested that modernization of the traditional sector would come about through the flow of new technologies and new psychological orientations from the city to the countryside. This called for measurement of differences in psychological orientations along the route from the traditional toward the modern sector (Kahl, 1968) and to seek to determine what it was in the experience of individuals that led them to modernize their world view.

Related to modernization are studies tracing the spread of innovation in terms of person-to-person networks (Rogers, 1962).

The modernization and innovation studies, like the community-development literature, suffer from the same theoretical weakness: social psychological analysis in a structural vacuum—seeking to explain changes in individual behavior and psychological orientations in terms of the immediate interpersonal experience of the subject.

The innovation studies suffer from two further defects. Focus on a particular item of new technology implies that progress takes place by individuals adopting some new thing, entirely divorced from any social, economic, or technological context. As Arthur Mosher (1969) has pointed out, it is rare indeed that the poor farmer can better his lot by adopting any single innovation. The farmer is likely to need not just better seeds but also fertilizer and insecticides, perhaps more irrigation water, plus information on using the new technology, plus credit, plus access to the market under improved conditions, and so on. Unless the farmer can put all of these potential aids together—and in the right time sequences—he is unlikely to get much benefit from any one of them.

The innovation studies also fail to make any distinction among types of change. The implicit assumption is that a change is a change is a change. Later in this chapter, we will show how different types of changes involve different motivational problems and require different organizational strategies.

Our studies suggest that it is fruitless to study the attitude change that accompanies modernization or the interpersonal pathways for the spread of new ideas unless we place these concerns within a structural context. To be sure, the individual's behavior and attitudes are products of his experience, and the other people with whom he interacts form a major part of that experience, but these interactions take place within a structural framework. The social structure and the distribution of power tend to block certain activities and facilitate others, tend to inhibit the formation of certain types of relationships and foster the development of other types.

Unless we give close attention to structural constraints and facilitating factors, we many find ourselves recommending lines of action that are bound to fail. If we are serious about improving the welfare of the people at the bottom, then we must think in terms of a strategy for structural change.

STRUCTURE AND PROCESS

The focus on structure and power is important, but we must warn against a common tendency in Latin America to see all of social, economic, and political life in power terms. Those so fixated on power tend to think that all the gains they seek will be won once the distribution of power has shifted markedly in their favor.

Our position is that a change in the distribution of power may be a *necessary* condition for bringing about certain social and economic changes, but it will never be a *sufficient* condition. The best demonstration of this point is found in the structural change from hacienda to peasant community. Little could have been done to better the lot of the

Indians within the framework of the monolithic structure of power of the traditional sierra hacienda. Progress for the Indians required destruction of their semifeudal dependence upon the hacendado. But the defeat of the hacendado did not enable the peasants to live happily every after. The power shift opened up new opportunities for the peasants, but it also faced them with new problems. Let us put these problems in the form the peasants typically faced.

In the struggle for liberation from serfdom, the hacenado provides a common enemy around whom social solidarity can be built. Without the hacendado as a focal point for the organization of their activities, the peasants must deal with a more diffuse and complex political and economic structure.

The first problem is that of distributing the lands won from the hacendado. Shall the distribution be carried out so as to maintain the existing inequalities among peasant families? Or shall all lands be redistributed on the basis of equal sharing? In Yanamarca, this issue precipitated a long and bitter political struggle.

When the peasants take their produce to the market instead of selling only to the hacendado, they get better prices than before, but they find it hard to go beyond the immediate improvement. The individual peasant has only small amounts to sell, and it may be costly to get his produce to the market. Intermediaries will take his goods to the market for him, but he is likely to find that they absorb too much of his profits.

The obvious solution is to form a cooperative to give the peasants the price advantage of volume purchases of supplies and sales of produce. But the cooperative must carry out a much more complex set of activities than does a union, which focuses upon the withholding of labor. The cooperative pools funds so that a few individuals will have control over more money than any single comunero controls. Who is to be trusted with the funds, and what procedures will safeguard the money? It may even be hard to get anyone to serve as treasurer because he fears he will be suspected of stealing whenever the coop's affairs go badly.

How is the coop to get the produce to the market? Why not advertise for competitive bids and sign a contract with the man who offers the best terms? That way the coop would not have to tie up its funds in vehicles. But this is a United States style solution. Its viability depends upon the ability of the peasants to secure enforcement of the contract, in case the middleman does not make good on his commitments. The peasants

250

would expect the middleman to cheat them, and they would not expect going to court to result in anything except additional expenses.

So the coop buys its own truck on credit. This transaction is costly, especially in a country where interest rates are high.

If there is no experienced truck driver in the community, an outsider may be hired, but can he be trusted? Hiring a member of a community contributes to the local economy but accentuates other problems. The Peruvian sierra must be one of the world's worst places to learn to drive a truck. The roads are rough, the inclines steep, the curves sharp—and guardrails are unknown. The novice driver can hardly be encouraged by the wooden crosses along the road to mark where other drivers have plunged to their deaths.

But the driving problem is not so difficult as the maintenance problem. If the driver has neither the knowledge nor the equipment to repair his vehicle, the community will have to arrange for such service even when the truck is at home base. Getting a vehicle repaired is likely to involve much more waiting time in rural Peru than in an industrialized country. The truck may be out of service when it is most urgently needed. And around the world, people who don't understand auto mechanics are likely to be overcharged by repairmen.

In the peasant world, depreciation is an unknown concept. For some months, it may appear that the truck operation is successful—yielding more than its costs. But if no depreciation reserve has been accumulated, the community may be without funds to cover the increasing maintenance costs on an aging vehicle or the purchase price on a new one. Back to square 1.

Under the monolithic power structure of the traditional hacienda, the serf did not need to concern himself with the politico-administrative structure of the country. As far as he was concerned, the hacendado was mayor, chief of police, bishop, etc. When peasants gained the political status of Indian (peasant) community, they found themselves at the bottom of a dual and overlapping structure of local government.

The municipality depends primarily upon an annual subsidy from the national government, since local license fees, fines, etc., make up only a small fraction of its budget. The peasant community generally has a much smaller income (rental of communal property, grazing fees and fines), but it has a traditional means of getting public work done through faenas.

251

When the leaders of the two local government structures work together, we observe a useful complementarity. The municipality pays for materials and services not available locally, and the community provides the labor to carry out the project. If cooperation breaks down, the municipality's money will not begin to cover the labor costs, and work will stop—unless the municipality can get more money from the national government. But money from the national government does not come without costs. The village may need to finance delegations to Lima and to entertain visiting national and departmental officials.

Getting the two governmental structures to work for the people depends, in large measure, upon the effectiveness of local organization. Solidarity is important—but in terms of what social unit? Intercommunity disputes over land ownership have been endemic in rural Peru, and many such disputes go on for years and consume far more money than the land is worth. A struggle with a neighboring community is a means of building solidarity within your own community, but most municipalities or political districts contain more than one peasant community. In case of a dispute among communities within the same municipality, the outcome may depend upon which community is also the capital of the municipality. If village X is the district capital, and if the same political faction is in control of both the municipal council of the district and the junta comunal of the community, then X will make its labor available to projects financed by the municipal council—while communties Y and Z are likely to say "to hell with it."

Even within a given community, there are likely to be serious conflicts. These generally revolve around land ownership and water-use rights. As communities become further differentiated occupationally, the members come to share fewer common interests, so it becomes more difficult for them to work together. However, with occupational differentiation is likely to go superior access to power figures outside the community.

THE CHARACTERISTICS OF CHANGE PROJECTS

It is customary to think of improvement projects in physical and financial terms: a school, a road, a new irrigation channel, etc., and the amount of labor and money required. Such a classification is useful for some purposes, but it tells us nothing about motivation and organizational problems. For those problems, we need a psychological and structural framework.

The psychological aspects of the problem are well known and have been dealt with extensively elsewhere (Whyte and Williams, 1968), so they are only summarized here.

The individual puts out effort and resources in expectation of receiving rewards. The amounts he is willing to put out will depend upon the following factors:

1. *The Investment-Reward Ratio*. The resources the individual invests will depend on his estimate of the value of the reward. If he makes a large investment for a reward that turns out to be small, he is discouraged from further efforts. If the reward turns out to be large in relation to his investment, he is stimulated to make further investments along the same line.

2. *The Risk*. The individual learns to estimate not only the investment-reward ratio but also the probability that any reward at all will be forthcoming. If the potential reward appears to be very large but the probability of getting it seems small, the individual is unlikely to make the investment.

3. *Alternative Opportunities*. Men generally have alternative uses for their investments. A man is more likely to invest in a high-risk–high-payoff scheme if he has sufficient surplus so that commitment to that scheme does not prevent him from pursuing alternative opportunities. The peasant does not have such surpluses. Therefore he is likely to prefer a moderate-risk–moderate-reward scheme over a high-risk–high-reward alternative.

4. *The Time Span of Rewards*. Except for sports, games, and parties, few human activities yield immediate rewards. The individual must plan in terms of how long a time can be expected to elapse between making his investment and collecting his reward. This factor is not unrelated to *risk* for, in general, the longer the time span to the reward, the greater the likelihood that unforeseen circumstances will prevent the individual from collecting the payoff.

   Peasants in Peru have generally been accustomed to a span of three to six months between the beginning of their investment (preparing the land for planting) and the reaping of the reward

253

(bringing in the harvest for sale and home consumption). Fruit trees may require five to seven years after planting before the payoffs begin. Eucalyptus trees in the sierra require 15 years to reach maturity. The returned migrants of Lampián had already had several years of experience in farm labor in the fruit groves, with opportunities to observe the handsome payoffs, before they made such investments themselves. In the applied anthropology project at Kuyo Chico, Oscar Núñez del Prado got the Indians interested in the eucalyptus project only after a series of successful experiences on projects with quick- to moderate-term payoffs (Núñez del Prado, 1973). Subsistence farmers can be expected to make investments for a long-run payoff only if they first have some successful experience at short- and then medium-term–payoff projects.

5. *The Social-Comparison Effect.* Judgments as to the desirable relationships between investments and rewards are not made in a social vacuum. The individual judges what is good for him to some extent in terms of what others in similar circumstances are getting out of a given amount of investment. He is more likely to continue making that investment if he finds he has been getting returns comparable to those of people around him. If his investment-reward ratio falls below that standard, he will feel agrieved and will be discouraged from continuing such investment.

The last point moves the analysis into the social realm. Projects differ in the required patterns of investment and reward distribution. To some extent, these patterns are inherent in the nature of the project; to some extent, they are subject to shaping by those who promote the projects. Our studies suggest the following typology of cases:

1. *Individual-Direct.* Here the payoff is to the individual or to his family in direct relationship to the investment made. Such is the case with an innovation on land owned by the individual family. The returned migrants in Lampián, once they had taken over the land allotted to them, could make their investments in fruit growing with the assurance that they would reap the rewards. The same was true for the returned migrants who turned to truck gardening in Pucará. In neither case did the innovators have to secure the

cooperation of anyone outside of the family, nor did they have to share the rewards with others.

2. *Individual through Group, with Equitable Sharing in Investments and Rewards.* In this type of project, it is impossible for the individual to achieve the improvement by himself, and the payoffs cannot be monopolized. It is only through group efforts that the project can be successfully carried out. Traditional community faenas are of this type—or else it is impossible to maintain them.

In the peasant struggle against the hacendado, the establishment of a school was both a primary demand and a major rallying point for community solidarity. Even those families with children beyond school age shared in the conviction that peasants could progress only through education. Thus, they were able to make extraordinary collective efforts against very heavy odds.

An electric lighting system and a community reservoir have the same broad appeal. They may differ in the controllability of access to benefits. Those families that fail to cooperate on the electric power project will not be allowed to connect their homes to the system. If plans called for running water in the homes, the same sanctions would be available as in the electricity case, but many peasant communities are not ready to support the labor and financial costs of such an extensive piping system. The project may therefore be limited to one or more spigots in public places. In that case, access to noncooperators can hardly be denied, although if the noncooperators are concentrated in one section of the village, the communal government may deny that section a public water spigot.

Of course, a project does not have to be only for general public benefit or for private benefit. Various combinations are possible. For example, the Huayopampa water system was designed primarily to provide public water spigots. Several families had running water in their homes. They were allowed to connect to the community system by supplying the piping and paying the costs of the private installation. Since there was no shortage of potable water, families could secure these private benefits without reducing those available to the rest of the community.

Under most conditions, it is not necessary to mobilize all

families in a village in order to carry out a project of general community benefit. If a small minority refuses to participate, the project may nevertheless proceed, provided there is some way to penalize the nonparticipants or at least to exclude them from the full benefits of the project. However, some communal projects cannot be successful unless participation is 100 percent or close to that figure. Such a project presents very formidable problems of community organization.

In some cases, consolidation of land ownership will be needed before the advances of modern agricultural knowledge and technology can be applied. But consolidation calls for inclusive community action. If even a few families refuse to go along with a redistribution of land, they may block the program. It may not always be possible to carry out such consolidations on a purely voluntary basis. Experience suggests that this is a most difficult problem requiring a combination of community participation, economic incentives, and government sanctions against holdouts (Smock, 1966).

Consolidation also involves a question of equity: whether each family is getting a fair equivalent for what it is giving up. If the project is seen as benefitting the community broadly and if the leaders appear to have made honest efforts to allocate costs and benefits fairly, they may gain widespread cooperation even if the villagers recognize that exact equality has not been attained.

The extent of agreement of members will depend upon the structure of the project and the skill of community leaders, but consensus and commitment will depend also upon factors inherent in the structure of the community. If the community is homogeneous in its activities and occupations, the members are likely to share a broad range of common interests. As the community becomes more differentiated, the range of common interests tends to narrow.

Huayopampa and Pacaraos illustrate this point. Huayopampinos were predominantly dedicated to fruit growing, and the income range was far smaller than in Pacaraos. The truckers and store owners held the dominant positions in Pacaraos, and their interests were far different from those of the farmers.

In Pucará, we have seen conflicts arise as the truck gardeners challenged the power of the traditional farmers. In San Agustín de

Cajas, we traced the growth of conflict between the brickmakers and the traditional farmers.

3. *The Differential Impact Project*. In this type, the success of the project promises to benefit some members of the community more than others, or some stand to gain and others to lose. Some projects fall into this type for their inherent characteristics, whereas others, planned as type 2 projects, fall into type 3 because of the inability of leaders to resolve organizational problems or because of unforeseen physical obstacles.

An example of the inherent type 3 project is provided by a large-scale planting of eucalyptus trees carried out in Vicos (personal communication from Mario Vázquez). Those who worked on the tree planting received compensation, so there was equitable sharing of rewards in this respect. However, the project eliminated a substantial area of grazing land. This was of no concern to most of the families, but it was a matter of real consequence to several families owning large herds. Opposition to the project was concentrated among these families.

The project to recover church lands in Cajas fell into type 3 because the lands were rented by some members of the community, who stood to lose if the community took over the lands and worked out some other arrangement. It was the good fortune of Pucará that the church lands within its boundaries were being rented to members of the rival community of Zapallanga, which made the campaign to reclaim the lands a type 2 project—as far as Pucará was concerned.

As it achieves success, the peasant movement is likely to find itself facing more type 3 projects than it did in earlier stages. When all actions are directed against the hacendado, any investment can be seen as an equitable sharing in costs in the expectation of an equitable sharing of benefits. Once the hacendado is defeated, the peasants face the problem of distributing his lands. Two competing principles then emerge: Distribute so as to equalize total holdings among families or distribute so as to leave more or less intact the preexisting differences among peasant families. The observer should not need social science techniques in order to predict which families will take which side of this issue.

Examples of noninherent type 3 cases are found in the Cajas

reservoir project and the Pucará secondary school project. In both cases, there was a broad and general commitment to the project in principle. Agreement broke down over the location question.

The moral of this discussion is not that type 3 projects are to be avoided. It is naïve to think that peasant communities should progress only through projects in which there is a direct relationship between the individual's investments and his rewards (type 1) or where there is equitable community-wide sharing in costs and benefits (type 2).

For the change agent, the moral is to recognize that type 3 projects present much more difficult *political* problems than do types 1 and 2 and therefore require different *political* strategies. It should also be recognized that a type 3 project entails costs in the reduction of community solidarity, which may make it more difficult to carry through even those projects intended to fall into type 2.

In some cases, it may be possible to avoid the conflicts apparently attached to type 3 projects by restructuring the project without abandoning the general development objective. For example, when Allan Holmberg and his associates assumed control of Hacienda Vicos, they did not divide the lands among the Indian families but retained them to be worked collectiely with the benefits to be shared, and this system was maintained after Cornell relinquished control. Thus the Vicosinos could use the collectively owned lands as a focal point for increasing resources and building community solidarity.

Often, it will not be possible to transform a type 3 into a type 2 project. In such cases, there is no avoiding a political struggle, and the development problem must be seen in these terms.

4. *The Project Requiring Control of Individual Interests in Favor of Group Interests.* If the community as a whole is to benefit, individual members must be restrained from doing what otherwise would be rewarding to them. Assume that a village depends upon cattle for its economic existence. Let us say further that there are too many cattle for the available pasturage, and they are beginning to eat the grass to the roots and destroy the land cover.

From a technical point of view, what needs to be done is clear.

A breeding program must be introduced to improve the quality of the cattle. The available pasturage must be increased or the size of the herd must be reduced.

Which animals are to be bred with which and which animals not allowed to breed must be established. There must be control of people and animals and of a large land area.

In village cattle culture, the grazing lands are usually communal. The villagers have to decide what the rules shall be and how they shall be enforced.

For the welfare of the community as a whole, it may be important to exclude inferior animals from the breeding pool; yet it is in the interest of their owners to breed them with better-quality animals. In herd limitation, we also face a conflict between individual and community interests. Each owner wants as many animals as possible, but if each follows his own interests, the results will be disastrous for the whole community.

We speak of a "structural" approach to incentives, for it is clear that response to incentives should be interpreted against the structural properties of the innovation. In the case of the individual family farm, no new structural problem is presented. If the individual farmer can be persuaded to try out the innovation and it pays off, he will naturally continue. Furthermore, the practice is likely to enter into the channels of diffusion, as his neighbors observe his success.

In a type 2 project, it is necessary to mobilize a group, but there is little problem in the distribution of costs and benefits, so that execution of the project may serve to strengthen group solidarity.

In a type 3 project, a built-in conflict exists, and the village must find some way of coping with it.

A type 4 situation poses the most difficult structural problem of all. To be effective, the organization must include all cattle owners. They must not only participate; they must also submit to control. In such cases, it is probably misleading to think in terms of a cooperative. Unless those operating the program have coercive powers, we can expect the owners to follow their individual interests. The villagers may have to build—or fit into—a powerful organization with which they have not had previous experience.

259

THE POLITICS OF RURAL DEVELOPMENT

Our studies make it obvious that political processes are important in rural development but that recognition is only the beginning of analysis. Here we seek general conclusions on local and national politics, faith in local government, law and social change, and the influence of ideologies.

1. *Local and National Politics*. In the literature on political behavior, there is a great gap between studies of politics at the national level and at the local level. Students of national politics have generally had little information upon how events at this level influence behavior in rural communities, and students of local politics generally provide only fragmentary information on national political developments.

   With the research strategies previously used, this gap is inevitable. The researcher concentrating on the national level cannot at the same time trace out the impacts of national events upon village life throughout the countryside. The researcher in a single community will encounter some effects of national political events, but data from one community hardly provide a foundation for a systematic treatment of local-national relations.

   Our program included studies of a number of communities and haciendas and also provided information on two peasant movements. From this broad base on the countryside, as we pull together the traces of national events, we can point out a pattern of local-national politics during several time periods.

   A part of this story has already been told in our analysis of the historical bases for the political (and economic) differences between the Mantaro valley and Cuzco and of the different line of development followed by Mito compared with Cajas and Pucará. Here we will emphasize political processes from the 1940s onward.

   The APRA party and ideology became important in cities and coastal rural areas in the late 1920s and early 1930s. APRA achieved the height of its power and national influence with its participation in the Bustamante government (1945–1948). We have seen APRA influences spreading into the highlands most dramatically in the case of Lampián, where José de Verón Marquina conducted a dynamic educational and political campaign, leading to basic structural changes in the community. In Huayopampa, APRA influence was pervasive but produced less dramatic results. In more traditional and remote Pacaraos, few traces of APRA influence were to be found.

In the 1940s, people committed to the APRA party and ideology played leading roles in stimulating social change and economic progress in the Mantaro valley. In rural Cuzco, where a more rigid power structure prevailed, few traces of APRA were to be found in the 1940s and 1950s. By the time peasant movements gained momentum in the south and central highlands, APRA had become just another party to the politically active citizens in rural communities. Especially as APRA allied itself with the conservative government of Manuel Prado (1956–1962), advocates of social reform shifted their allegiance to Belaúnde and his Popular Action party or to Marxist political organizations. By the 1960s, students representing one or another Marxist faction controlled the student bodies in most universities, and the most articulate leaders of peasant movements were Marxists. This did not mean that they had close ties to Moscow or Peking, but it did mean that several versions of Marxism had become rallying points for those committed to drastic changes in the social structure and distribution of power.

The Belaúnde government aroused great expectations in the countryside. Feeling at last that they had a national government sympathetic to their cause, peasants living in wide areas of the central and southern highlands took land reform into their own hands, organizing invasions of hacienda lands and forming colonos into unions to take the haciendas from the landlords.

Belaúnde hoped to carry out land reform through legal and administrative processes, but his legislation was delayed and watered down by the opposition-controlled congress. The president hoped that his community development agency, Cooperación Popular, would relieve popular pressures and stimulate rural prog-

261

ress. Belaúnde tried to get around this congressional blockage by getting AID funds for rural development, but Washington decreed that AID funds would be held up until Belaúnde resolved the problem of the International Petroleum Corporation.

To further reduce the political impact of Cooperación Popular, the congressional majority developed its own program of doling out money for local improvement projects. While Cooperación Popular offered diminishing assistance, in the form of technical service and equipment and supplies in programs that required major local commitments for labor and materials, the congressional coalition handed out money grants that required no labor from the recipients. In the case of Cajas, local APRA leaders, after losing one election, staged a comeback and took over power largely on the strength of grants their APRA congressmen secured for them.

Thus, duality at the national level was matched at the local level. We have noted the strengths of local government when community and municipality work together, with the community providing labor and the municipality providing funds. When municipal officials were appointed by the national government, the lines of control were clear. When leaders of community and municipality disagreed, the community could bargain through offering or withholding labor. If this strategy failed, community leaders could hardly expect success in appealing to the national officials who had appointed the local officials.

When municipal elections were held in a situation of divided powers in Lima, the complementarity of municipality and community could survive as long as the same faction controlled both organs of government. When different political factions were in control of the two units, they were not forced to settle their differences on the local level. Leaders of each local unit could attempt to get the support of one of the two powers in Lima. We thus observe an apparent paradox: the increase in democracy through voting at the municipal level, in conditions of divided leadership at both local and national levels, led local officials to depend even more upon central authority for support. (But note that there was no tradition for local taxation to support local projects.)

The existence of a dual authority in Lima also made it difficult to resolve internal community problems. In the village of Yanamarca,

262

no resolution of the local conflict over distribution of the hacendado's lands could be achieved as long as the defeated party could appeal to its political supporters in Lima. It was not until the establishment of the military government, in 1968, that a final decision became possible.

2. *Decline of Faith in Local Government.* This dualism at both national and local levels contributed to a decline of the peasants' faith in local government. Belaúnde's establishment of municipal elections, in late 1963, was greeted with universal enthusiasm, and some of this euphoria was probably reflected in our survey responses in mid-1964.

In Chapter 13, we have traced the growing frustration of Mantaro valley villages with their local governments. We do not have as full data on the internal politics of the other villages in the 1964–1969 period, but the survey responses tend to show the same general decline of faith in local government.

Our analysis suggests that the national politico-administrative structure plays an important role in the functioning of local government; however, our surveys suggest that the peasants were inclined to take out their frustrations on the local governments. (A complementary interpretation is that the military government could hardly be held responsible for frustrations up to 1968.)

These findings suggest that when a national government first institutes elections for local officials, citizens are likely to respond with high expectations. If this increasing popular participation is accompanied by continued dependence upon the national government, then people's faith in local government will depend, in large measure, upon the effectiveness of relations between national and local governments. We have shown how fairly evenly balanced power rivalries at the national and local levels tended to accentuate and perpetuate conflict within the villages.

3. *Law and Social Change.* Students of social change have been inclined to look upon the law, lawyers, and the courts as forces supporting the status quo. Since Peru has long had constitutional provisions and laws that prohibit the traditional hacienda labor system, one is inclined to regard these laws as simply ornamental: symbols of Peru's respect for universally acknowledged human rights with no relation to the actual behavior of hacendados.

Our analysis suggests that it is a mistake to look upon the law and legal processes simply as a support to the status quo. When the peasants are unorganized and have no upward linkages except through those individuals and groups that traditionally have dominated them, then legal processes are important for the maintenance of the status quo. But when the peasants begin to organize and form linkages outside the traditional dominance channels, they can use the tools of law to promote social change. And when they do reach out, they find lawyers, politicians, and union leaders willing and able to help them in their struggle.

4. *Ideology and Development.* North Americans tend to be ill at ease with ideologies. The United States cultural background makes us suspicious of global philosophical formulations and more comfortable with what we consider empirical and pragmatic matters. This suggests that ideologies, being far removed from day-to-day events, are either superfluous intellectual baggage or else sets of prejudices that stand in the way of a realistic explanation of behavior.

The behavioral scientist finds himself pushed toward another view as he examines events in rural communities. There he finds changes in agricultural practices, local political organization, and the psychological orientation of the villagers intimately linked with national political organizations and ideologies. We have traced the marked impact of the APRA ideology, especially upon Huayopampa and Lampián and, to a lesser extent, upon the communities of the Mantaro valley during the 1930s and 1940s. We have seen the ideology of communism playing a role during the 1960s in the peasant movement of the Convención valley and in the interventions of the new generation of schoolteachers in the Pisaq area.

The hacendados and newspapers were indiscriminate in calling peasant leaders Communists. Probably the number of party members was small, and yet communism as a humanitarian ideal had a strong appeal when posed against a rural society that appeared to be organized for the exclusive benefit of the hacendados.

Since the peasant leaders had a set of grievances and a set of objectives, why did they also need an ideology, whether Aprismo or communism? The answer to that question must be speculative, but let us venture one.

When men live for long periods under punishing conditions, with few rewards, they need something more than the lessons of experience to lead them to struggle for major changes in their lives. At least part of that something appears to be political ideology. Ideology enables man to go beyond responding to immediate rewards and punishments. It provides a rationale for continuing to hope for a transformation of society even against great odds, and it helps political actors to feel that their day-to-day actions are advancing them and their fellows toward long-range goals.

On the Integration of 21
Research Methods

Our research program was launched on the basis of a combination of methods: the survey, characteristically used by sociologists and social psychologists, and the interviewing/observational methods commonly used by social anthropologists. As we went along, we found ourselves also gathering extensive historical, economic, and political-behavior data.

This chapter presents what we have learned through the use of this array of methods. We seek to show not only the benefits of the use of such a combination of methods but also some of the shortcomings of our efforts, so that other behavioral scientists can learn from both our successes and our failures.

COMBINING SURVEYS AND
ANTHROPOLOGICAL FIELD METHODS

Surveys and anthropological methods are customarily looked upon as rival research strategies (Whyte, 1964). (For convenience, we will call interviewing/observational techniques "anthropological methods," recognizing, of course, that they are used also by some sociologists and by some other behavioral scientists.) We believe that these two methods should be seen as complementary: the weaknesses of one are the strengths of the other.

The great value of the questionnaire is that it provides us with a large quantity of data at a relatively low cost (in comparison with other methods) and in a readily quantifiable form. But it is not an all purpose instrument. Generally it offers us data of two types: (1) demographic: sex, age, marital status, occupation, years of residence in the community, etc., for each respondent; and (2) the subjective state of the respondent: his attitudes, beliefs, and values regarding himself, his community, and the world around him.

The questionnaire generally gives us very little information regarding the particular events which make up the social processes of community life. The questionnaire can tell us how much confidence the respondents have in their municipal council. It cannot tell us how the councillors have acted to produce this degree of confidence.

Anthropological methods have two great values. They enable a good field worker to develop a relationship with his informants that permits him to penetrate their thoughts and to discover the sentiments that may not be expressed in response to standardized questions. They make possible a description of human activities and interactions and are thus essential for the examination of social processes and the social structure. . . .

With anthropological methods, quantification and standardization are not impossible, but we constantly face this dilemma: when we quantify and standardize, are we not in some way sacrificing the "richness" of the flow of human events, which led us in the first place to use anthropological methods? However, this dilemma is serious only if we are committed to the exclusive use of anthropological field techniques.

If we use anthropological techniques for examining the culture, social processes, and the social structure and rely upon questionnaires to measure attitudes, values, and beliefs of our respondents, we will be using each method for the special contribution it can make.

The two methods offer different types of data, so that the validity of one type often cannot be fully tested by the other type, but in many cases the data from the two methods fit well together. We then have more confidence in our conclusions than we would have if we had depended solely on a single method. Apparent contradictions should not lead us to try to determine which method is telling us "the real story."

We use contradictions as exercises in research methods, trying to understand the discrepancies, and seeking new data which may permit us to resolve problems of interpretation (Matos Mar and Whyte, 1966).

This combination of methods has proven useful in four stages of research: (1) developing the research design and instruments, (2) interpreting preliminary results, (3) determining future data-gathering needs, and (4) developing a theoretical framework.

Many of the survey items were designed to tap aspects of peasant life as they had been described in anthropological studies. The logic of the survey also led us toward comparative studies of a number of communities—although that logic, of course, did not determine how many communities would provide the necessary variety.

Two examples will illustrate the use of the two methods in the interpretation of preliminary results.

As one example, let us consider the responses in Pacaraos to the item, "How much power does the junta comunal have to solve the problems of this village?" In Pacaraos, 23 percent respond, "all the power necessary" and 40 percent respond, "the power to do certain things but not others." Do these figures suggest that the people of Pacaraos have much or little confidence in the power of their junta comunal? It might be argued that when 63 percent of the villagers feel that the junta has either all the power necessary or the power to do some things but not others, this is a substantial vote of confidence in this local government institution. But when we look at the figures for Huayopampa and find that 90 percent say that their junta has "all the power necessary," we get a more valuable perspective on our figures. We still cannot say whether the Pacareños are expressing much or little confidence in the power of their junta, but we can say that the Huayopampinos have much greater confidence in the power of theirs. In other words, the responses to a survey item are not very useful until we compare one village with another, and such comparison requires some degree of standardization, which a survey provides.

As another example, as noted in Chapter 17, past surveys had indicated that dynamic communities could be expected to show less respect for age and old people than stagnant ones. The finding that age was more respected in Huayopampa than in Pacaraos led us to speculate that the dynamism of Huayopampa was not a recent phenomenon and that people now old had played leading roles in moving that village ahead.

But note that in neither of these two cases did the survey data tell us the whole story. The item on the junta comunal did not tell us *why* respondents in the two communities perceived such great differences in the power of their local government. To answer that question, we had to observe the junta in action, examine community records, and interview comuneros about their local government. Similarly, regarding respect for age, we had to use anthropological methods to confirm our interpretation of survey measures and to trace the economic and social development of Huayopampa.

Our concern with the decline of cooperation and the rise of conflict in Huayopampa illustrates the value of our strategy both for determining future data gathering needs and for developing a theoretical framework. A key problem for research design in any field is the determination of priorities. Especially in a broad-ranging research program such as ours, there is no problem in finding "interesting things" to study. The problem is to make rational decisions regarding the relative importance of these many interesting things.

This is a problem both of data and of theory. If we had not had the 1964–1969 data on perceptions of conflict and cooperation in Huayopampa, we would not have recognized the magnitude of the changes that had taken place in that community. But these survey data by themselves did not influence our research priorities. When we reviewed the comparative marginals for all communities in the fall of 1969, we did indeed note these conflict-cooperation changes, but our response to that finding was simply, "Isn't that interesting." At the time, we did not find the changes interesting enough to make further research in Huayopampa a matter of high priority.

It was only in 1973, after we had placed Huayopampa in our four-box conflict-cooperation framework, that we came to recognize the exceptional nature and the importance of the changes that had taken place in that community. And the four-box framework itself depended upon a combination of research methods. Although several of our anthropological field reports might have suggested the possibility of communities that were low in both conflict and cooperation or high in both characteristics, given the past unreliability of anthropological descriptions of peasant communities, we would hardly have rejected the single-continuum model solely on the basis of anthropological reports by student fieldworkers. Only as we turned to survey measures of conflict and cooperation did we see the possibility of developing the four-box model that has provided the framework for our interpretation of peasant communities.

ON HARD AND SOFT DATA

In expositions on methods, it is customary to encounter the distinction between quantitative and qualitative, or betweeen *hard* and *soft*, data. We are likely then to find that quantitative, or hard, data are those derived from a questionnaire or survey, whereas qualitative, or soft, data are those derived from the fieldwork of the anthropologist. People who make such distinctions are ready to credit the anthropologist with "insights" that might point the real scientist toward new types of hard data, but they are inclined to consider the anthropologist more an artist than a scientist.

Applying this logic, we find that an individual's attitudes and opinions expressed in response to survey questions, when they have been coded and punched into cards, become hard data, whereas the fieldworker's observations of the actual behavior of the same individual are considered soft data. Of course this is ridiculous.

What is involved here is not the question of hard versus soft data but rather the ease with which data can be quantified. Except for open-ended items, a questionnaire is so structured that responses automatically fit into quantitative form. The behavior the fieldworker observes does not fall so readily into standard categories. The observer must establish his own categories or use categories established by others and then persuade critics that the observational guide permits a reasonable degree of objectivity and that another observer with the same observational guide (if conscientious and well trained) would categorize the same behavior in a similar way.

Although establishing categories and coding behavior within these categories is more difficult than placing survey responses into predetermined alternatives, various investigators have worked out methods that meet the test of reliability—producing similar results when the same method is applied by different observers (see, among others, Chapple et al., 1955 and Bales, 1950). The quantitative data gathered by anthropology students in our program have depended less upon the direct observation of behavior by fieldworkers than upon official records of behavior of importance to the community: who did (and who did not) turn out for a given faena, who did (and who did not) attend the monthly community meeting, who did (and who did not) pay the fines levied for noncompliance with community obligations, and so on. Since these items of behavior were of considerable importance to community members and leaders, we assume that the records kept would be accurate, and, indeed, on-the-spot observation by our fieldworkers confirmed this assumption. The most "hard-nosed" survey expert can hardly deny that these are hard data. And they cannot be dismissed as trivial, for they provide us with essential information regarding community solidarity and the capacity of local government to implement its decisions.

The fieldworkers in Huayopampa and Pacaraos also developed a body of quantitiative economic information: amount of land owned by each family, number of cows and sheep per family, occupation of family members, and income from farming and other sources. These data enabled us not only to measure the average difference in income between Huayopampa and Pacaraos but also to note the different shapes of the incomes pyramids for both communities.

PROBLEMS IN THE INTEGRATION OF METHODS

When reviewing the first reports submitted by the team of anthropology students after their intensive study of Huayopampa, Whyte was impressed by two aspects of their work: (1) the anthropological data confirmed the survey findings in all important respects, and yet (2) the students make no references to the survey data.

When Whyte raised these points in discussion with the team, one of the fieldworkers replied:

Yes, we did know about the survey, and we looked at it before we started our field work. But we couldn't believe that answers to a questionnaire in a peasant village would have any real meaning, so we just decided to forget about the questionnaire when we did our anthropological study.

Whyte pointed out that it was not too late to reexamine the survey so that their final report could draw upon both types of data. They agreed; yet, aside from token efforts, they did nothing to provide for such an integration.

Only a few of the students developed interest and competence in the analysis of both types of data. Many more students demonstrated their ability to produce first-rate anthropological field reports, but what integration of the two types of data we have been able to provide is based almost exclusively upon the work of senior staff members.

This problem is by no means limited to Peru. In the United States, students of sociology tend to have little interest in the soft data provided by anthropologists, and students of anthropology have distrusted the numbers coming out of surveys.

Nor were our shortcomings in methodological integration found solely on the side of anthropology. We now recognize that it was possible to make far more use of our anthropological field studies in order to link survey responses to social structure.

Although we did not have enough money or enough able students in all of our communities to make the intensive studies of family income and economic activities carried out in Huayopampa and Pacaraos, we could have built out of these studies short-cut methods to apply in other communities. For example, after a preliminary field study, with the help of key informants, the researcher could have identified the socioeconomic levels generally perceived in the community and representative families that fit into each level. If there were thought to be five levels, he could have undertaken to make intensive studies of the family economies of one family at each level. He could then have had key informants in the village place each respondent in the proposed survey in terms of the five levels and five representative families. When the respondent was surveyed, this socioeconomic placement could have been recorded on the questionnaire and punched into the data cards, along with information given by the respondent himself. The allocation of respondents in terms of these socioeconomic levels could then have led to estimates of average income at each level. These estimates would have been much cruder than those derived from studies of each family, but they would have been

272

better than information gotten directly from respondents by surveys, since questions from relative strangers about income, land and cattle ownership, etc., in a peasant community are likely to stir suspicion and give rise to inaccurate answers.

The approach outlined above would need to be field-tested. It is not presented here as a full answer to the methodological problems posed but rather as an illustration of the way we can learn from our field experience to devise short-cut methods that may produce more effective interdesciplinary research.

ON THE POTENTIALITIES OF
ANTHROPOLOGICAL FIELD METHODS

Our emphasis upon the integration of methods may lead the reader to assume much more uniformity within anthropological methods than in fact exists. Social anthropologists generally gather their data through interviewing and observation, but there are, of course, enormous variations among them in what they are trying to find out and in the ways they work.

Let us make explicit the characteristics of our own use of anthropological methods. Many anthropologists are concerned with the study of culture, but we were primarily interested in the study of behavior.

Culture is a concept subject to a board range of interpretations, so we shall have to specify the contrast we have in mind. One important line of anthropological work on culture focuses attention upon the beliefs and practices of a people as they explain them to each other and to outsiders. This leads to a normative emphasis—but the judgments are supplied by the informants and not superimposed by the anthropologists. The fieldworker seeks to elicit from informants a picture of how their society *ought* to operate; of the values they hold dear; of the obligations they recognize to kinsmen, to clan members, to the community, and so on.

An anthropologist with such interests observes that people's values and beliefs are acted out and reinforced in characteristic social and ceremonial activities. He observes and describes these activities. If several communities in the same general area share many beliefs and values and participate in similar social and ceremonial activities, he concludes that they share in a common culture and continues his efforts to describe the main features of that culture.

273

Such a focus on culture masks the differences among communities that are to be found at the behavioral level. In the Chancay highlands, there were 27 officially recognized indigenous communities. The similarities among them were important enough to justify considering all of them to be of one type. Spanish was the language spoken, there being few individuals who knew more than a few words of Quechua. They were all predominantly agricultural communities. They all had the same basic political structure: personero, junta comunal, monthly community meetings, etc. Each community had at least one patron saint and a fiesta system combining Catholic and folk religious elements. Each community had a system of communal labor known as the faena. In each community there existed a similar set of beliefs on how people ought to behave.

Such similarities are certainly important. An outsider who deals with any of these communities will need to have some knowledge regarding the ways in which they resemble each other. But if he fails to recognize significant differences among these communities, he makes a serious error. Huayopampa and Pacaraos differed from each other in such important ways as to present the prospective change agent with markedly different sets of problems, possibilities, and limitations. Lampián had differed from both of these in the severity of its generational conflict.

The same statement can be made regarding the Mantaro valley. That the villages have much in common has long been recognized, yet we found striking differences between Mito, on the one hand, and Pucará and Cajas, on the other. Even between these latter two, differences in occupational structure and in the types of tenancy of church-owned lands, among other factors, contributed to differences in effectiveness in carrying out community projects. In our fourfold conflict-cooperation diagram, each of the three communities falls in a different box.

We must also deal with variability within a given village. The anthropologist dare not assume that interviews with any single individual will represent "the true picture." Nor is it sufficient to recognize differences in attitudes and behavior that accompany age and sex differences. Some of the peasant communities we have studied are highly differentiated in terms of occupation, size of land holdings, and other factors. These lines of differentiation tend to be associated with differences in perceptions and beliefs as to what is good for the community and, therefore, with factional alignments.

274

We are not denying the existence of uniformities. We are saying that if the investigator begins with the assumption of homogeneity within communities and among communities in a given area, subsequent studies will reveal so much variability as to force him to start all over again. If that is the case, then it is better to start with the assumption of variability and then seek to discover the uniformities that lie beneath the variability.

The uniformities of concern to us are to be found on the level of behavior. Many of the elements generally considered in cultural studies will enter our analysis insofar as they tend to specify the conditions of behavior and to categorize the individuals who are behaving. It is unprofitable to seek to generalize about these cultural elements as such.

This focus on behavior requires a sharp distinction between *what is* and *what ought to be*—whether the moral judgement is applied by the investigator or by members of the community under study. It is not enough to know what members of the community are supposed to do when the junta comunal decides upon a project for a faena. Conformity is not automatic. Whenever men's actions involve costs in time, effort, and/or resources, they cannot be elicited and maintained without a system of rewards for compliance and penalties for failure to comply.

Approval or disapproval by one's fellows can be a powerful sanction, but compliance will also depend upon material or physical sanctions for use on those who are not sufficiently motivated by the thoughts and feelings of others. We are not suggesting that man acts solely in order to gain an immediate reward or to escape an immediate penalty. Social psychologists speak on the *internalization* of values. Through prior experience, the individual learns to do what he feels is right even when he perceives no offer of reward or threat of penalty. At the same time, the individual is aware of the extent to which those around him are meeting or failing to meet their obligations. An occasional and isolated failure of others will have little effect upon the individual's own conception of his obligations. But when increasing numbers of people are failing to comply, Person asks himself "Why should I carry the load?" and soon we find him among the noncompliers. Evasion of duties becomes contagious, and social control breaks down.

It is of little scientific value to know how people think they and others should behave. In some communities (Huayopampa, for example), we found a high degree of correspondence between expressed norms and observed behavior. In others (Pacaraos, for example), we found striking discrepancies between expressed norms and behavior.

Nor is it enough to note such differences from community to community, if we are interested in the prediction and/or control of behavior. We must ask: What sanctions are available to support normative behavior? When someone deviates from the norms, who brings sanctions to bear, how, and with what results?

We are not dealing simply with a schedule of rewards and penalties. We must determine also in what ways and how effectively these sanctions are *applied*, as we have noted in comparing the effectiveness of Huayopampa and Pacaraos in collecting fines for the same types of offenses.

This emphasis upon the study of behavior and its variability has been well stated by Frank Cancian in the following words:

> The use of extensive samples of individual behavior may be contrasted with two other approaches to the study of social structure: (1) the approach that generalizes about social structure on the basis of intensive analysis of a few "crucial" cases, and therefore carries little information about the actual proportion of the population that follows any particular pattern; and (2) the approach that generalizes about social structure on the basis of information about norms, and therefore carries virtually no information about what people actually do. Many anthropologists are able to argue convincingly that the proper goal of a field study is the production of a report showing how the native system makes coherent sense as a way of looking at the world and a way of living. I cannot object to this goal, but I think that the usual way of attaining it leaves too much to the imagination of the anthropologist. The more powerful his intellect and imagination, the more likely the anthropologist is to use this power to create coherence, whatever the actual situation. Careful attention to extensive samples of behavior may help avoid these dangers (1955:2–3).

ON RESTUDIES AND TEAM RESEARCH

In most cases, a study of a given community has been carried out by a single student, but in the Chancay valley project, with Huayopampa and Pacaraos, we had teams of four to five people in the community at the same time. The results have been sufficiently encouraging as to suggest the value of team efforts. A team can provide for a division of labor, with one individual examining the records of the communal government, observing junta meetings, and interviewing about local government activities while another student concentrates on the organization of the economic activities and upon the measurement of income. A team effort also provides for protection against the biases of a single individual. The members learn from each other as they spend hours, in the course of the field period, discussing and comparing their findings and arguing about their interpretations. For example, in the course of what was our *third* fieldwork period on this village, five able students spent six months in Huayopampa. We suspect that this team approach produced better results than would have come from the investment of the equivalent of two and one-half man-years on the part of an equally able single investigator.

We had originally hoped that during 1964 we would complete not only the surveys but also the anthropological studies in each of our villages. We did get several first-rate anthropological reports, but even the best of the reports had serious deficiencies. We recognized then that our original plan had been unrealistic. Although we had planned each year after 1964 for additional fieldwork in these villages, these new efforts were to be only brief expeditions for the purpose of checking anything that might have changed from the previous study during the year. However, instead of simply bringing each village up to date, we carried out full-scale restudies, designed to check the original findings, to fill in gaps, and to reexamine interpretations made on the basis of the original study.

In some cases, restudies revealed serious errors of the original studies. Our first study of one community described an unusual type of committee functioning under the local government. The restudy provided no information on this committee. When we checked with the research team of the restudy, we found that the committee in question did not exist and in fact had never existed. How could such a mistake be made? The student who did the first study described the committee on the basis of information given him by a single informant. This informant had a record for urging changes that frequently were not carried out. The minutes of the meetings of local government do record the establishment of the committee, but the idea was never implemented.

In another community, after making a much more careful and systematic examination of the economic aspects of community life, our restudy team developed figures to indicate that the first study's family income estimate was twice as large as it should have been.

It might be argued that such errors can be avoided by a single good anthropologist if he uses good methods. We agree that a well-trained and experienced anthropologist will bring in more adequate field data than beginning students, but the history of social anthropology should raise doubts about the wisdom of relying entirely upon the field reports of a single anthropologist, no matter how well trained or how large his professional reputation. In Chapter 20, we examined cases in which two well-known and highly respected anthropologists gave sharply conflicting interpretations of the same community.

The checking and rechecking process also stimulated our students to raise their standards as to quality of their data. They explained to us, "The information you had was simply wrong because the man who made the study got it from a single informant and did not check it with anybody else." Or: "Those original income estimates were just based on sloppy methods. We have talked with Fulano, and he himself has admitted that this part of his study was no good." As students recheck the work of their predecessors, they have the incentive to raise their own standards of performance. As they prepare their reports, they must be inclined to look over their shoulders not only at the professors who will read their reports but also at future students who will follow them and check up on their work.

The quality of our studies has been improved by the writing of comparative descriptions and analyses about pairs or sets of communities. When a research director reads over reports on communities A and B, deficiencies may escape his attention until he is required to write a chapter comparing the two communities. He then finds that he has excellent information on one aspect of life in community A, but the information from community B on this aspect does not refer to some points considered important by the writers of the A report. For example, impressed by the Pacaraos report on the low frequency of collection of fines, we looked for comparable data in the Huayopampa monograph—and did not find any. Since Huayopampinos paid 100 percent of their fines, collection did not seem a problem there and thus was not reported. When we compared the two villages, Huayopampa's success in collecting fines was clearly as important as Pacaraos's failure. Thus, the task of comparison enriched our understanding of the data needed for analyzing the dynamics of community life.

ON THE USES OF HISTORICAL DATA

In the original outline for the field studies in anthropology. Whyte proposed that history be used simply to provide general background and that we should not trace the historical record beyond the last 50 years. Our students had too much interest in history to abide by this limitation. We now have data on land ownership and changes in tenure in the delta of the Chancay valley going back to the conquest of Peru. Similarly, the fieldworkers traced the history of Huayopampa and Pacaraos back to the conquest and developed an historical record of increasing detail for each subsequent century. This work has produced information of value in a neglected field, the development of rural Peru, but has it contributed anything beyond "general background" to our present studies? We can point to several important contributions of history to our current understanding of these villages—and all of these go back beyond our original 50-year limit.

In the literature of sociology, anthropology, and community development, we generally find the rural community presented as a passive entity in relation to dynamic urban centers. Particularly if it is far removed from an urban center, the village is seen as a tradition-bound unit, conserving its own culture and being inclined to resist interventions from the city. We doubt this picture even for more remote parts of rural Peru. The village records show that as much as 100 years ago, the people of Huayopampa and Pacaraos were making strenuous efforts to develop an educational system that would put them in touch with the modern world. The records provide frequent statements to the effect that the village should make such and such a change in order to put itself in harmony with modern (city) methods. History does indeed provide examples of men from the cities intervening in the local community, but in these cases it is clear that for at least 100 years, Huayopampinos and Pacareños have sought to integrate themselves more closely with the nation.

A striking example of the uses of history is provided by study of land distribution in Huayopampa and Pacaraos. By coincidence, final distribution of communal lands was begun in both villages in the year 1902. Whereas Pacaraos distributed this land to permanent ownership, Huayopampa retained title to the land and rented it out. We see, therefore, that the difference in the strength of community organization in the two villages can be traced back at least to the fateful decisions of 1902.

A researcher who looked only at the material resources available for development today would find no clues to the decadence and stagnation of Mito and the dynamism of Pucará and Cajas. It was only as Alberti traced the political decline and dismemberment of Mito and the gain in political position of Pucará and Cajas that the differences in present conditions and future prospects became understandable.

We find history an important corrective for a form of myopia common among behavioral scientists. The most popular research techniques focus upon present-time data and provide the researcher with a static picture of the scene under study. Since the researcher knows that human beings act through time, he seeks to infer from his data what may have happened in the past, but he is on shaky ground when he tries to draw dynamic conclusions from static data. History is a discipline organized in terms of time sequences. Few historians try to establish the generalizations of interest to the behavioral scientist, but we can exploit the diachronic focus of history to bring to life the social processes that are vital to our understanding to community life.

POTENTIALS FOR A NATIONAL PROGRAM

Let us finally consider the extent to which our experience might contribute to the planning of national rural research and development programs.

Our own program was ambitious: surveys of 23 villages and 3 haciendas in 1964, surveys of 12 villages and 6 haciendas in 1969, and anthropological and historical studies of many of these units through this period and beyond. Nevertheless, our work covered only a small fraction of rural Peru.

Covering all or most of the rural areas of a country of any size would not only require much more money than we had to spend. If we had had national ambitions and unlimited funds, we would simply have buried ourselves in unanalyzed data. A major expansion of our research design would also require modifications in plans both for the anthropological-historical studies and for the surveys.

For a national program, the most serious limitation of anthropological-historical village and area studies is that they are costly in time and talent. It took two fieldworkers a couple of weeks or less to execute the survey in a village, but the anthropological-historical study required the immersion of one or more fieldworkers for months. It would clearly be impractical to plan to study a large sample of communities on such an intensive basis. Even if the planners did not run out of money, they would soon run out of able fieldworkers and of supervisors capable of giving direction to such complex and far-flung enterprises.

For surveys, gathering the data is much less costly, and computer analysis goes fast, yet there we face important limitations in the value of the analysis. By surveying and resurveying five years later, we planned to measure changes and through the anthropological studies, to explain these changes. Although this combination proved fruitful, we found that it did not focus on the change process as well as we had hoped.

The basic problem was that in only 2 out of the 12 villages for which we had surveys for both years were the years 1964 and 1969 critical periods of change. In 1964, Huayopampa showed the highest perceived level of cooperation and an extremely low level of conflict, and the 1969 survey of Huayopampa showed a sharp drop in cooperation and an even more marked increase in conflict. These shifts clearly signaled that the community had gone through a crisis. In the case of Kuyo Chico, the 1969 survey was carried out a month after the abrupt termination of a government-supported applied anthropology project that had stimulated a remarkable surge of development. It was important to learn that the villagers' faith in the national government had sharply dropped whereas their confidence in their own ability to handle village problems had remained at a high level.

For the other 10 villages, the problem was that the years 1964 and 1969 did not happen to bracket change processes important enough to show up in our surveys. In some cases, 1964–1969 simply involved the continuation of change processes begun earlier, whereas other cases probably involved the beginning of changes that would not show any marked effects until well after 1969. In retrospect, it appears that we were lucky to achieve a sharp change focus on even 2 out of 12 villages.

If we were now utilizing our experience for national planning, we would begin by selecting a sample of 6 to 10 villages in each of the major regions of the country. Then in region X, we would survey villages A and B, repeating the process with pairs of villages in the other regions.

We would not undertake any anthropological studies until we had completed the first-year surveys and scanned the patterns of responses. We would then pick out a few villages whose response patterns appeared to be particularly interesting for theoretical and/or policy purposes: for example, villages very high or very low in confidence in their ability to solve village problems, villages with very high or very low levels of cooperation and/or conflict or villages high in both conflict and coopera- tion, villages manifesting very high or very low levels of interpersonal trust, and so on. We would design our anthropological fieldwork in these villages in order to probe for the social processes underlying the survey findings.

In the second year, in region X, we would survey villages C and D, repeating the procedures outlined above. For the third year, we would survey E and F, and so on. Whether we go back to A and B the fourth year or take on G and H, and so on, would depend upon a decision on a three-year or longer cycle between surveys and resurveys.

When we do resurveys, new research possibilities open up, as the direction of intensive studies is no longer limited to what looks interest- ing for a given village at a given time. Let us say that the survey of village A yields no pattern of responses interesting enough to justify an- thropological fieldwork there; nevertheless, we record the responses and deposit the tape in our data bank. Three to five years later, we compare the village A resurvey with the original survey. If we find major changes in dimensions of interest to us, we direct an intensive anthropological study at that village to explain the changes revealed in the comparison of the two surveys.

Our survey-resurvey program would enable us to focus the more costly anthropological methods where we would gain the greatest leverage in discovering the dynamics of social change. If we could develop and maintain such a research system for 10 to 15 years, behavioral scientists would have an extraordinarily rich body of data for the building of better theories of rural development. For the first time, we would be able to build the time dimension into our studies on the basis of currently gathered survey data fortified by the current and retrospective field studies of anthropologists.

The system should also provide government planners with more solidly grounded research findings leading to more effective rural-development policies. For example, if some of the villages in the sample turn out to be targets for the intervention of directed change projects, over the period of several years surveys and anthropological studies could determine the extent, nature, and direction of the changes produced. Similarly designed studies of villages developing primarily in response to internally generated forces would also help planners to discover the roots of indigenous development in order to be able to design government policies that would strengthen such internal development tendencies.

Such a program would also provide extraordinary educational opportunities for professionals and students involved in the fieldwork, data analysis, and report writing.

Science and Styles of 22
Social Research

In the course of a decade of research on rural Peru, our ideas on theory and science have undergone marked changes. In this chapter, we trace the evolution of our ideas and use this experience to draw conclusions on science and styles of social research. By way of contrast, we begin by describing what we take to be the standard sociological strategy.

THE STANDARD SOCIOLOGICAL STRATEGY

According to the prevailing standards regarding research design, the researcher is expected to think in terms of discrete variables, which are to be measured with as much precision as possible. Before he gathers his data, the researcher is expected to specify his independent and dependent variables and to predict how they are going to be related to each other—that is, to state hypotheses regarding the degree and direction (positive or negative) of association among variables.

Some elementary qualifications are, of course, necessary. Correlation simply establishes a satistical relationship between variables and does not tell us that one variable *causes* variation in a second variable, nor does it rule out the possibility that both variables may vary in response to another variable that we may or may not have measured. Furthermore, labeling one variable "independent" does not mean that it necessarily has causal influence on another variable that is labeled "dependent"— only that, for the purposes of a particular analysis, the researcher is interested in determining to what extent variations in the independent variable are associated with variations in the dependent variable.

With due regard to these reservations, the researcher seeks to draw certain causal inferences from the correlations he finds. He is expected to hypothesize certain relations among variables in terms of some theoretical framework. He then reports the relationships that were found as predicted and attempts to account for the relationships that did not fit the predictions. In a sense, the hypotheses that turn out to be supported tell the researcher what he thought he already knew, simply adding to his confidence in this knowledge, whereas the relationships that do not come out as predicted point to deficiencies either in the theoretical framework, in the methods of measurement, or in both.

The standard research strategy involves the implicit assumption that the problem has been so sharply and correctly defined that a tight research design is called for. If the nature of the problem is not at all clear, then a research strategy involving a tight design is likely to give a spurious impression of scientific procedures. And a series of studies along the same line may simply lead to conclusions whose neatness is matched by their sterility.

Furthermore, at best such a strategy is compatible only with survey research, where variables and relationships can be specified and measured with all of the precision of modern statistical techniques. This strategy is much more difficult to apply when one is dealing with observational/interview data on social structure and social processes. In much of such research, the important variables have not been previously established, and prevailing theoretical orientations may be misleading. Thus, as in our case, the major problem is conceptual: to develop a theoretical

285

framework that would enable us to diagram some aspects of social structure, to trace sequences of events and social processes, and to link together structure and process.

PRELIMINARY RESEARCH DESIGN

The initial plans for our research program grew out of Whyte's 14 months in Peru from 1961 to 1962. That project called for a series of in-plant interview/observational studies of human problems of industrial development. From this base, the project branched out into a survey in one industrial firm and into a values questionnaire applied to male high school seniors in 12 Lima schools and in schools in 5 provincial cities (Whyte: 1963b; 1965). When John Hickman took some of our high school questionnaire items for his own survey in highland villages, his findings stirred our interest in further work along this line.

Experience up to this point convinced us of the desirability of combining surveys and anthropological methods in the same project. The opportunity was suggested to us by the presidential campaigns of 1962 and 1963, during which Belaúnde stressed his commitment to agrarian reform and rural community development. If President Belaúnde was indeed going to launch a major program designed to change rural Peru, it would be important to lay down baseline measures in order later to measure the impact of government-induced changes as well as to study the change process.

To get this baseline down in a fair number of communities as soon as possible, we concentrated first on surveys. For several reasons, we made no effort to pick a national sample of communities. Given the wide range of regional differences, a national sample would have been so large as to be far beyond our resources and available personnel. Furthermore, studying widely scattered communities would have been far more costly than studying the same number in clusters. We were further constrained by the practical requirement of selecting study areas accessible to students and professors from Lima or from a provincial university and by the possibilities of establishing collaborative arrangements with Peruvian professors competent to direct the fieldwork.

These practical limitations ruled out the study of "representative" villages, but we were able to work on villages providing a wide range of differences in wealth, education, occupation, and accessibility to cities. This wide range made it possible to maintain continuity in our program even as we made major changes in theory and research methods.

One of the most important changes involved our conception of the nature of peasant communities. As we look back on our experience, we now recognize that we ourselves were once believers in the myth of the passive peasant. The urgency of our effort to achieve wide survey coverage as soon as possible was based upon the implicit assumption that the only changes we were likely to see in the peasant villages were those due to outside (government) intervention. Therefore if we did not get our baseline down on time, we would miss the boat.

TOWARD A MORE DYNAMIC FRAMEWORK

Having worked on our survey data analysis at Cornell, Alberti went to Peru in mid-1967 to study intervillage systems in the Mantaro valley, following the framework of Frank Young. Because the research in that valley progressed faster than he had anticipated, Alberti decided to take on another intervillage system in the neighboring Yanamarca valley. Since that decision led to a turning point in our conception of peasant society, we quote here part of Alberti's letter to Whyte (September 1967):

> We have come across a fantastic area for study of social change: la parte alta [the high part] of the Yanamarca Valley, north of Jauja. The hacienda system was predominant there up to a few years ago and still today a very small number of haciendas have survived. . . . In a visit to a community, Tingo, while talking to some autoridades [local officials], I learned that only recently they won their independence from the feudal rule of the hacendado. This of course aroused my curiosity, and I wanted to know how the transformation took place. First I asked if I could see the house which was the residence of the hacendado and also the houses in which they used to live during the hacienda days. After visiting the dwelling of both the hacendado and peones, we kept talking about their achievement. I was particularly interested in knowing more about the flow of events that led to the total transformation of the hacienda system into a completely new type of social organization. I kept formulating and reformulating the same question: what events forced the hacendado to leave his land? Of course, I could not expect the comuneros to

287

give me a full explanation. I simply asked them to remember what happened shortly before the hacendado left for Jauja. Three autoridades were speaking at the same time. However, I managed to record a few facts that seem to have been crucial in bringing about this important instance of social change.

Whyte had read about Hugo Blanco and the Convención valley movement of 1961 and 1962, but at the time, it had seemed like an interesting but isolated phenomenon. Alberti's letter on Yanamarca raised more general questions for Whyte: How long has this sort of thing been going on? And how widely has this been going on?

These questions did not provoke any immediate change in plans. Alberti completed his thesis on intervillage systems, and the rest of us in the program went ahead with analysis of the 1964 surveys, review of the village anthropological studies, and planning of the 1969 resurveys. Nevertheless, having once discovered the peasant movement in the Yanamarca valley, we could not just confine fragments of that story to the research files. When we had completed the 1969 survey program, Alberti and his student assistants returned to the central highlands to gather the data reported in Chapter 11. We ourselves undertook no new fieldwork in the Convención valley, but we found the year-long study by Fioravanti and the army's own account of military intervention there extending and deepening the early account by Wesley Craig (1967).

Our growing interest in peasant movements also led us to realize the inadequacy of our original orientation toward modernization research. In fact, we came to see the myth of the passive peasant as part of the modernization theoretical package. In that framework, the problem is primarily one of the psychological orientation of peasants: their fatalism, traditionalism, resistance to change, etc. Therefore research should focus on measurement of peasant attitudes and values and on peasant contact with the dynamic, modern urban centers.

Our original research design provided ample data for the analysis of modernization. Each village could serve as a separate unit of analysis, with respondents being sorted out on the modernism-traditionalism dimension. Surveys and resurveys could measure changes in this dimension and guide us toward the influences that were producing these changes.

In terms of the original design, the clustering of village studies in particular areas was simply a matter of convenience. To be sure, we had to provide some information about the area of each cluster of villages, but that was only to give ourselves and our readers *background*. Similarly, in order to understand each village during the period of our research, we had to provide some historical information, but again we saw this as simply background material.

As we began to see peasants as men and women in action and began focusing on changes in the distribution of power within communities, areas, and regions, what had been background moved to the forefront of our analysis. Villages were no longer our central concern but had become simply convenient locations for the study of social structure and social processes. In order to make sense out of what was happening in a given village, we had to place it within its context of space, time, and the distribution of power and resources. We needed to compare not only individual villages but also areas and regions.

Our studies in the central highlands precipitated our shift of historical data from background for description to essential elements in analysis. Earlier, we had picked up historical information that seemed important in explaining the development of particular villages (the history of education in Huayopampa, the 1902 land-distribution decisions in Huayopampa and Pacaraos). Now Alberti came upon the Espinosa study (1973) that explained the absence of large haciendas in the Mantaro valley in terms of events that occurred in the early decades after the Spanish conquest. Until Alberti had traced the history of Mito, Pucará, and Cajas, the stagnation of one and the dynamism of the other two remained incomprehensible. This work also helped us to recognize the need to link together space and time, for the decline of Mito was accompanied by spatial changes: the return of migrants from the mines and the subsequent mobilization of the people of the anexos.

The preceding discussion has indicated how we changed our sense of direction in the course of the research program. Let us now move on to trace the origins of some of our key ideas.

THE TRIANGLE WITHOUT A BASE

The triangle without a base was born one morning in the fall of 1966, during the period when Julio Cotler was visiting Cornell. Participating in the discussion, along with Cotler, were J. Oscar Alers, then Cornell's research associate with IEP; Giorgio Alberti, then a graduate student; Lawrence K. Williams, and William Whyte.

We had finished our discussion of progress and plans and had gone on to consider theoretical ideas that might help us in interpreting our data. Cotler had been especially concerned with examining the structure of the traditional sierra hacienda. While he was putting into words his conception of the power structure, Cotler stepped up to the blackboard and drew the four-line figure illustrated below.

This simple figure represented two important ideas: the hacendado as monopolist, having full control of the resources the peasants needed and also of their lines of communication beyond the hacienda, and the lack of lines linking the peasants, indicating their unorganized state.

The birth of the triangle without a base produced an immediate *Eureka* experience. We felt that the diagram gave us a sharper and clearer view of social structure and social problems for sierra peasants. From this point on, we found ourselves thinking within this general structural framework. We also began to recognize that this diagram had applications beyond the rural sierra. It seemed to represent the situation in the traditional Peruvian organization, where the boss was all-powerful, saw to it that each subordinate had a personal relationship with him, and discouraged the formation of social bonds among peers. We also saw the traditional Peruvian middle- or upper-class family in these terms. In such a family, the father was the absolute boss and distributed favors and penalties among his sons and daughters in such a way as to keep them dependent upon him and prevent them from getting together to do anything on their own. This pattern of relationships helped to explain an important weakness in the hacendado's position. In Tingo, in an earlier generation, the father of the family had been the patriarch, with firm control over both his family and his peasants. The authoritarian pattern of relationships created friction and mistrust among the patriarch's children, but as long as the father lived, the conflict remained submerged. When the old man died, the conflict broke out into the open. This seems a common situation in the traditional Peruvian family.

Any structural diagram drawn to represent a large number of social situations must necessarily be an oversimplification. Although the triangle without a base highlighted important structural problems of the traditional hacienda, we came to see the necessity of further elaboration of this model as we studied cases in which the peasants had been able to break out of the monolithic structure. It was evident that the closing of the base of the triangle would be a necessary step in the changing of the distribution of power, and yet it was hard to believe that this closing of the base could take place without any other changes in the society. As we examined cases of successful peasant mobilization, we recognized that other important changes were indeed taking place at the same time and perhaps were even preceding the closing of the base.

We found individual peasants and groups of peasants going outside of the triangle to establish direct links with the world beyond the hacienda. We traced these links to economic middlemen, lawyers, politicians, union leaders, the Agricultural Development Bank, and officials of the Ministry of Labor and the Ministry of Education. These cases suggested that the closing of the base was likely to take place only if it were accompanied by the establishment of outside and upward linkages by the peasants. At the same time, these outside and upward linkages could not have been exploited by unorganized peasants, so that a community-solidarity movement was a necessary element in the change of the power structure.

In the reasoning described thus far, we had been looking at the problem from the vantage point of the peasants: that is, considering the changes that would strengthen their position. It now occurred to us to look at the problem from the vantage point of the hacendado: to ask what changes might weaken his position. If one considers the triangle without a base as a closed system, then it follows that any increase in power of the peasant means a decrease in the power of the hacendado, but the cases suggested that the loss in hacendado power was not limited to the hacendado-peasant relationship. The cases showed clearly that the hacendado's power over the peasants depended, in large measure, upon the linkages the hacendado held with those in superior power positions

291

and also with friends and relatives, who might support him in a crisis situation. No sooner had we begun to look for forces outside of the triangle tending to weaken the hacendado's position that it became apparent that we had the evidence already in hand from our studies showing deteriorating relationships between the hacendado and his upward and horizontal linkages.

At a later point, it became evident that we would have to rethink relationships inside the triangle. The triangle seemed useful as a general model, but whenever we sought to apply it to an actual hacienda system, we recognized that the fit was not good enough. In most cases, the hacendado's direct contacts with serfs were infrequent. The hacendado had usually been an absentee owner or renter, making only occasional visits to his property. The man in charge on a full-time basis was the administrator. But even he did not directly supervise the work of the colonos. The functionary immediately below the administrator might be hired from the outside; the supervisors at lower levels were drawn from among the colonos themselves. As we traced these additional lines between hacendado and colonos, we saw the structural basis for the well-known fact that the hacendado did not treat all colonos alike but rather maintained his control through favoring some at the expense of others. This favoritism was expressed structurally through the appointment of first- and second-line supervisors. These individuals were excused from manual labor and favored also in other ways such as having large plots of land for family cultivation, a larger herd of cattle on the hacendado's range, and so on.

This elementary exercise of filling out the typical lines of authority on the hacienda called to our attention important gaps in our knowledge. As yet, we know rather little regarding the role of the administrator. Since the hacendado is present on the property so seldom, the administrator must have considerable latitude in directing the work. In order to make life easier for himself or to salve his own conscience, he may make concessions to the peasants which would not have been granted by the hacendado. Alternatively, he can try to push the peasants harder than the hacendado intends in order to gain unauthorized benefits for himself.

The more elaborate diagram we now use points to the critical role of lower-level supervisors between administrators and colonos. Since we reached this conclusion about these supervisors after the end of our fieldwork, we have been able only to speculate on the role played by these intermediaries in peasant movements.

While acknowledging such gaps in our data, we can also use this case to illustrate the uses of theory. We depend on theory to guide us toward answers to questions. It is also important to recognize that theory can reveal to us new questions for which we must seek answers.

The most general lesson to be drawn from this account of our theoretical exploration can be put in this form. If indeed it is important for behavioral scientists to study social structure and social processes, then we must go beyond words and seek to *diagram* the essential relationships of a particular social system. A simple diagram may lead us to conclusions otherwise beyond our reach. As we continue seeking to apply the diagram to empirical reality, we will need to modify and further elaborate the original diagram. This process of modification and elaboration, as we go back and forth from drawing to thinking about our data, leads us to adopt new ways of organizing and analyzing existing data and also leads us to recognize important gaps in our information.

THE EVOLUTION OF THE
FOUR-BOX FRAMEWORK

Although we had long been interested in the anthropological debate on the nature of the peasant community, in our first publication containing discussion of this issue (Matos Mar et al., 1969) we had not gone beyond saying that Foster's image of the limited good looked interesting but nevertheless we had found wide differences among communities in the prevalence of conflict, distrust, and envy.

Four years passed before we were able to take the next step in the development of a new theoretical framework. The initial impetus came out of Whyte's reading of an anthropological field report regarding the village of Mito. The writer called Mito a community that had a low level of cooperation and also a low level of conflict. Earlier, Whyte had read this report casually, but now he was writing a monograph on the Mantaro valley, and he paused to consider the implications of the statement.

How could a community be low in both conflict and cooperation? The first step toward an answer involved checking of data that would support or refute the general statement. Whyte turned to the marginals for questions on conflict and cooperation to compare Mito with Pucará and Cajas. The figures indeed revealed that Miteños perceived their community as lower in both conflict and cooperation than did respondents in the two comparison villages.

Two lines of work now seemed to be required: reconceptualization of the conflict-cooperation problem and quantitative analysis of the survey data to determine the patterns that emerge as we go beyond these three communities.

Whyte asked himself why he had been surprised to find a community that was described as being low in both conflict and cooperation. This surprise suggested that we had been assuming that a community low in conflict must be high in cooperation and vice versa. How could that assumption be represented in a theoretical model? That question led Whyte to the single-continuum model in which cooperation and conflict would be at opposite poles. The discovery of a community that was low in both conflict and cooperation tended to cast doubt on the single-continuum model. Was Mito just a fluke that could be disregarded, or did this community point in an important new theoretical direction? As a first step in answering that question, Whyte asked a further question, Could there be a community that was relatively high in both conflict and cooperation? A rough inspection of the marginals for 1969 revealed that indeed there were two such communities.

This step led us in two quick jumps to both the two-continua model and then to the four-box model which is reached simply by placing the two continua perpendicular to each other.

Both of these models represent the conclusion that cooperation and conflict, as perceived by community members, are separate and independent. The next step was to verify this conclusion statistically through correlating responses on the two items with each other. As noted in Chapter 19, we found that the correlations were so close to zero as to indicate that the two dimensions were unrelated to each other.

Ordinarily, the behavioral scientist formulates his theoretical ideas in terms of relationships he expects to find and is then disappointed if the predicted correlations do not materialize. Here was a case in which a correlation approximating zero confirmed an idea that has led us toward the building of a new theoretical framework for the interpretation of peasant communities.

The next step was to place each of the 12 communities for which we had survey data for the 2 years into the two-dimensional space provided by our measures of conflict and cooperation. This placement confirmed the pattern that we thought we saw from an inspection of the marginals: there were indeed cases that fell in each of the four boxes created by drawing perpendicular lines for the mean values of cooperation and of conflict for a given year.

We were excited by the pattern revealed by the simple arithmetic operations, but we were not content to stop with the quantitative findings. We asked, What does the pattern mean?

We sought to answer that question in two ways. First, since it had generally been assumed that conflict and cooperation are opposite poles of the same continuum, we had to show how it could be possible to find perceived levels of both conflict and cooperation high or both levels low in a given community. We found the answer in looking at projects for community improvement. For example, a community having no change projects under way would lack a focal point for organizing cooperative activities and would also lack a focal point for developing community conflict, in which case we would expect the perceived levels of both conflict and cooperation to be low.

The next step was to ask whether the placement of the 12 communities among the four boxes made sense. We considered the communities in a given box and asked ourselves in what ways do these communities resemble each other? In what ways do they differ from communities in the other three boxes? These questions led us to the interpretive descriptions of each community which we have presented in Chapter 19.

We then asked whether we could generalize on characteristics of communities within a given box and distinguish them from communities in the other boxes. There was also further quantitative work to be done to be sure that the findings were not due primarily to size or differentiation. The mechanical operation of locating each village for 1964 and 1969 focused our attention upon the five communities that had changed boxes and especially upon Huayopampa.

One critic, reviewing our work, interpreted our research strategy as suggesting "that the relationship of ethnographic observation to survey research is that linking theory generation to theory testing. The thought process described starts with the ethnography as a source of ideas and then tests them against survey data."

In other words, research is a two-step process: the researcher begins with soft methods to develop ideas; he then moves on to the hard scientific methods of testing those ideas. After that, he starts over, with another project, and goes through the same old one-two.

That is the conventional wisdom in sociology—and it is dead wrong. It distorts reality and understates the value of *both* research methods.

Whyte did indeed get the germ of a theoretical idea from reading the anthropological report on Mito, but it was only when he checked the marginals for the surveys on the three Mantaro valley communities that he realized he might have an idea worth *developing* as well as testing. Indeed, although the 1969 survey data provided a replication of the 1964 statistical pattern of conflict-cooperation and thus a powerful scientific test of our theoretical reformulation, it is important to note that the resurvey also served to focus our attention upon communities that had changed markedly in perceived conflict-cooperation. Finding that the shift for Huayopampa was unique both in direction and magnitude led us back to that community for further anthropological fieldwork.

MICRO- AND MACROLEVELS OF ANALYSIS IN A STRUCTURAL-HISTORICAL FRAMEWORK

In seeking to explain behavior at the village level, we have found it necessary to search for the links between the microlevel and the macrolevel of regional and national politics and economic development. It is not enough to assume that these macrolevel developments are important for understanding local life; we must seek the empirical data that link the two levels. For example, we began our examination of the central highlands with the historical events of the early colonial period which resulted in the elimination of large haciendas from the Mantaro valley. We showed how the economic and political rivalry between Huancayo and Jauja through the nineteenth and early twentieth centuries shaped the development of villages that fell within the orbit of each of the two cities. We then followed the transformation of the Mantaro and Yanamarca valleys through the development of the mines of Cerro de Pasco, which in themselves represented a major intervention of foreign capital and managerial talent backed by political power at the highest level of the nation. We traced the role played by some members of the elite of the traditional city of Jauja in recruiting the labor force for the mines from among hacienda colonos and village peasants. We saw how the building of a mass labor force for the mines precipitated a union movement in which former peasants and colonos developed working-class loyalties and an ideology of collective solidarity. Finally, we noted how growing peasant mobilization, together with other changes, transformed the power structure of the Jauja area, so that the children of those who had recruited labor for the mines lost the power once held by their fathers and grandfathers.

We have tried to demystify the concept of power by showing how it is manifested by those who wield it and those who have it wielded against them. Focusing upon the level of individual, group, community, and organizational behavior, we run the risk of giving the impression that the forces motivating, guiding, and controlling behavior are all operating within the local social system. Even if we look first within that social system, we soon encounter events that can be explained only by their links to macrolevel developments.

For example, the efforts of the colonos in the Convención valley to form a union naturally led to counteractions by the hacendados. The peasants knew that the hacendados were appealing to the national government to support them by sending in troops. The hacendados waited and the peasants waited, and the troops did not come. The peasants were learning from both what did and what did not happen that the power of the hacendados was not what it had been in earlier generations. By examining political and economic developments at the national level, we have explained the declining power of the rural landed aristocracy, and at the level of the Convención valley, we have shown how the peasants and their leaders discovered the nature of the power shift and proceeded to shift the balance further in their favor.

In developing our structural-historical analysis of social change, we have adapted to our purposes some of the leading ideas of Marxism. We follow Marx in giving great weight to economic interests and class conflict, but we find that, today, the analytical class labels *bourgeoisie* and *proletariat* are commonly used as reifications of reality and, as such, are of little use for scientific purposes. Within the bourgeoisie of Peru, we have seen competing and conflicting fractions: the traditional landholding elite and the modernizing owners and managers of commercial farming plantations, with their growing economic activities outside of agriculture; those controlling export enterprises and those controlling firms oriented to the national market (with, more recently, the emergence of an interest group promoting "nontraditional exports" to set themselves apart from those exporting agricultural crops and raw materials); those allied with one network of financial, industrial, and commercial organizations and those allied with a rival network; and so on. Leaders of such fractions sometimes get together on a common policy, but such bourgeois solidarity is not to be taken for granted. It is more realistic to view the national bourgeoisie in terms of potential lines of internal cleavages among different factions that are often in competition and conflict with each other. It is often the shifting nature of these alliances and conflicts that provides the fluidity necessary to enable dominated class groups to enter into the struggle for power and thus eventually to bring about major changes in the power structure.

The same problem of reification occurs with the terms *proletariat* and *peasantry*. As to the first term, beyond the obvious distinction between organized and unorganized industrial workers, there are differences of skill, pay, and occupation that sometimes lead workers to cooperate or conflict with each other according to conditions that must be empirically determined.

As to the peasantry, we must recognize important socioeconomic differences among hacienda colonos, sharecroppers, farm laborers, and small independent farmers. Even among small farmers, there are some who have more and better land and better access to water than others. Then, too, there are small farmers who work part of their time on haciendas and others who are not so dependent on the hacendado.

Under certain conditons, a peasant solidarity movement serves to unite these people in resistance to a common enemy, and the differences among them are submerged in the common cause. But when the hacendado retires from the scene, objective differences (rooted in relations of production) emerge to form the substance of the process of political competition and intergroup negotiation.

We have also noted that although disputes over the distribution of costs and benefits often provide the issues for conflict within peasant communities, the cleavages may be also structured by noneconomic factors, such as differences in neighborhood, culture, religion, age, and so on. These are important differences, and their relationship to the economic base of the class structure must be taken into account if we do not want to use the term *class* as a blanket concept that hides reality rather than helping us to understand it.

Another line of uncritical and demagogic use of the term class is revealed in an otherwise valuable study by Juan Martínez Alier, who directed against us the following statement. He criticizes

North American and Peruvian sociologists and anthropologists who have used the concept of "pluralism" (which is a way of avoiding the use of "social class") and of "domination," in the sense of unlimited power of the hacendados to impose their interests, facilitated by the absence of "horizontal" communication and the existence of only "vertical" communication (which enables them to avoid using the concept of "class struggle") (1974:81).

Thus Martínez invokes the concepts of *social class* and *class struggle* as panaceas for solving all theoretical and empirical problems.

In the first place, the lines we have drawn are not intended to indicate simple paths of communication. To say that on the traditional hacienda colonos do not communicate with each other is obviously absurd. The absence of a line linking them is simply intended to depict their *unorganized* state. There may be better ways of drawing such diagrams, but whatever the deficiencies in this symbolization, it is important to recognize that we are studying not patterns of communication but organization and the distribution of power.

In the second place, our critic is apparently offended because in a previous publications we did not use common Marxist terminology. This book is full of discussions of social class and the social-class differences, but to examine these differences in terms of the global categories of the bourgeoisie and the proletariat is more confusing than helpful. Nor do we reject the concept of the class struggle—except that we must relate it to the empirical realities we have been studying. We are concerned with class struggle in the sense of seeking to determine the conditions under which members of a lower class gain power and economic resources at the expense of members of a higher class. We do not see this struggle in terms of class against class but in terms of *organization* of specific groups of people with common interests. Defenders of the status quo see the organization of society in terms of *vertical* solidarity: those in dominant class positions take care of the interests of lower-class people in ways that suit dominant class interests. A successful peasant movement depends upon disrupting this vertical organization and building *horizontal* solidarity with lower-class people organizing to take care of their own interests in their own ways. This kind of change does not depend simply upon the existence of different social classes with antagonistic interests. That condition existed in rural Peru long before the successful peasant movements. Therefore we need to go beyond global class categories to discover the conditions that made it possible for peasants to organize themselves in terms of their class interests and bring about significant changes in the distribution of power and resources.

These reflections lead us to build what we might call a structural-historical theoretical framework. We are concerned with behavior at the microlevel of hacienda and community, but we regard these entities as being convenient locations for study rather than as enjoying independent existence. We are concerned with behavior at the macrolevel of region and nation, but we are not content with assuming that power exercised at these levels *must* affect local units in certain ways; we require ourselves to discover and trace the impacts of macrolevel events upon microlevel events and vice versa (for if local events occur similarly in many locations or involve large numbers of people, they may influence actions on the national level). We are concerned with the study of social processes and with the micro- and macrolevel elements of social structure that tend to facilitate or limit their development—and we are concerned also with the way social processes tend to reshape those structural elements.

This means that *time* is an essential dimension in our studies. The structural elements we see influencing current social processes are the product of the past interplay between structure and process, with structure shaping process and process shaping structure. This means that we cannot be content with a present-time picture of hacienda or community. To grasp the dynamics of social change, we must identify the major structural elements currently shaping society at macro- and microlevels and then trace changes in these elements back into recent, and even more remote, history. Only as we carry out such a structural-historical study can we understand the processes of change at the local level.

BIBLIOGRAPHY

Adams, Richard N.

1959   *A Community in the Andes: Problems and Progress in Muquiyauyo*. Seattle: University of Washington Press.

Alberti, Giorgio

1970   Los Movimientos Campesinos. In Robert G. Keith et al., *El Campesino en el Peru*. Lima: Instituto de Estudios Peruanos.

1972   The Breakdown of Provincial Urban Power Structure and the Origins of Peasant Movements. In Benno Galjart (ed.), *Rural Sociology*. Netherlands: Sociologia Ruralis.

1973   Peasant Movements in the Yanamarca Valley. In David Chaplin (ed.), *Change and Development in Peru*. New Brunswick, N.J.: Transaction Books.

———, **and Julio Cotler**

1969–1970   *Estructura Social y Reforma Agraria, La Revista del Museo Nacional*. Lima: Instituto de Estudios Peruanos.

| 1972 | *Aspectos Sociales de la Educación Rural en el Peru*. Lima: Instituto de Estudios Peruanos. |

1972   *Aspectos Sociales de la Educación Rural en el Peru*. Lima: Instituto de Estudios Peruanos.

1973   Agrarian Reform in the Sugar Plantations of Northern Peru. In Jorge Dandler (ed.), *Nationalism and Revolution in the Andes: Chile, Peru and Bolivia*. New York: Anchor-Doubleday.

Alberti, G. and Rodrigo Sánchez

1974   *Poder y Conflicto Social en el Valle del Mantaro*. Lima: Instituto de Estudios Peruanos.

Alers, J. O. and R. Applebaum

1968   Migraciones en el Peru: Un Inventario de Proposiciones. Lima: Bulletin of *Centro de Estudios de Población y Desarrollo*.

Bales, R. Freed

1950   *Interaction Process Analysis*. Cambridge, Mass: Addison-Wesley.

Béjar, Héctor

1969   *Peru 1965: Notes on a Guerrilla Experience*. New York: Monthly Review Press.

Blanco, Hugo

1972   *Land or Death: The Peasant Struggle in Peru*. New York: Pathfinder Press.

Blau, Peter

1964   *Exchange and Power in Social Life*. New York: Wiley.

Bonachea, Ramón L. and Marta San Martín

1974   *The Cuban Insurrection: 1952–1959*. New Brunswick, N.J.: Transaction Books.

Cancian, Frank

1955   *Economics and Prestige in a Maya Community: The Religious Cargo System in Zinacantan*. Palo Alto: Stanford University Press.

Castillo, Hernán

1964   *Mito: The Orphan of its Illustrious Parents*. Ithaca: Cornell University Department of Anthropology.

Celestino, Olinda

1972   *Migración y Cambio Estructural: La Comunidad de Lampián*. Lima: Instituto de Estudios Peruanos.

Chapple, Eliot D. (with Conrad M. Arensberg)

1940   *Measuring Human Relations: An Introduction to the Study of Interactions of Individuals*. Genetic Psychology Monograph no. 22. Provincetown, Mass.: The Journal Press.

Chapple, Eliot D., Martha F. Chapple, and Judith A. Repp
1955   Behavioral Definitions of Personality and Temperament Characteristics. *Human Organization* 13:4.

Coser, Lewis
1956   *The Functions of Social Conflict*. New York: Free Press.

Cotler, Julio
1967–1968   The Mechanics of Internal Domination and Social Change in Peru. *Studies in Comparative International Development* 3:12.

1968   Haciendas y Comunidades Tradicionales en un Contexto de Movilización Política. Mimeographed. Lima: Instituto de Estudios Peruanos.

Craig, Wesley
1967   From Hacienda to Community: An Analysis of Solidarity and Social Change in Peru. Ph.D. dissertation, Cornell University.

1969   The Peasant Movement of La Convención, Peru: Dynamics of Rural Labor Organization. In Henry A. Landsberger (ed.), *Latin American Peasant Movements*. Ithaca: Cornell University Press.

Debray, Régis
1967   *Revolution in the Revolution? Armed Struggle and Political Struggle in Latin America*. New York: Monthly Review Press.

Degregori, Carlos Ivan and Jurgen Golte
1973   *Dependencia y Disintegración Estructural en la Comunidad de Paracaos*. Lima: Instituto de Estudios Peruanos.

Dobyns, Henry, Paul L. Doughty, and Harold Lasswell
1971   *Peasants, Power, and Applied Social Change: Vicos as a Model*. Beverly Hills: Sage Publications.

Einaudi, Luigi
1969   *The Peruvian Military: A Summary Political Analysis*. Santa Monica: The Rand Corp.

Elias Minaya, José F.
1969   *Las Hacienda en el Valle de Virú—1969*. Lima: report in files of Instituto de Estudios Peruanos.

Escobar, Alberto, José Matos Mar, and Giorgio Alberti
1975   *Peru: País Bilingue?* Lima: Instituto de Estudios Peruanos.

Espinosa, Waldemar
1973   *Los Huancas, Aliados de la Conquista*. Lima: Casa de la Cultura.

303

Fioravanti, Eduardo
1974   *Latifundio y Sindicalismo Agrario en el Perú: Estudio del Caso de los Valles de la Convención y Lares*. Lima: Instituto de Estudios Peruanos.

Foster, George
1960–1961 Interpersonal Relations in Peasant Society. *Human Organization* 19:4.
1966   Peasant Society and the Image of the Limited Good. *American Anthropologist* 67:4.

Fuenzalida, Fernando, José Villarán, and Teresa Valiente
1968   *Huayopampa: Estructuras Tradicionales y Economía de Mercado*. Lima: Instituto de Estudios Peruanos.

Gallegos Venero, Enrique
1973   Un Combate Victoriosa en Guerra Contrarevolucionaria. *Oíga*, March 9.

Greaves, Thomas Custer
1968   The Dying Chalan: Case Studies of Four Haciendas of the Peruvian Coast. Ph.D. dissertation, Cornell University.

Guevara, Che
1968   *The Diary of Che Guevara*. New York: Bantam Books.

Handelman, Howard
1975   *Struggle in the Andes: Peasant Political Mobilization in Peru*. Austin: Texas University Press.

Haya de la Torre, Victor Raúl
1936   *El Antimperialismo y el Apra*. 2d. ed., Santiago, Chile: Ediciones Ercilla.

Inkeles, Alex and David H. Smith
1974   *Becoming Modern: Individual Change in Six Developing Countries*. Cambridge; Harvard University Press.

Kahl, Joseph
1968   *The Measurement of Modernism*. Austin: Texas University Press.

Kellert, S., L. K. Williams, W. F. Whyte, and G. Alberti
1967   Culture Change and Stress in Rural Peru: A Preliminary Report. *Milbank Memorial Fund Quarterly* 45:4. (Published in Spanish by Instituto de Estudios Peruanos in Lima in 1968.)

Landsberger, Henry A. (ed.)
1969   *Latin American Peasant Movements*. Ithaca: Cornell University Press.

Lenski, Gerhard
1966   *Power and Privilege*. New York: McGraw-Hill.

Lewis, Oscar
1951   *Life in a Mexican Village: Tepoztlán Restudied*. Urbana: University of Illinois Press.

Martínez Alier, Juan
1973   *Los Huacchilleros del Perú*. Lima: Instituto de Estudios Peruanos.

Matos Mar, José, Augusto Salazar Bondy, Alberto Escobar, Jorge Bravo Bresani, and Julio Cotler
1968   *Perú Problema: 5 Ensayos*. Lima: F. Moncloa Editores.

Matos Mar, José and William F. Whyte
1966   *Proyecto de Estudios de Cambios en Pueblos Peruanos*. Lima: Instituto de Estudios Peruanos.

Matos Mar, José, W. F. Whyte, J. Cotler, L. K. Williams, J. O. Alers, F. Fuenzalida, and G. Alberti
1969   *Dominación y Cambios en el Perú Rural*. Lima: Instituto de Estudios Peruanos.

Mosher, Arthur T.
1969   *Creating a Progressive Rural Structure*. New York: Agriculture Development Council.

Núñez del Prado, Oscar, with the collaboration of W. F. Whyte
1973   *Kuyo Chico: Experiment in Applied Anthropology*. Chicago: University of Chicago Press.

Orlove, Benjamin Sebastian
1975   Alpacas, Sheep, and Men: The Wool Export Economy and Regional Society in Southern Peru. Ph.D. dissertation, University of California at Berkeley.

Paige, Jeffrey M.
1975   *Agrarian Revolution: Social Movements and Export Agriculture in the Underdeveloped World*. New York: Free Press.

Pitt-Rivers, Julian
1960–1961   Comment on Foster: Interpersonal Relations in Peasant Society. *Human Organization* 19:180–183.

Portugal, José
1966   La Irrigación La Esperanza del Valle de Chancay. Mimeographed. Lima; Instituto de Estudios Peruanos.

Redfield, Robert
1930   *Tepoztlán: A Mexican Village*. Chicago: University of Chicago Press.

Rogers, Everett M.
1962   *Diffusion of Innovations*. New York: Free Press.

Smock, David
1966   Rural Development in Eastern Nigeria. New York: Mimeo-graphed report to the Ford Foundation.

Whyte, William F.
1963a   Culture, Industrial Relations, and Economic Development: the Case of Peru. *Industrial and Labor Relations Review* 16:4.

1963b   Toward an Integrated Approach for Research in Organizational Behavior. Proceedings of the 16th Annual Meeting: Presidential Address of the Industrial Relations Research Association.

1964   High Level Manpower for Peru. In C. Myers and F. H. Harbison (eds.), *Manpower and Education: Country Studies*. New York: McGraw-Hill. (Published as SENATI bulletin in Spanish in Peru.)

1965   Common Management Strategies in Industrial Relations—Peru. In W. H. Form and A. A. Blum (eds.), *Industrial Relations and Social Change in Latin America*. Gainesville: University of Florida Press.

1967   Models for Building and Changing Organizations. *Human Organization* 26:1–2.

1968   Imitation or Innovation: Reflections on the Institutional Development of Peru. *Administrative Science Quarterly* 13:3. (Published in Spanish by Instituto de Estudios Peruanos in Lima in 1967.)

1969a   The Role of the U.S. Professor in Developing Countries. *The American Sociologist* 4:1.

1969b   Rural Peru—Peasants as Activists. *Trans-Action* 7:1.

1975a   Conflict and Cooperation in Andean Communities. *American Ethnologist* 2:2.

1975b   *Organizing for Agricultural Development*. New Brunswick: Transaction Books.

———— **and Robert Braun**
1966   Heroes, Homework and Industrial Growth. *Columbia Journal of World Business* 1:2.

———— **and L. K. Williams**
1963   Supervisory Leadership: An International Comparison. CIOS International Management Congress, XIII.

1968   *Toward an Integrated Theory of Development: Economic and Non-Economic Variables in Rural Development*. Ithaca, New

York State School of Industrial and Labor Relations, Paperback 5.

Williams, L. K.
1973   Some Developmental Correlates of Scarcity. *Human Relations* 26:1.

————, **William F. Whyte, and Charles S. Green**
1966   Do Cultural Differences Affect Workers' Attitudes? *Industrial Relations* 5:3

Wils, Fritz
1975   *Industrialists, Industrialization, and the Nation State in Peru.* Amsterdam, Netherlands: privately printed.

Young, Frank
1964   Location and Reputation in a Mexican Intervillage Network. *Human Organization* 23:36–41.